Study Guide

Essentials of Modern Business Statistics
with Microsoft® Excel
THIRD EDITION

David R. Anderson

University of Cincinnati

Dennis J. Sweeney

University of Cincinnati

Thomas A. Williams

Rochester Institute of Technology

Prepared by

John S. Loucks
St. Edward's University

THOMSON

SOUTH-WESTERN

Australia · Brazil · Canada · Mexico · Singapore · Spain · United Kingdom · United States

THOMSON

SOUTH-WESTERN

Study Guide to accompany Essentials of Modern Business Statistics with Microsoft ® Excel, Third Edtion
David R. Anderson, Dennis J. Sweeney, Thomas A. Williams

VP/Editorial Director:
Jack W. Calhoun

Editor-in-Chief:
Alex von Rosenberg

Sr. Acquisitions Editor:
Charles McCormick, Jr.

Sr. Developmental Editor:
Alice Denny

Sr. Marketing Manager:
Larry Qualls

Sr. Production Project Manager:
Deanna Quinn

Manager of Technology, Editorial:
Vicky True

Technology Project Editor:
Kelly Reid

Web Coordinator:
Scott Cook

Sr. 1st Print Buyer:
Diane Lohman

Printer:
West Group
Eagan, MN

Art Director:
Stacy Jenkins Shirley

Cover Designer:
Patti Hudepohl

Cover Image(s):
© Getty Images

For permission to use material from this text or product, submit a request online at http://www.thomsonrights.com.

For more information about our products, contact us at:

Thomson Learning Academic Resource Center

1-800-423-0563

Thomson Higher Education
5191 Natorp Boulevard
Mason, OH 45040
USA

Preface

The <u>Study Guide to Accompany Essentials of Modern Business Statistics with Microsoft Excel, 3rd Edition</u> has been written with several objectives in mind. The objectives are:

1. To <u>provide a list of learning objectives</u> for each chapter that students can use as a checklist to ensure they have an understanding of the key concepts covered in the parent text.

2. To <u>organize and summarize the material</u> in the parent text in a structured review section.

3. To <u>categorize examples and exercises</u> according to the statistical concept involved so that students can focus on the concepts where they need the most practice.

4. To <u>illustrate the basic concepts</u> of the parent text in detail through the presentation of 93 illustrated examples.

5. To <u>reinforce the basic concepts</u> by providing 103 additional exercises and 210 objective and fill-in-the-blank questions with answers at the end of each chapter.

6. To <u>challenge students</u> by including several exercises requiring more than simple, straightforward application of the techniques of the chapter.

7. To <u>illustrate business applications</u> areas in which statistical methodologies may be applied.

8. To <u>provide Excel worksheets</u> that students can use as templates for solving the exercises in the study guide and textbook.

To accomplish these goals, each chapter has been divided into seven basic parts:

1. Learning Objectives:
   Each chapter starts with a check-list of the learning objectives that should be achieved by the student upon completion of the chapter. This allows students to assess their proficiency and identify areas needing additional attention.

2. Review:
   This section summarizes point by point the theoretical foundations, terminology, formulas, and methodologies for every topic area of the chapter. This provides an excellent outline for understanding the essential points of the chapters.

3. Key Concepts:
   This section notes the main topic areas of each chapter and denotes which examples illustrate the concept, and which answered exercises require the use of the concept in its solution. Examples that illustrate the use of an Excel spreadsheet are clearly marked. Every major concept of the text is illustrated in at least one example worked out in detail and in at least one exercise with its answer provided at the end of the chapter.

4. Examples:
   These are problems worked out in full, giving the step-by-step details as the problem is worked through to completion. For the majority of these examples, an Excel spreadsheet approach to solving the problem is demonstrated. The Excel worksheets presented in these examples can be used as templates for completing the exercises in the study guide and the textbook.

5. Exercises:
   These problems are for students to do on their own with the answers provided at the end of the chapter. This enables students to test themselves on the individual concepts with brief answers to validate their results.

6. Self Test:
   Each chapter contains fifteen questions – 5 true/false, 5 fill-in-the-blank, and 5 multiple choice – designed to reinforce the theoretical concepts of the chapter.

7. Answers:
   This section contains the answers to all of the self-test questions (true/false, fill-in-the-blank, and multiple choice), as well as the exercises, in the chapter.

We hope you find this study guide instructive and a useful supplement in your study of business statistics.

John S. Loucks
St. Edward's University
Austin, Texas 78704
johnsl@admin.stedwards.edu

Contents

CHAPTER 1

Data and Statistics

Applications in Business and Economics

Data

Data Sources

Descriptive Statistics

Statistical Inference

Statistical Analysis Using Microsoft Excel

LEARNING OBJECTIVES

1. Obtain an appreciation for the breadth of statistical applications in business and economics.

2. Understand the meaning of the terms elements, variables, and observations as they are used in statistics.

3. Understand that data are obtained using one of the following scales of measurement: nominal, ordinal, interval, and ratio.

4. Obtain an understanding of the difference between qualitative, quantitative, cross-sectional and time series data.

5. Learn about the sources of data for statistical analysis both internal and external to the firm.

6. Be aware of how errors can arise in data.

7. Know the meaning of descriptive statistics and statistical inference.

8. Be able to distinguish between a population and a sample.

9. Understand the role a sample plays in making statistical inferences about the population.

REVIEW

Applications in Business and Economics
*   Public accounting firms use statistical sampling procedures when conducting audits for their clients.
*   Financial advisors use a variety of statistical information, including price-earnings ratios and dividend yields, to guide their investment recommendations.
*   Electronic point-of-sale scanners at retail checkout counters are being used to collect data for a variety of marketing research applications.
*   A variety of statistical quality control charts are used to monitor the output of a production process.
*   Economists use statistical information in making forecasts about the future of the economy or some aspect of it.

Data, Data Sets, Elements, Variables, and Observations
*   Data are the facts and figures that are collected, summarized, analyzed, and interpreted.
*   The data collected in a particular study are referred to as the data set.
*   The elements are the entities on which data are collected.
*   A variable is a characteristic of interest for the elements.
*   The set of measurements collected for a particular element is called an observation.
*   The number of observations is always the same as the number of elements.
*   The total number of data values in a data set is the number of elements multiplied by the number of variables.

Scales of Measurement

- Nominal scale: applies to data consisting of labels or names used to identify an attribute of the element. Data can be non-numeric or numeric.
- Ordinal scale: applies to data showing the properties of nominal data and the order or rank of the data is meaningful. Data can be non-numeric or numeric.
- Interval scale: applies to data showing the properties of ordinal data and the interval between values is expressed in terms of a fixed unit of measure. Data are always numeric.
- Ratio scale: applies to data showing the properties of interval data and the ratio of two values is meaningful. Data are always numeric.

Qualitative and Quantitative Data

- The statistical analysis that is appropriate depends on whether the data for the variable are qualitative or quantitative.
- Qualitative data are labels or names used to identify an attribute of each element.
- Quantitative data indicate either how much or how many.
- Quantitative data are always numeric.
- Qualitative data can be either numeric or nonnumeric.
- Ordinary arithmetic operations are meaningful only with quantitative data.

Cross-Sectional and Time Series Data

- Cross-sectional data are collected at the same or approximately the same point in time.
- Example of cross-sectional data: data detailing the number of building permits issued in December 2004 in each of the counties of Texas.
- Time series data are collected over several time periods.
- Example of time series data: data detailing the number of building permits issued in Travis County, Texas in each of the last 36 months.

Data Sources: Existing

- Companies maintain databases about their customers, employees, and operations.
- More and more companies are creating web sites and providing public access to them.
- Firms like Dun & Bradstreet and Dow Jones & Company offer database services to clients.
- Most government agencies, like the Census Bureau (www.census.gov), make their data available through a web site.
- Data are also available from industry associations and special interest organizations.

Data Sources: Statistical Studies

- In experimental studies the variables of interest are first identified. Then one or more factors are controlled so that data can be obtained about how the factors influence the variables.
- In observational studies no attempt is made to control or influence the variables of interest.
- A survey is perhaps the most common type of observational study.

Data Acquisition Considerations

- Time Requirement: Searching for information can be time consuming. Information might no longer be useful by the time it is available.
- Cost of Acquisition: Organizations often charge for information even when it is not their primary business activity.
- Data Errors: Using any data that happens to be available or that were acquired with little care can lead to poor and misleading information.

Descriptive Statistics
- Summaries of data are referred to as descriptive statistics.
- Tabular Summary: An example is a table showing frequencies for a variable.
- Graphical Summary: An example, for qualitative data, is a bar graph. An example, for quantitative data, is a histogram.
- Numerical Summary: The most common numerical descriptive statistic is the average (or mean).

Statistical Inference
- Statistical inference is the process of using data obtained from a small group of elements (the sample) to make estimates and test hypotheses about the characteristics of a larger group of elements (the population).

Using Excel for Statistical Analysis
- Statistical analysis typically involves working with large amounts of data.
- Computer software is typically used to conduct the analysis.
- Frequently the data that is to be analyzed resides in a spreadsheet.
- Spreadsheet packages are capable of data management, analysis, and presentation.
- MS Excel is the most widely available spreadsheet software in business organizations.
- In using Excel for statistical analysis, three tasks might be necessary:
  - Enter Data: Select cell locations for the data and appropriate labels, and then enter the data and labels.
  - Enter Functions and Formulas: Select cell locations, enter Excel functions and formulas, and provide descriptive material to identify the results.
  - Apply Tools: Use Excel's tools for data management, data analysis, and presentation.

KEY CONCEPTS

CONCEPT	EXAMPLES	EXERCISES
Elements, Variables, and Observations	1	1
Qualitative and Quantitative Data	2	2
Scales of Measurement	3	3
Cross-Sectional and Time Series Data	4	4,5
Experimental and Observational Studies	5	6
Data Sets and Excel Worksheets	⑥	7
Descriptive Statistics and Statistical Inference	7	8

◯ Excel Used

EXAMPLES

EXAMPLE 1

Elements, Variables, and Observations

Laura Naples, Manager of Heritage Inn, periodically collects and tabulates information about a sample of the hotel's overnight guests. This information aids her in planning and scheduling decisions she must make.

The table below lists data on ten randomly selected hotel registrants, collected as the registrants checked out. The data listed are:
- Number of people in the group
- Date of birth of person registering
- Shuttle service used: yes or no
- Total telephone charges incurred
- Reason for stay: business or personal

Name of Registrant	Number in Group	D.O.B (mm/dd/yy)	Shuttle Used	Telephone Charges ($)	Reason for Stay
Adam Sandler	1	05/07/59	yes	0.00	personal
Michelle Pepper	4	11/23/48	no	12.46	business
Claudia Shepler	2	04/30/73	no	1.20	business
Annette Rodriquez	2	12/16/71	no	2.90	business
Tony DiMarco	1	05/09/39	yes	0.00	personal
Amy Franklin	3	09/14/69	yes	4.65	business
Tammy Roberts	2	04/22/66	no	9.35	personal
Edward Blackstone	5	10/28/54	yes	2.10	personal
Mary Silverman	1	11/12/49	no	1.85	business
Todd Atherton	2	01/30/62	no	5.80	business

a) How many elements are there in the data set?

b) How many variables are there in the data set?

c) How many observations are there in the data set?

d) What are the observations for the second element listed?

e) What is the total number of measurements in the data set?

SOLUTION 1

a) There are 10 elements (registrants) in the data set.

b) There are 5 variables (number in party, DOB, shuttle used, telephone charges, and reason for stay).

c) There are 10 observations (one for each registrant) in the data set.

d) The observations for the second element are: 4, 11/23/48, no, 12.46, and business.

e) The total number of measurements in the data set is 50 (10 elements X 5 variables).

EXAMPLE 2

Qualitative and Quantitative Data

Refer to the Heritage Inn guest data presented in Example 1.

a) Which variables are quantitative?

b) Which variables are qualitative?

SOLUTION 2

a) There are two quantitative variables - number in party and telephone charges. Ordinary arithmetic operations such as computing an average value are meaningful for these variables.

b) There are three qualitative variables - DOB, shuttle used, and reason for stay. DOB contains numeric values, but it is considered a qualitative variable. We cannot directly perform any ordinary arithmetic operation on the DOB data. We can derive the age of each registrant from the DOB data and age would be considered a quantitative variable.

EXAMPLE 3

Scales of Measurement

Refer to the Heritage Inn guest data presented in Example 1. What is the scale of measurement for each of the variables.

SOLUTION 3

Number in group – ratio scale.
Date of birth – ordinal scale.
Shuttle use – nominal.
Telephone charge – ratio scale.
Reason for stay – nominal scale.

EXAMPLE 4

Cross-Sectional and Time Series Data

Refer again to the Heritage Inn guest data presented in Example 1. Does the data set represent cross-sectional or times series data? Explain the reason for your answer. What characteristic is lacking in the data set that, if it were present, would cause you to choose the other category as your answer? What is a potential shortcoming of this type of data?

SOLUTION 4

The data set represents cross-sectional data. The data might have been collected over several time periods (weeks or months), but the data is not sorted by time period. To use a photography analogy, the Heritage Inn data is a snapshot and not a movie.

The fact that it is a snapshot of conditions/circumstances at approximately one point in time might be a shortcoming, even if the sample was chosen in a purely random, unbiased manner. If the manager is interested in the ongoing status of the variables, this data set might not be representative.

EXAMPLE 5

Experimental and Observational Studies

Refer again to the Heritage Inn guest data presented in Example 1. Does the data set represent an experimental or an observational study? Explain the reason for your answer. How might the study be altered in order for you to categorize the study differently?

SOLUTION 5

The data set represents an observational (nonexperimental) study. There is no indication that an attempt was made to control or influence the variables of interest.

As an example of an experimental study, a controllable variable could be introduced and its effect on telephone charges could be examined. Such a controllable variable might be whether or not a guest party is given a discount on the telephone billing rate. Data on telephone charges could be collected for each group (guests given the discount and guests not given the discount). Statistical analysis of the experimental data could help determine the effect of lower telephone rates on charges guests incur.

EXAMPLE 6

Data Sets and Excel Worksheets

Refer again to the Heritage Inn guest data presented in Example 1. Enter the Heritage Inn data set, with appropriate labels, in an Excel worksheet. Compute the average number of guests in a group, the average telephone charge per group, and the average telephone charge per guest.

SOLUTION 6

Using Excel's *AVERAGE* Function

The two or three (depending on the problem) tasks involved with using Excel for statistical analysis are: 1) enter data, 2) enter functions and formulas, and/or 3) apply tools.

Enter Data: The appropriate labels for the columns of data are entered in cells A1:F1. The data are entered in cells A2:F11.

Enter Functions and Formulas: Excel's AVERAGE function can be used to compute the average number of guests in a group and the average telephone charge per group. For example, to compute the average number of guests in a group, the following formula is entered into cell B13:

$$=AVERAGE(B2:B11)$$

The average telephone charge per group is computed in a similar manner. To compute the average telephone charge per guest, it is not necessary or appropriate to use the AVERAGE function. The average telephone charge per guest is:

Average telephone charge per guest = Average telephone charge per group / Average number of guests in a group

$$B15 = B14/B13$$

To identify the results, appropriate labels are entered in cells A13:A15.

Formula Worksheet

	A	B	C	D	E	F
1	**Name of Registrant**	**Number in Group**	**D.O.B (mm/dd/yy)**	**Shuttle Used**	**Telephone Charges ($)**	**Reason for Stay**
2	Adam Sandler	1	05/07/59	yes	0.00	personal
3	Michelle Pepper	4	11/23/48	no	12.46	business
4	Claudia Shepler	2	04/30/73	no	1.20	business
5	Annette Rodriquez	2	12/16/71	no	2.90	business
6	Tony DiMarco	1	05/09/39	yes	0.00	personal
7	Amy Franklin	3	09/14/69	yes	4.65	business
8	Tammy Roberts	2	04/22/66	no	9.35	personal
9	Edward Blackstone	5	10/28/54	yes	2.10	personal
10	Mary Silverman	1	11/12/49	no	1.85	business
11	Todd Atherton	2	01/30/62	no	5.80	business
12						
13	**Average Number in Group**			=AVERAGE(B2:B11)		
14	**Average Telephone Charge Per Group**			=AVERAGE(E2:E11)		
15	**Average Telephone Charge PerGuest**			=D14/D13		

Value Worksheet

	A	B	C	D	E	F
1	Name of Registrant	Number in Group	D.O.B (mm/dd/yy)	Shuttle Used	Telephone Charges ($)	Reason for Stay
2	Adam Sandler	1	05/07/59	yes	0.00	personal
3	Michelle Pepper	4	11/23/48	no	12.46	business
4	Claudia Shepler	2	04/30/73	no	1.20	business
5	Annette Rodriquez	2	12/16/71	no	2.90	business
6	Tony DiMarco	1	05/09/39	yes	0.00	personal
7	Amy Franklin	3	09/14/69	yes	4.65	business
8	Tammy Roberts	2	04/22/66	no	9.35	personal
9	Edward Blackstone	5	10/28/54	yes	2.10	personal
10	Mary Silverman	1	11/12/49	no	1.85	business
11	Todd Atherton	2	01/30/62	no	5.80	business
12						
13	Average Number in Group				2.30	
14	Average Telephone Charge Per Group				4.03	
15	Average Telephone Charge PerGuest				1.75	

EXAMPLE 7

Descriptive Statistics and Statistical Inference

Refer again to the Heritage Inn guest data presented in Example 1.

a) Example 6 above involved computing several averages for the Heritage Inn guest data. Do these calculations fall under the heading of Descriptive Statistics or Statistical Inference methods?

b) Give two examples of descriptive statistics methods that could be applied to the Heritage Inn data.

c) Give two examples of statistical inference methods that could be applied to the Heritage Inn data.

SOLUTION 7

a) Calculating and reporting an average is an example of descriptive statistics. When an average pertaining to a sample is used to estimate a population average, statistical inference is being conducted.

b) Computing the proportion of the registrants in the sample who were staying at the hotel for business reasons is an example of descriptive statistics. Another example of a descriptive statistics method is constructing a histogram that shows the frequency of one guest in a group, two guests in a group, and so on.

c) One example of statistical inference is stating that the estimate of the proportion of all Heritage Inn registrants using the Inn's shuttle service is 0.4 with a margin of error of +/- .03. Another example is inferring that the overall average telephone expense per guest at the Heritage Inn is $1.75.

EXERCISES

EXERCISE 1

Elements, Variables, and Observations

Tony Zamora, a real estate investor, has just moved to Clarksville and wants to learn about the city's residential real estate market. Tony has randomly selected 25 house-for-sale listings from the Sunday newspaper and collected the data listed below.

Segment of City	Selling Price ($000)	House Size (00 sq. ft.)	Number of Bedrooms	Number of Bathrooms	Garage Size (cars)
Northwest	290	21	4	2	2
South	95	11	2	1	0
Northeast	170	19	3	2	2
Northwest	375	38	5	4	3
West	350	24	4	3	2
South	125	10	2	2	0
West	310	31	4	4	2
West	275	25	3	2	2
Northwest	340	27	5	3	3
Northeast	215	22	4	3	2
Northwest	295	20	4	3	2
South	190	24	4	3	2
Northwest	385	36	5	4	3
West	430	32	5	4	2
South	185	14	3	2	1
South	175	18	4	2	2
Northeast	190	19	4	2	2
Northwest	330	29	4	4	3
West	405	33	5	4	3
Northeast	170	23	4	2	2
West	365	34	5	4	3
Northwest	280	25	4	2	2
South	135	17	3	1	1
Northeast	205	21	4	3	2
West	260	26	4	3	2

a) How many elements are there in the data set and what are they?

b) How many variables are there in the data set and what are they?

c) How many observations are there in the data set?

d) What are the observations for the third element listed?

e) What is the total number of measurements in the data set?

EXERCISE 2

Qualitative and Quantitative Data

Refer again to the real estate data presented in Exercise 1.

a) Identify the variables that are quantitative?

b) What type of analysis can be done with the qualitative data?

EXERCISE 3

Scales of Measurement

Suppose the current weather report for your area contains the following information. Specify the measurement scale for each of the variables.

a) Temperature: 84°

b) Wind Speed: 10 mph

c) Wind Direction: (from the) South

d) Sky Description: Sunny

e) Molds Level: High

EXERCISE 4

Cross-Sectional and Time Series Data

Refer again to the real estate data presented in Exercise 1. Is the data set cross-sectional or time series data? Explain.

EXERCISE 5

Cross-Sectional and Time Series Data

Molly Porter owns and operates two convenience stores, one on the East side of the city and the other on the South side. She has workforce-planning decisions to make and has collected some recent sales data that are relevant to her decisions. Listed below are the monthly sales ($000) at her two stores for the past six months.

Store	March	April	May	June	July	August
East	102	100	103	105	109	103
South	72	74	81	86	92	95

a) Is the data set cross-sectional or time series data? Explain.

b) Comment on any apparent patterns you see in the data.

EXERCISE 6

Experimental and Observational Studies

Refer again to the convenience store sales data presented in Exercise 5. Does the data set represent an experimental or an observational study? Explain the reason for your answer.

EXERCISE 7

Data Sets and Excel Worksheets

Refer again to the real estate data presented in Exercise 1. Enter the data set, with appropriate labels, in an Excel worksheet. Compute the average selling price of a house, average number of bedrooms per house, and average garage size.

EXERCISE 8

Descriptive Statistics and Statistical Inference

Refer again to the real estate data presented in Exercise 1.

a) What is the population being studied?

b) What are the population characteristics of interest to Tony Zamora?

c) What is the sample size?

d) Make an inference about the average garage size for a house in Clarksville.

e) Develop a descriptive statistic that can be used as an estimate of the percentage of houses in Clarksville that have four or more bedrooms.

SELF-TEST

TRUE/FALSE

_____ 1. In an observational study, an attempt is made to control the variables of interest.

_____ 2. The total number of data items in a complete data set is equal to the number of elements multiplied by the number of variables.

_____ 3. The cost of data acquisition and the subsequent statistical analysis should not exceed the savings generated by using the information to make a better decision.

_____ 4. A survey is a common form of observational study.

_____ 5. Cross-sectional data are data collected over several time periods.

FILL-IN-THE-BLANK

1. When _____ data are recorded as numeric values, performing arithmetic operations on the values – such as computing the average value – provide meaningless results.

2. _____ are the entities on which data are collected.

3. The process of making estimates or testing hypotheses about the characteristics of a population is referred to as _____.

4. The data collected in a particular study are referred to as the _____ for the study.

5. _____ data indicates either how much or how many.

MULTIPLE CHOICE

___ 1. How many observations are there in a complete data set having 10 elements and 5 variables?
   a) 2
   b) 5
   c) 10
   d) 50

___ 2. Which of the following is an example of qualitative data?
   a) a social security number
   b) a score on a multiple-choice exam
   c) the height, in meters, of a diving board
   d) the number of square feet of carpet laid

___ 3. Unusually large and small values in a data set are called
   a) errors
   b) cross-sectional data
   c) qualitative data
   d) outliers

___ 4. Which one of the following is not an example of descriptive statistics?
   a) a histogram depicting the age distribution for 30 randomly selected professors
   b) an estimate of the number of Alaska residents who have visited Canada
   c) a table summarizing the data collected in a sample of new-car buyers
   d) the proportion of mailed-out questionnaires that were completed and returned

___ 5. Which one of the following is an example of quantitative data?
   a) the number on a baseball uniform
   b) the serial number on a one-dollar bill
   c) the part number of an inventory item
   d) the number of cell phones a family has

ANSWERS

EXERCISES

1) a) 25 elements (houses for sale)
   b) 6 variables (segment of city, selling price, house size, number of bedrooms, number of bathrooms, garage size)
   c) 25 observations (one for each element)
   d) Northeast, 170, 19, 3, 2, 2
   e) 150 (25 elements X 6 variables)

2) a) All are quantitative except Segment of City
   b) We can provide counts and compute the proportion or percentage of the houses being in each segment of the city.

3) a) interval   b) ratio   c) nominal   d) nominal   e) ordinal

4) Cross-sectional data. The data describe the six variables for the 25 houses at the same point in time.

5) a) Time series data for two variables: monthly sales for East store and monthly sales for South store.
   b) Both stores have been experiencing an overall rise in sales during the past six months. The South store's increase in sales (as a percentage of sales) has been greater than the East store's increase. The increases might be temporary, due to the seasonal nature of demand. It is also possible that the increases will continue.

6) The data set represents an observational (nonexperimental) study. There is no indication that an attempt was made to influence the sales from month to month for either store.

7) $261,800; 3.92 bedrooms; 2.00 cars

8) a) all of the houses in Clarksville
   b) the six variables on which Tony has collected data
   c) 25 houses
   d) the sample suggests that the average garage size for all houses in Clarksville is 2.00 cars
   e) the percentage of houses in the sample with 4 or more bedrooms (76%)

TRUE/FALSE

1) False
2) True
3) True
4) True
5) False

FILL-IN-THE-BLANK

1) qualitative
2) Elements
3) statistical inference
4) data set
5) Quantitative

MULTIPLE CHOICE

1) c
2) a
3) d
4) b
5) d

CHAPTER 2

Descriptive Statistics: Tabular and Graphical Presentations

Summarizing Qualitative Data

Summarizing Quantitative Data

Exploratory Data Analysis:
The Stem-and-Leaf Display

Crosstabulations and Scatter Diagrams

LEARNING OBJECTIVES

1. Learn how to construct and interpret summarization procedures for qualitative data such as: frequency and relative frequency distributions, bar graphs and pie charts.

2. Be able to use Excel's COUNTIF function to construct a frequency distribution and the Chart Wizard to construct a bar graph and pie chart.

3. Learn how to construct and interpret tabular summarization procedures for quantitative data such as: frequency and relative frequency distributions, cumulative frequency and cumulative relative frequency distributions.

4. Be able to use Excel's FREQUENCY function to construct a frequency distribution and the Chart Wizard to construct a histogram.

5. Learn how to construct a histogram and an ogive as graphical summaries of quantitative data.

6. Be able to use and interpret the exploratory data analysis technique of a stem-and-leaf display.

7. Learn how to construct and interpret cross tabulations and scatter diagrams of bivariate data.

8. Be able to use Excel's Pivot Table Report to construct a cross tabulation and the Chart Wizard to construct a scatter diagram.

REVIEW

Summarizing Qualitative Data

Frequency Distribution
- A frequency distribution is a tabular summary of data showing the frequency (or number) of items in each of several nonoverlapping classes.
- The objective is to provide insights about the data that cannot be quickly obtained by looking only at the original data.

Relative Frequency Distribution
- The relative frequency of a class is the fraction or proportion of the total number of data items belonging to the class.
- A relative frequency distribution is a tabular summary of a set of data showing the relative frequency for each class.

Percent Frequency Distribution
- The percent frequency of a class is the relative frequency multiplied by 100.
- A percent frequency distribution is a tabular summary of a set of data showing the percent frequency for each class.

Bar Graph

- A bar graph is a graphical device for depicting qualitative data that have been summarized in a frequency, relative frequency, or percent frequency distribution.
- On the horizontal axis we specify the labels that are used for each of the classes.
- A frequency, relative frequency, or percent frequency scale is used for the vertical axis.
- Using a bar of fixed width drawn above each class label, we extend the height appropriately.
- The bars are separated to emphasize the fact that each class is a separate category.

Pie Chart

- The pie chart is a commonly used graphical device for presenting relative frequency distributions for qualitative data.
- First draw a circle; then use the relative frequencies to subdivide the circle into sectors that correspond to the relative frequency for each class.
- Since there are 360 degrees in a circle, a class with a relative frequency of .25 would consume .25(360) = 90 degrees of the circle.

Summarizing Quantitative Data

Frequency Distribution

- With quantitative data we have to be careful in defining the nonoverlapping classes to be used in the frequency distribution.
- The three steps necessary to define the classes are:
  - Determine the number of nonoverlapping classes.
  - Determine the width of each class.
  - Determine the class limits.
- The guidelines for selecting number of classes are:
  - Use between 5 and 20 classes.
  - Larger data sets usually require a larger number of classes.
  - Smaller data sets usually require fewer classes.
- The guidelines for selecting the width of classes are:
  - Use classes of equal width.
  - Approximate Class Width =

$$\frac{\text{Largest Data Value} - \text{Smallest Data Value}}{\text{Number of Classes}}$$

Histogram

- A common graphical presentation of quantitative data is a histogram.
- The variable of interest is placed on the horizontal axis and the frequency, relative frequency, or percent frequency is placed on the vertical axis.
- A rectangle is drawn above each class interval with its height corresponding to the interval's frequency, relative frequency, or percent frequency.
- Unlike a bar graph, a histogram has no natural separation between rectangles of adjacent classes.

Cumulative Distributions
- The cumulative frequency distribution shows the number of items with values less than or equal to the upper limit of each class.
- The cumulative relative frequency distribution shows the proportion of items with values less than or equal to the upper limit of each class.
- The cumulative percent frequency distribution shows the percentage of items with values less than or equal to the upper limit of each class.

Ogive
- An ogive is a graph of a cumulative distribution.
- The data values are shown on the horizontal axis.
- Shown on the vertical axis is one of the following: cumulative frequency, cumulative relative frequency, or cumulative percent frequency.
- The frequency (one of the above) of each class is plotted as a point.
- Straight-line segments connect the plotted points.

Exploratory Data Analysis
- The techniques of exploratory data analysis consist of simple arithmetic and easy-to-draw pictures that can be used to summarize data quickly.
- One such technique, for quantitative data, is the stem-and-leaf display.

Stem-and-Leaf Display
- A stem-and-leaf display shows both the rank order and shape of the distribution of the data.
- It is similar to a histogram on its side, but it has the advantage of showing the actual data values.
- The first digit(s) of each data item are arranged to the left of a vertical line.
- To the right of the vertical line we record the last digit for each item in rank order.
- Each line in the display is referred to as a stem.
- Each digit on a stem is a leaf.

Relationship Between Two Variables
- Often a manager is interested in tabular and graphical methods that will help understand the relationship between two variables.
- Crosstabulation and a scatter diagram are two methods for summarizing the data for two variables simultaneously.

Crosstabulation
- A crosstabulation is a tabular summary of data for two variables.
- The two variables might both be qualitative, both be quantitative, or be one of each.
- The classes for one variable are represented by the rows; the columns represent the classes for the other variable.
- Converting the entries in the table into row percentages or column percentages can provide additional insight about the relationship between the variables.
- When two or more crosstabulations are combined into one summary crosstabulation, the conclusion drawn about the relationship between two variables in the summary crosstabulation can be incorrect …. an occurrence known as Simpson's paradox.

Scatter Diagram

- A scatter diagram is a graphical presentation of the relationship between two quantitative variables.
- One variable is shown on the horizontal axis and the other variable is shown on the vertical axis.
- A positive relationship, negative relationship, or no relationship might be apparent to a manager with the aid of a scatter diagram.

KEY CONCEPTS

CONCEPT	EXAMPLES	EXERCISES
Summarizing Qualitative Data		
Frequency Distribution	①	1
Relative Frequency Distribution	②	1
Percent Frequency Distribution	②	1
Bar Graph	③	2
Pie Chart	④	2
Summarizing Quantitative Data		
Frequency Distribution	⑤	3
Relative Frequency Distribution	⑤	3
Percent Frequency Distribution	⑤	3
Histogram	⑥	4
Cumulative Distributions	⑦	5
Ogive	⑧	5
Exploratory Data Analysis		
Stem-and-Leaf Display	9	6
Relationship Between Two Variables		
Crosstabulation	⑩	7
Scatter Diagram	⑪	8

◯ Excel Used

EXAMPLES

EXAMPLE 1

Frequency Distribution – Qualitative Data

Guests staying at Marada Inn were asked to rate the quality of their accommodations as being excellent, above average, average, below average, or poor. The ratings provided by a sample of 20 quests are shown below.

Below Average	Average	Above Average	Above Average
Above Average	Above Average	Above Average	Below Average
Below Average	Average	Poor	Poor
Above Average	Average	Above Average	Average
Excellent	Above Average	Average	Above Average

Provide a frequency distribution showing the number of occurrences of each rating level in the sample.

SOLUTION 1

Using Excel's COUNTIF Function for Frequency Distributions

Enter Data: The label Rating Given and the data for the 20-guest sample are entered into cells A1:A21. (*Note:* Misspelled data will not be counted as it should. Misspelling includes typing any spaces before or after the phrases.)

Enter Functions and Formulas: Excel's COUNTIF function can be used to count the number of times each rating level appears in cells A2:A21.

(*Note:* It is a good idea to total your frequency count as a partial check of the accuracy of your data and function entries. We know from our sample size that the total frequency should be 20.)

Formula Worksheet:

	A	B	C	D
1	**Rating Given**		**Quality Rating**	**Frequency**
2	Above Average		Poor	=COUNTIF($A$2:$A$21,C2)
3	Below Average		Below Average	=COUNTIF($A$2:$A$21,C3)
4	Above Average		Average	=COUNTIF($A$2:$A$21,C4)
5	Average		Above Average	=COUNTIF($A$2:$A$21,C5)
6	Average		Excellent	=COUNTIF($A$2:$A$21,C6)
7	Above Average		Total	=SUM(D2:D6)
8	Above Average			
20	Excellent			
21	Poor			

Note: Rows 9-19 are hidden.

Value Worksheet:

	A	B	C	D
1	**Rating Given**		**Quality Rating**	**Frequency**
2	Above Average		Poor	2
3	Below Average		Below Average	3
4	Above Average		Average	5
5	Average		Above Average	9
6	Average		Excellent	1
7	Above Average		**Total**	20
8	Above Average			
20	Excellent			
21	Poor			

Note: Rows 9-19 are hidden.

EXAMPLE 2

Relative and Percent Frequency Distributions – Qualitative Data

Refer to the quality ratings data in Example 1. Construct a relative frequency distribution and percent frequency distribution for the data.

SOLUTION 2

Using Excel's COUNTIF Function

For a data set with n observations, the relative frequency of each class is computed as:

Relative Frequency of a Class = (Frequency of the Class)/n

Enter Data: We will continue with the worksheet shown in the solution to Example 1. We now enter the label "Relative Frequency" in cell E1 and "Percent Frequency" in cell F1.

Enter Functions and Formulas: See the formula worksheet below.

Formula Worksheet

	C	D	E	F
1	**Quality Rating**	**Frequency**	**Relative Frequency**	**Percent Frequency**
2	Poor	=COUNTIF($A$2:$A$21,C2)	=D2/$D$7	=E2*100
3	Below Average	=COUNTIF($A$2:$A$21,C3)	=D3/$D$7	=E3*100
4	Average	=COUNTIF($A$2:$A$21,C4)	=D4/$D$7	=E4*100
5	Above Average	=COUNTIF($A$2:$A$21,C5)	=D5/$D$7	=E5*100
6	Excellent	=COUNTIF($A$2:$A$21,C6)	=D6/$D$7	=E6*100
7	**Total**	=SUM(D2:D6)	=SUM(E2:E6)	=SUM(F2:F6)

Note: Columns A and B are not shown.

Value Worksheet

	C	D	E	F
1	**Quality Rating**	**Frequency**	**Relative Frequency**	**Percent Frequency**
2	Poor	2	0.10	10
3	Below Average	3	0.15	15
4	Average	5	0.25	25
5	Above Average	9	0.45	45
6	Excellent	1	0.05	5
7	Total	20	1.00	100

Note: Columns A and B are not shown.

EXAMPLE 3

Bar Graph

Refer to the quality ratings data in Example 1. Display the frequencies (computed in Example 1) graphically with a bar graph.

SOLUTION 3

Using Excel's CHART WIZARD for Bar Graphs

Continuing with the worksheet shown in the solution to Example 1, we can construct the bar graph using Excel's Chart Wizard. A third task (in addition to Enter Data and Enter Functions and Formulas) is now necessary: Apply Tools.

Enter Data: The data set was entered in Example 1.

Enter Functions and Formulas: The functions and formulas for the frequencies we want to graph were entered in Example 1.

Apply Tools: The following steps describe how to use Excel's Chart Wizard to construct a bar graph using the frequency distribution appearing in cells C1:D6.

Step 1 Select cells C1:D6
Step 2 Select the **Chart Wizard** button
Step 3 When the **Chart Wizard-Step 1 of 4-Chart Type** dialog box appears:
      Choose **Column** in the **Chart type** list
      Choose **Clustered Column** from the **Chart sub-type** display
      Click **Next >**
Step 4 When the **Chart Wizard-Step 2 of 4-Chart Source Data** dialog box appears
      Click **Next >**
Step 5 When the **Chart Wizard-Step 3 of 4-Chart Options** dialog box appears:
      Select the **Titles** tab and then
          Type **Marada Inn Quality Ratings** in the **Chart title** box

Enter **Quality Rating** in the **Value (X)** axis box
Enter **Frequency** in the **Value (Y)** axis box
Select the **Legend** tab and then
Remove the check in the **Show Legend** box
Click **Next >**
Step 6 When the **Chart Wizard-Step 4 of 4-Chart Location** dialog box appears:
Specify the location for the new chart (we chose cell C9)
Click **Finish**

You can alter the graph initially produced by Excel to look like the one below or to suit your personal preferences. A right-click on almost any item in the chart will bring up a menu of alteration options.

Bar Graph

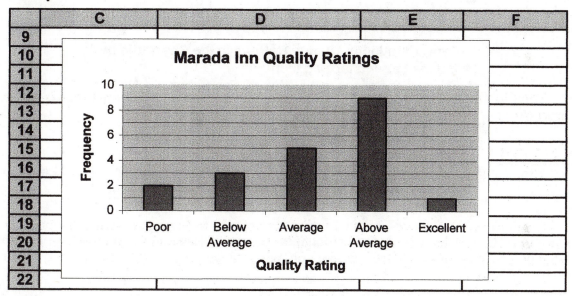

EXAMPLE 4

Pie Chart

Refer to the quality ratings data in Example 1. Display the percent frequencies (computed in Example 2) graphically with a pie chart.

SOLUTION 4

Using Excel's CHART WIZARD for Pie Charts

Excel's Chart Wizard provides a general tool for constructing graphical displays such as pie charts. Extending the worksheet shown in the solution to Example 2, we can construct the pie chart.

Enter Data: The data set was entered in Example 1.

Enter Functions and Formulas: The functions and formulas for the percent frequencies we want to graph were entered in Example 2.

Apply Tools: The following steps describe how to use Excel's Chart Wizard to construct a pie chart using the percent frequency distribution appearing in cells C1:C6 and F1:F6.

Step 1   Select cells C1:C6 and F1:F6 (To select nonadjacent cells, select cells C1:C6 and then press the Control key while selecting cells F1:F6.)

Step 2   Select the **Chart Wizard** button

Step 3   When the **Chart Wizard-Step 1 of 4-Chart Type** dialog box appears:
   Choose **Pie** in the **Chart type** list
   Choose **Pie** from the **Chart sub-type** display
   Click **Next >**

Step 4   When the **Chart Wizard-Step 2 of 4-Chart Source Data** dialog box appears
   Click **Next >**

Step 5   When the **Chart Wizard-Step 3 of 4-Chart Options** dialog box appears:
   Select the **Titles** tab and then
      Type **Marada Inn Quality Ratings** in the **Chart title** box
   Select the **Legend** tab and then
      Remove the check in the **Show Legend** box
   Select the **Data Labels** tab and then
      Select **Show Label and percent**
      Select **Show leader lines**
   Click **Next >**

Step 6   When the **Chart Wizard-Step 4 of 4-Chart Location** dialog box appears:
   Specify the location for the new chart (we chose cell C9)
   Click **Finish**

You can alter the chart initially produced by Excel to look like the one below or to suit your personal preferences. A right-click on almost any item in the chart will bring up a menu of alteration options.

Pie Chart

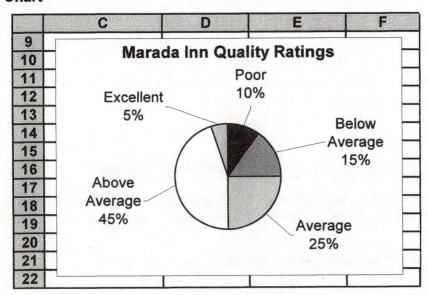

EXAMPLE 5

Frequency Distribution – Quantitative Data

The manager of Hudson Auto Repair would like to get a better picture of the distribution of costs for new parts used in the engine tune-up jobs done in the garage. A sample of 50 customer invoices for tune-ups has been taken and the costs of parts, rounded to the nearest dollar, are listed below.

91	78	93	57	75	52	99	80	73	62
71	69	72	89	66	75	79	75	72	76
104	74	62	68	97	105	77	65	80	109
85	97	88	68	83	68	71	69	67	74
62	82	98	101	79	105	79	69	62	73

Develop a frequency distribution for these cost data. Use your own judgment to determine the number of classes and class width that provide a distribution that will be meaningful and helpful to the manager.

SOLUTION 5

Using Excel's FREQUENCY Function

First, we must define the nonoverlapping classes to be used in the frequency distribution. The data is in dollars and most people will think in increments of $5, $10, $20, and so on. We should consider using one of these increments as the class width.

If we round <u>up</u> the largest data value (109) to 110 and we round <u>down</u> the smallest data value (52) to 50, we have a range of 110 – 50 = 60 for the frequency distribution to span. If we choose 10 as the class width, the result will be 60/10 = 6 classes, which is a reasonable number of classes.

The data is in integer dollar amounts. If we set the lower limit of the first class at 50, the upper limit of the first class will be 59 (not 60). There are 10 dollar amounts between 50 and 59, inclusively. The second class will have limits of 60 and 69, and so on.

Enter Data: The label Parts Cost and the cost data from the 50 customer invoices are entered into cells A1:A51. Descriptive labels are entered into cells C1, D1, and E1. The class limits 50-59, 60-69, and so on, are entered into cells C2:C7. The class upper limits used by the FREQUENCY function are entered into cells D2:D7.

Enter Functions and Formulas: The FREQUENCY function is not a "simple" Excel function. FREQUENCY is capable of providing multiple values and for this reason it is called an <u>array formula</u>. An array formula must be entered in a special way.

<u>Entering the Necessary Array Formula</u>

Step 1 Select cells E2:E7 (where the frequencies will appear)
Step 2 Type, but do not enter, the following formula:
=FREQUENCY(A2:A51,D2:D7)
Step 3 Press CTRL + SHIFT + ENTER and the array formula will be entered into each of the cells D2:D7.

Formula Worksheet:

	A	B	C	D	E
1	Parts Cost		Parts Cost	Upper Limit	Frequency
2	91		50-59	59	=FREQUENCY(A2:A51,D2:D7)
3	71		60-69	69	=FREQUENCY(A2:A51,D2:D7)
4	104		70-79	79	=FREQUENCY(A2:A51,D2:D7)
5	85		80-89	89	=FREQUENCY(A2:A51,D2:D7)
6	62		90-99	99	=FREQUENCY(A2:A51,D2:D7)
7	78		100-109	109	=FREQUENCY(A2:A51,D2:D7)
8	69				
50	74				
51	73				

Note: Rows 9-49 are hidden.

Value Worksheet:

	A	B	C	D	E
1	Parts Cost		Parts Cost	Upper Limit	Frequency
2	91		50-59	59	2
3	71		60-69	69	13
4	104		70-79	79	16
5	85		80-89	89	7
6	62		90-99	99	7
7	78		100-109	109	5
8	69				
50	74				
51	73				

Note: Rows 9-49 are hidden.

EXAMPLE 6

Histogram

Refer to the auto parts cost data in Example 5. Display the frequency distribution (constructed in Example 5) graphically with a histogram.

SOLUTION 6

Using Excel's CHART WIZARD for Histograms

Enter Data: The data set was entered in Example 5.

Enter Functions and Formulas: The functions and formulas for the frequencies we want to graph were entered in Example 5.

Apply Tools: The following steps describe how to use Excel's Chart Wizard to construct a histogram.

Step 1 Select cells E2:E7

Step 2 Select the **Chart Wizard** button on the Standard toolbar

Step 3 When the **Chart Wizard-Step 1 of 4-Chart Type** dialog box appears:
    Choose **Column** in the **Chart type** list
    Choose **Clustered Column** from the **Chart sub-type** display
    Click **Next >**

Step 4 When the **Chart Wizard-Step 2 of 4-Chart Source Data** dialog box appears
    Select the **Series** tab and then
        Click in the **Category (X) Axis Labels** box
        Select cells C2:C7.
    Click **Next >**

Step 5 When the **Chart Wizard-Step 3 of 4-Chart Options** dialog box appears:
    Select the **Titles** tab and then
        Type **Hudson Auto Parts Costs** in the **Chart title** box
        Type **Parts Cost ($)** in the **Category (X)** axis box
        Type **Frequency** in the **Value (Y)** axis box
    Select the **Legend** tab and then
        Remove the check in the **Show Legend** box
    Click **Next >**

Step 6 When the **Chart Wizard-Step 4 of 4-Chart Location** dialog box appears:
    Specify the location for the new chart (we chose cell C10)
    Click **Finish**

Initial Histogram:

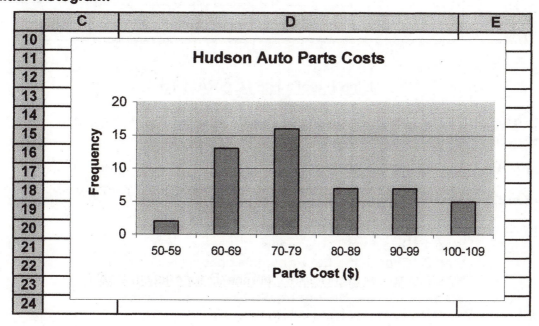

Eliminating Gaps Between Rectangles

Step 1 Right click on any rectangle in the column chart
Step 2 Select the **Format Data Series** option
Step 3 When the **Format Data Series** Option dialog box appears:
Select the **Options** tab and then
Enter **0** in the **Gap width** box
Click **OK**

You can alter the chart initially produced by Excel to look like the one below or to suit your personal preferences. A right-click on almost any item in the chart will bring up a menu of alteration options.

Finished Histogram:

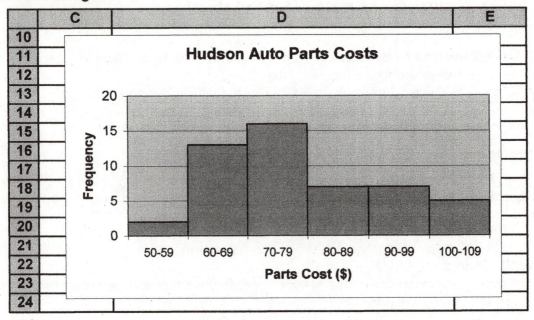

Using Excel's HISTOGRAM Tool

Excel also provides a set of data analysis tools, including the Histogram tool for constructing frequency distributions and histograms.

Enter Data: The data set was entered in Example 5.

Enter Functions and Formulas: No functions and formulas are needed.

Apply Tools: Follow these steps to use Excel's Histogram tool:
Step 1. Select the **Tools** menu
Step 2. Choose the **Data Analysis** option
Step 3. Choose **Histogram** from the list of Analysis Tools
Step 4. Fill in the **Histogram** dialog box as follows:

Histogram Dialog Box:

Histogram:

The histogram produced using the Histogram tool will look very similar to the initial histogram produced using the Chart Wizard (see above). Some editing of it is required. Follow these steps:

Step 1. Right click on the legend title (Frequency) and select **Clear**

Step 2. Left click on the horizontal axis title (Upper Limit), type **Parts Cost**, and press **Enter**

Step 3. Remove the gaps between the bars the same way we did using Chart Wizard

EXAMPLE 7

Cumulative Distributions

Refer to the auto parts cost data in Example 5. Develop a cumulative frequency distribution and a cumulative percent frequency distribution for this data.

SOLUTION 7

Using Excel's for Cumulative Distributions

Extending the worksheet shown in the solution to Example 5, we can construct the cumulative frequency and cumulative percent frequency distributions for the cost data.

Enter Data: The data set was entered in Example 5.

Enter Functions and Formulas: The functions and formulas for the frequencies we need were entered in Example 5. The first cumulative frequency (2) is simply the frequency for the first class. The second cumulative frequency (15) is equal to the frequency of the second class (13) plus the prior cumulative frequency (2), and so on.

To compute the cumulative percent frequency distribution, we must convert each cumulative frequency value to a cumulative relative frequency value and then multiply it by 100.

Formula Worksheet:

	A	B	C	D	E	F	G
1	Parts Cost		Parts Cost	Upper Limit	Frequency	Cumulative Frequency	Cumulative % Frequency
2	91		50-59	59	2	=E2	=F2/$E$8*100
3	71		60-69	69	13	=E3+F2	=F3/$E$8*100
4	104		70-79	70	16	=E4+F3	=F4/$E$8*100
5	85		80-89	89	7	=E5+F4	=F5/$E$8*100
6	62		90-99	99	7	=E6+F5	=F6/$E$8*100
7	78		100-109	109	5	=E7+F6	=F7/$E$8*100
8	69			Sum	=SUM(E2:E7)		

Note: Rows 9-51 are not shown.

Value Worksheet:

	A	B	C	D	E	F	G
1	Parts Cost		Parts Cost	Upper Limit	Frequency	Cumulative Frequency	Cumulative % Frequency
2	91		50-59	59	2	2	4
3	71		60-69	69	13	15	30
4	104		70-79	70	16	31	62
5	85		80-89	89	7	38	76
6	62		90-99	99	7	45	90
7	78		100-109	109	5	50	100
8	69			Sum	50		

Note: Rows 9-51 are not shown.

EXAMPLE 8

Ogive

Refer to the auto parts cost data in Example 5. Construct an ogive showing the cumulative percent frequency distribution for the data.

SOLUTION 8

Using Excel's CHART WIZARD for Ogives

We will continue with the worksheet shown in the solution to Example 7 to develop the ogive. We need to modify the worksheet in two ways before we can apply the Chart Wizard tool.

First, we will insert a new row between existing rows 1 and 2. The reason for a new row is that we need a starting point for the ogive showing that no data values fall below the 50-59 class. In other words, we need to create a 40-49 class with a cumulative percent frequency equal to 0.

Second, we need to change the class upper limit values. Because the class limits are 50-59, 60-69, and so on, there appear to be one-unit gaps from 59 to 60, 69 to 70, and so on. These gaps are eliminated by plotting points, on our ogive, at the midpoints of the gaps. Thus, 59.5 is used as the upper limit for the 50-59 class, 69.5 is used for the 60-69 class, and so on.

Enter Data: The data set was entered in Example 5.

Enter Functions and Formulas: The formulas for the cumulative percent frequencies we need were entered in Example 7. Now, in order to enter the new 40-49 class in the worksheet we must free up a row. To do this, we drag cells C2:G8 down one row to cells C3:G9. This frees up cells C2:G2 for the new 40-49 class information. Next, we type in the new upper limit values.

The worksheet will now look like this:

	A	B	C	D	E	F	G
1	Parts Cost		Parts Cost	Upper Limit	Frequency	Cumulative Frequency	Cumulative % Frequency
2	91		40-49	49.5	0	0	0
3	71		50-59	59.5	2	2	4
4	104		60-69	69.5	13	15	30
5	85		70-79	70.5	16	31	62
6	62		80-89	89.5	7	38	76
7	78		90-99	99.5	7	45	90
8	69		100-109	109.5	5	50	100
9	74			Sum	50		

Apply Tools: Follow these steps:

Step 1 Select cells D2:D8 and G2:G8 (To select nonadjacent cells, select cells D2:D8 and then press the Control key while selecting cells G2:G8.)

Step 2 Select the **Chart Wizard** button

Step 3 When the **Chart Wizard-Step 1 of 4-Chart Type** dialog box appears:
   Choose **XY (Scatter)** in the **Chart type** list
   Choose **Scatter with data points connected by lines** from the **Chart sub-type** display
   Click **Next >**

Step 4 When the **Chart Wizard-Step 2 of 4-Chart Source Data** dialog box appears
    Click **Next >**
Step 5 When the **Chart Wizard-Step 3 of 4-Chart Options** dialog box appears:
    Select the **Titles** tab and then
        Type **Hudson Auto Parts Costs** in the **Chart title** box
        Enter **Parts Cost ($)** in the **Value (X)** axis box
        Enter **Cumulative Percent Frequency** in the **Value (Y)** axis box
    Select the **Legend** tab and then
        Remove the check in the **Show Legend** box
        Click **Next >**
Step 6 When the **Chart Wizard-Step 4 of 4-Chart Location** dialog box appears:
    Specify the location for the new chart (we chose C12)
    Click **Finish**

Ogive:

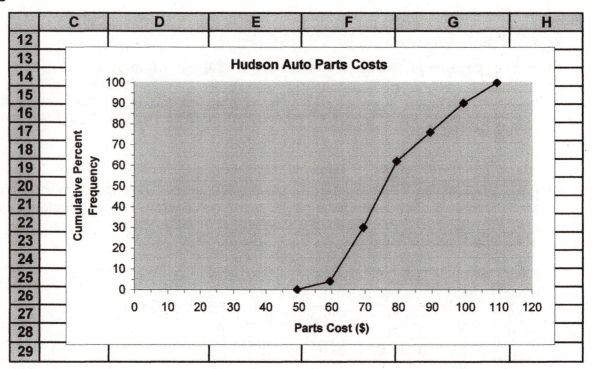

EXAMPLE 9

Stem-and-Leaf Display

Refer to the auto parts cost data in Example 5.

a) Develop a stem-and-leaf display showing both the rank order and shape of the data set.

b) Develop a stretched stem-and-leaf display using two stems for each leading digit(s).

c) Which display is better at revealing the natural grouping and variation in the data?

SOLUTION 9

a) To develop a stem-and-leaf display, we first arrange the leading digits (all but the last digit) of each data value to the left of a vertical line. To the right of the vertical line, we record the last digit for each data value as we pass through the observations in the order they are recorded. The last digit for each data value is placed on the line corresponding to its first digit.

At this point, the display will look like this:

```
 5 | 7 2
 6 | 2 9 6 2 8 5 8 8 9 7 2 9 2
 7 | 8 5 3 1 2 5 9 5 2 6 4 7 1 4 9 9 3
 8 | 0 9 0 5 8 3 2
 9 | 1 3 9 7 7 8
10 | 4 5 9 1 5
```

Next, we sort (in ascending order) the digits on each line. The result is the finished stem-and-leaf display.

```
 5 | 2 7
 6 | 2 2 2 2 5 6 7 8 8 8 9 9 9
 7 | 1 1 2 2 3 3 4 4 5 5 5 6 7 8 9 9 9
 8 | 0 0 2 3 5 8 9
 9 | 1 3 7 7 8 9
10 | 1 4 5 5 9
```

b) If we believe that our stem-and-leaf display has condensed the data too much, we can stretch the display by using two stems for each leading digit(s). All data values ending in 0, 1, 2, 3, and 4 are placed on one line, and all values ending in 5, 6, 7, 8, and 9 are placed on a second line.

The resulting stretched stem-and-leaf display will look like this:

```
 5 | 2
 5 | 7
 6 | 2 2 2 2
 6 | 5 6 7 8 8 8 9 9 9
 7 | 1 1 2 2 3 3 4 4
 7 | 5 5 5 6 7 8 9 9 9
 8 | 0 0 2 3
 8 | 5 8 9
 9 | 1 3
 9 | 7 7 8 9
10 | 1 4
10 | 5 5 9
```

c) The stretched stem-and-leaf display in (b) does a better job of revealing the dispersion of the data.

EXAMPLE 10

Crosstabulation

Ithaca Log Homes manufactures four styles of log houses that are sold in kits. The price (in $000) and style of homes the company has sold in the past year are shown below.

Price	Style	Price	Style	Price	Style
≤99	Colonial	≥100	A-Frame	≥100	Colonial
≤99	Ranch	≥100	Split-Level	≤99	Colonial
≥100	Split-Level	≤99	Colonial	≤99	A-Frame
≥100	Split-Level	≥100	Ranch	≥100	Split-Level
≤99	Colonial	≥100	Colonial	≥100	Ranch
≤99	A-Frame	≤99	A-Frame	≤99	Split-Level
≤99	Split-Level	≤99	Split-Level	≥100	Split-Level
≤99	A-Frame	≤99	Split-Level	≥100	Colonial
≥100	Ranch	≤99	Colonial	≥100	Ranch
≥100	Split-Level	≤99	Ranch	≥100	Split-Level
≤99	A-Frame	≥100	Split-Level	≤99	Colonial
≤99	Colonial	≥100	Colonial	≥100	Colonial
≥100	Ranch	≤99	Split-Level	≤99	Split-Level
≤99	Colonial				

Prepare a crosstabulation for the variables price and style.

SOLUTION 10

Using Excel's PIVOTTABLE REPORT for Crosstabulation

On a new worksheet, enter the data in columns A, B, and C.

	A	B	C	D	E
1	Home	Price ($1000)	**Style**		
2	1	≤99	Colonial		
3	2	≤99	Ranch		
4	3	≥100	Split-Level		
5	4	≥100	Split-Level		
6	5	≤99	Colonial		
7	6	≤99	A-Frame		
8	7	≤99	Split-Level		
9	8	≤99	A-Frame		
10	9	≥100	Ranch		

Note: Rows 11-41 are not shown.

Changing the Default Order for the PivotTable Report

Step 1 Select the **Tools** pull-down menu
Step 2 Choose **Options**
Step 3 When the Options dialog box appears:
      Select the **Custom lists** tab
          In the **List entries:** box, type **≤99** and press Enter, and type **≥100**
      Select **Add**
      Click **OK**
We are now ready to use the PivotTable Report to construct a crosstabulation.

Using the PivotTable Report

Step 1 Select the **Data** menu
Step 2 Choose the **PivotTable and PivotChart Report**
Step 3 When the PivotTable and PivotChart Wizard Step 1 of 3 dialog box appears:
      Choose **Microsoft Office Excel list or database**
      Choose **PivotTable**
      Click **Next >**
Step 4 When the PivotTable and PivotChart Wizard Step 2 of 3 dialog box appears:
      Enter A1:C41 in the **Range** box
      Click **Next >**
Step 5 When the PivotTable and PivotChart Wizard Step 3 of 3 dialog box appears:
      Select **New Worksheet**
      Click **Layout**
      When the **PivotTable and PivotChart Wizard – Layout** diagram appears:
         Drag the **Price ($1000)** field button to the **ROW** section of the diagram
         Drag the **Style** field button to the **COLUMN** section of the diagram
         Drag the **Home** field button to the **DATA** section of the diagram
         Double click the **Sum of Home** field button in the data section
         When the **PivotTable Field** dialog box appears:
            Choose **Count** under **Summarized by**:
            Click **OK**
         Click **OK**
      When the PivotTable and PivotChart Wizard Step 3 of 3 dialog box reappears:
         Click **Finish**

Crosstabulation:

	E	F	G	H	I	J
1	Count of Home	Style				
2	Price ($1000)	Colonial	Ranch	Split-Level	A-Frame	Grand Total
3	≤99	8	2	6	5	21
4	≥100	5	5	8	1	19
5	Grand Total	13	7	14	6	40

EXAMPLE 11

Scatter Diagram

The Panthers football team is interested in investigating the relationship, if any, between interceptions made and points scored. The following data was collected for five recent games.

x = Number of Interceptions	y = Number of Points Scored
1	14
3	24
2	18
1	17
3	27

Develop a scatter diagram to show the relationship between the two variables, number of interceptions and number of points scored.

SOLUTION 11

Using Excel's CHART WIZARD for Scatter Diagrams

Enter Data: The appropriate labels and the data for the five football games are entered into cells A1:B6.

Data Worksheet:

	A	B	C
1	Number of Interceptions	Number of Points Scored	
2	1	14	
3	3	24	
4	2	18	
5	1	17	
6	3	27	
7			

Enter Functions and Formulas: No functions or formulas are needed.

Apply Tools: The following steps describe how to use Excel's Chart Wizard to produce a scatter diagram from the data in the worksheet.

Step 1 Select cells A1:B6
Step 2 Click the **Chart Wizard** button on the standard toolbar
Step 3 When the Chart Wizard Step 1 of 4 **Chart Type** dialog box appears:
      Choose **XY (Scatter)** in the Chart type list
      Choose **Scatter** from the Chart sub-type display
      Click **Next >**

Step 4 When the Chart Wizard Step 2 of 4 **Chart Source Data** dialog box appears
        Click **Next >**

Step 5 When the Chart Wizard Step 3 of 4 **Chart Options** dialog box appears:
        Select the **Titles** tab and then
            Type **Panthers' Interceptions and Points Scored** in the Chart title box
            Type **Number of Interceptions** in the **Value (X) axis:** box
            Type **Number of Points Scored** in the **Value (Y) axis:** box
        Select the **Legend** tab and then
            Remove the check in the **Show Legend** box
            Click **Next >**

Step 6 When the Chart Wizard Step 4 of 4 **Chart Location** dialog box appears:
        Specify the location for the new chart
        Click **Finish**

Scatter Diagram:

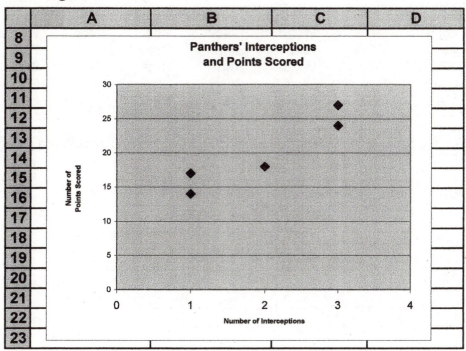

EXERCISES

EXERCISE 1

Frequency Distributions – Qualitative Data

It is time for Roger Hall, manager of new car sales at the Maxwell Ford dealership, to submit his order for new Mustang coupes. These cars will be parked in the lot, available for immediate sale to buyers who are not special-ordering a car. One of the decisions Roger must make is how many Mustangs of each color he should order. The new color options are very similar to the past year's options.

Roger believes that the colors chosen by customers who special-order their cars best reflect most customers' true color preferences. For that reason, he has taken a random sample of 40 special orders for Mustang coupes placed in the past year. The color preferences found in the sample are listed below.

Blue	Black	Green	White	Black	Red	Red	White
Black	Red	White	Blue	Blue	Green	Red	Black
Red	White	Blue	White	Red	Red	Black	Black
Green	Black	Red	Black	Blue	Black	White	Green
Blue	Red	Black	White	Black	Red	Black	Blue

Prepare a frequency distribution, relative frequency distribution, and percent frequency distribution for the data set.

EXERCISE 2

Bar Graph and Pie Chart

Refer to the Maxwell Ford data set in Exercise 1. Construct a bar graph showing the frequency distribution of the car colors. Also construct a pie chart showing the <u>percent</u> frequency distribution of the car colors.

EXERCISE 3

Frequency Distributions – Quantitative Data

Missy Walters owns a mail-order business specializing in clothing, linens, and furniture for children. She is considering offering her customers a discount on shipping charges for furniture based on the dollar-amount of the furniture order. Before Missy decides the discount policy, she needs a better understanding of the dollar-amount distribution of the furniture orders she receives.

Missy had an assistant randomly select 50 recent orders that included furniture. The assistant recorded the value, to the nearest dollar, of the furniture portion of each order. The data collected is listed below.

136	281	226	123	178	445	231	389	196	175
211	162	212	241	182	290	434	167	246	338
194	242	368	258	323	196	183	209	198	212
277	348	173	409	264	237	490	222	472	248
231	154	166	214	311	141	159	362	189	260

Prepare a frequency distribution, relative frequency distribution, and percent frequency distribution for the data set. Use your own judgment to determine the number of classes and class width that provide a distribution that will be meaningful and helpful to Missy in deciding the shipping discount policy.

EXERCISE 4

Histogram

Refer to the mail-order data in Exercise 3. Construct a histogram showing the <u>percent</u> frequency distribution of the furniture-order values in the sample.

EXERCISE 5

Cumulative Distributions and Ogive

Refer to the mail-order data in Exercise 3. Develop a cumulative frequency distribution and a cumulative percent frequency distribution for this data. Then construct an ogive showing the cumulative <u>percent</u> frequency distribution.

EXERCISE 6

Stem-and-Leaf Display

Refer to the mail-order data in Exercise 3. Develop a stem-and-leaf display for the data set. Employ the following tips to avoid having 38 stems and other shortcomings in your display.

Set the leaf unit equal to 10. In other words, convert the data to 10's of dollars. For example, the data value 226 would be treated as 22. The last digit, 6, is ignored. Stretch the display. That is, have two stems labeled 1, two stems labeled 2, and so on. Values 10-14 are entered on the first stem labeled 1, values 15-19 are entered on the second stem labeled 1, and so on.

EXERCISE 7

Crosstabulation

Tony Zamora, a real estate investor, has just moved to Clarksville and wants to learn about the local real estate market. He wants to understand, for example, the relationship between geographical segment of the city and selling price of a house, the relationship between selling price and number of bedrooms, and so on.

Tony has randomly selected 25 house-for-sale listings from the Sunday newspaper and collected the data listed below.

Segment of City	Selling Price ($000)	House Size (00 sq. ft.)	Number of Bedrooms	Number of Bathrooms	Garage Size (cars)
Northwest	290	21	4	2	2
South	95	11	2	1	0
Northeast	170	19	3	2	2
Northwest	375	38	5	4	3
West	350	24	4	3	2
South	125	10	2	2	0
West	310	31	4	4	2
West	275	25	3	2	2
Northwest	340	27	5	3	3
Northeast	215	22	4	3	2
Northwest	295	20	4	3	2
South	190	24	4	3	2
Northwest	385	36	5	4	3
West	430	32	5	4	2
South	185	14	3	2	1
South	175	18	4	2	2
Northeast	190	19	4	2	2
Northwest	330	29	4	4	3
West	405	33	5	4	3
Northeast	170	23	4	2	2
West	365	34	5	4	3
Northwest	280	25	4	2	2
South	135	17	3	1	1
Northeast	205	21	4	3	2
West	260	26	4	3	2

a) Construct a crosstabulation for the variables *segment of city* and *number of bedrooms.*

b) Compute the row percentages for your crosstabulation in part (a).

c) Comment on any apparent relationship between the variables.

EXERCISE 8

Scatter Diagram

Refer to the real estate data in Exercise 7. Develop a scatter diagram to show the relationship between the two variables *size of house* and *number of bathrooms*. Place the variable *number of bathrooms* on the horizontal axis.

SELF-TEST

TRUE/FALSE

_____ 1. The lines that connect the points plotted in an ogive cannot have a negative slope.

_____ 2. In a stem-and-leaf display, a single digit is used to define each leaf, while more than one digit can be used to define each stem.

_____ 3. At least one of the variables in a crosstabulation must be a quantitative variable.

_____ 4. There should be no gaps between adjacent bars in a histogram.

_____ 5. For a bar graph to be worthwhile, the data being displayed must involve at least two variables.

FILL-IN-THE-BLANK

1. The techniques of _____ consist of simple arithmetic and easy-to-draw graphs that can be used to summarize data quickly.

2. A _____ is a tabular summary of data showing the number of items in each of several nonoverlapping classes.

3. The last entry in a _____ distribution is always 1.00.

4. In general practice, cumulative frequency distributions are appropriate for summarizing _____ data and not _____ data.

5. Adjacent bars are touching in a histogram and are not touching in a _____.

MULTIPLE CHOICE

____ 1. Which one of the following graphical methods is most appropriate for qualitative data?
   a) ogive
   b) scatter diagram
   c) histogram
   d) pie chart

____ 2. A graphical method that will assist in the understanding of the relationship between two variables is a
   a) crosstabulation
   b) scatter diagram
   c) stem-and-leaf display
   d) bar graph

____ 3. A graphical method that can be used to show both the rank order and shape of a data set simultaneously is a
   a) relative frequency distribution
   b) pie chart
   c) stem-and-leaf display
   d) pivot table

____ 4. The proper way to construct a stem-and-leaf display for the data set {62,67,68,73,73,79,91,94,95,97} is to
   a) exclude a stem labeled '8'
   b) include a stem labeled '8' and enter no leaves on the stem
   c) include a stem labeled '(8)' and enter no leaves on the stem
   d) include a stem labeled '8' and enter one leaf value of '0' on the stem

____ 5. The graphical method presented in the chapter for displaying cumulative frequencies is
   a) an ogive
   b) a stem-and-leaf display
   c) a histogram
   d) a bar graph

ANSWERS

EXERCISES

1)

	C	D	E	F
1	Color of Car	Frequency	Relative Frequency	Percent Frequency
2	Black	12	0.300	30.0
3	Blue	7	0.175	17.5
4	Green	4	0.100	10.0
5	Red	10	0.250	25.0
6	White	7	0.175	17.5
7	Total	40	1.000	100.0

2) Bar Graph - Frequencies

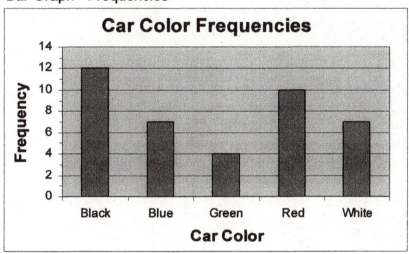

Pie Chart – Percent Frequencies

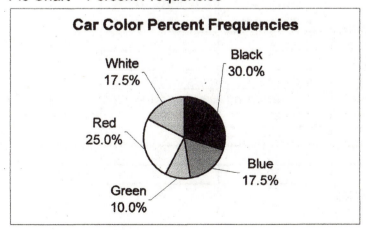

3)

	D	E	F	G
1	**Furniture Order**	**Frequency**	**Relative Frequency**	**Percent Frequency**
2	100-149	3	0.06	6
3	150-199	15	0.30	30
4	200-249	14	0.28	28
5	250-299	6	0.12	12
6	300-349	4	0.08	8
7	350-399	3	0.06	6
8	400-449	3	0.06	6
9	450-499	2	0.04	4

4)

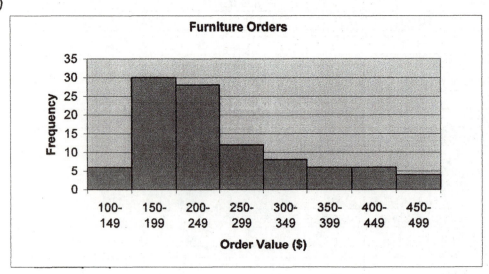

5)

	D	E	F	G
1	**Furniture Order**	**Frequency**	**Cumulative Frequency**	**Cumulative % Frequency**
2	100-149	3	3	6
3	150-199	15	18	36
4	200-249	14	32	64
5	250-299	6	38	76
6	300-349	4	42	84
7	350-399	3	45	90
8	400-449	3	48	96
9	450-499	2	50	100

6)

```
Leaf Unit = 10
1 | 2 3 4
1 | 5 5 6 6 6 7 7 7 8 8 8 9 9 9 9
2 | 0 1 1 1 1 2 2 3 3 3 4 4 4 4
2 | 5 6 6 7 8 9
3 | 1 2 3 4
3 | 6 6 8
4 | 0 3 4
4 | 7 9
```

7) a) Crosstabulation:

D	E	F	G	H	I
Count of Home	Number of Bedrooms				
Segment of City	2	3	4	5	Grand Total
Northeast	0	1	4	0	5
Northwest	0	0	4	3	7
South	2	2	2	0	6
West	0	1	3	3	7
Grand Total	2	4	13	6	25

b) Row Percentages:

D	E	F	G	H	I
Percent of Home	Number of Bedrooms				
Segment of City	2	3	4	5	Grand Total
Northeast	0.0	20.0	80.0	0.0	100.0
Northwest	0.0	0.0	57.1	42.9	100.0
South	33.3	33.3	33.3	0.0	100.0
West	0.0	14.3	42.9	42.9	100.1

c) We see that fewest bedrooms are associated with the South, and the most bedrooms are associated with the West and particularly the Northwest.

8)

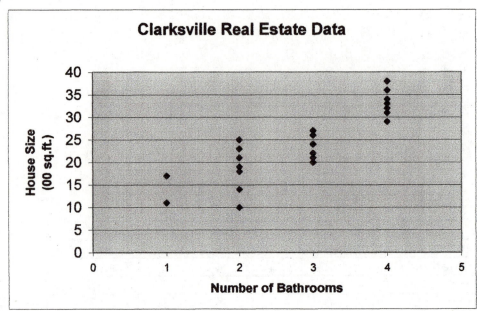

TRUE/FALSE

1) True
2) True
3) False
4) True
5) False

FILL-IN-THE-BLANK

1) exploratory data analysis
2) frequency distribution
3) cumulative relative frequency
4) quantitative, qualitative
5) bar graph

MULTIPLE CHOICE

1) d
2) b
3) c
4) b
5) a

CHAPTER 3

Descriptive Statistics: Numerical Methods

Measures of Location

Measures of Variability

Measures of Distribution Shape,
Relative Location and Detecting Outliers

Exploratory Data Analysis

Measures of Association
Between Two Variables

The Weighted Mean and
Working with Grouped Data

LEARNING OBJECTIVES

1. Understand the purpose of measures of location.

2. Be able to compute the mean, median, mode, quartiles, and various percentiles.

3. Understand the purpose of measures of variability.

4. Be able to compute the range, interquartile range, variance, standard deviation, and coefficient of variation.

5. Understand how to interpret skewness as a numerical measure of the shape of a distribution.

6. Understand how *z* scores are computed and how they are used as a measure of relative location of a data value.

7. Know how Chebyshev's theorem and the empirical rule can be used to determine the percentage of the data within a specified number of standard deviations from the mean.

8. Learn how to construct a 5-number summary and a box plot.

9. Be able to compute and interpret covariance and correlation as measures of association between two variables.

10. Be able to compute a weighted mean.

REVIEW

Measures of Location

Mean
- The mean of a data set is the average of all the data values.
- If the data are from a sample, the mean is denoted by $\bar{x}$.

$$\bar{x} = \frac{\sum x_i}{n}$$

- If the data are from a population, the mean is denoted by μ (mu).

$$\mu = \frac{\sum x_i}{N}$$

Median
- The median of a data set is the value in the middle when the data items are arranged in ascending order.
- If there are an odd number of items, the median is the value of the middle item.
- If there is an even number of items, the median is the average of the values for the middle two items.
- The median is most often reported for annual income and property value data because a few extremely large values can inflate the mean, making it misleading.

Mode
- The mode of a data set is the value that occurs with greatest frequency.
- The greatest frequency can occur at two or more different values.
- If the data have exactly two modes, the data are bimodal.
- If the data have more than two modes, the data are multimodal.

Percentiles
- The pth percentile of a data set is a value such that at least p percent of the items take on this value or less and at least $(100 - p)$ percent of the items take on this value or more.
  - Arrange the data in ascending order.
  - Compute index i, the position of the pth percentile.

$$i = (p/100)n$$

- If i is not an integer, round up. The pth percentile is the value in the ith position.
- If i is an integer, the pth percentile is the average of the values in positions i and $i + 1$.

Quartiles
- Quartiles are specific percentiles.
- First quartile = 25th percentile.
- Second quartile = 50th percentile = median.
- Third quartile = 75th percentile.

Measures of Variability

Range
- The range of a data set is the difference between the largest and smallest data values.
- It is the simplest measure of variability.
- It is very sensitive to the smallest and largest data values.

Interquartile Range
- The interquartile range of a data set is the difference between the third quartile and the first quartile.
- It is the range for the middle 50% of the data.
- It overcomes the sensitivity to extreme data values.

Variance
- The variance is the average of the squared differences between each data value and the mean.
- If the data set is a sample, the variance is denoted by s^2.

$$s^2 = \frac{\sum (x_i - \overline{x})^2}{n - 1}$$

- If the data set is a population, the variance is denoted by σ^2.

$$\sigma^2 = \frac{\sum (x_i - \mu)^2}{N}$$

Standard Deviation
- The standard deviation of a data set is the positive square root of the variance.
- It is measured in the same units as the data, making it more easily comparable, than the variance, to the mean.
- If the data set is a sample, the standard deviation is denoted s.

$$s = \sqrt{s^2}$$

- If the data set is a population, the standard deviation is denoted σ (sigma).

$$\sigma = \sqrt{\sigma^2}$$

Coefficient of Variation
- The coefficient of variation indicates how large the standard deviation is in relation to the mean.
- If the data set is a sample, the sample coefficient of variation is computed as:

$$\frac{s}{\bar{x}}(100)$$

- If the data set is a population, the population coefficient of variation is computed as::

$$\frac{\sigma}{\mu}(100)$$

Measures of Distribution Shape, Relative Location, and Detecting Outliers

Skewness
- An important measure of the shape of a distribution is skewness.
- For data skewed to the left, the skewness is negative; for data skewed to the right, the skewness is positive; if the data are symmetric, the skewness is zero.
- When the data are positively skewed, the mean will usually be greater than the median.
- When the data are negatively skewed, the mean will usually be less than the median.

z-Score
- The z-score is often called the standardized value.
- z denotes the number of standard deviations a data value x_i is from the mean.

$$z_i = \frac{x_i - \bar{x}}{s}$$

- A data value less than the sample mean will have a z-score less than zero.
- A data value greater than the sample mean will have a z-score greater than zero.
- A data value equal to the sample mean will have a z-score of zero.

Chebyshev's Theorem
- At least $(1 - 1/z^2)$ of the items in any data set will be within z standard deviations of the mean, where z is any value greater than 1.
- At least 75% of the items must be within $z = 2$ standard deviations of the mean.
- At least 89% of the items must be within $z = 3$ standard deviations of the mean.
- At least 94% of the items must be within $z = 4$ standard deviations of the mean.

Empirical Rule
- The empirical rule is based on the normal (bell-shaped) probability distribution.
- Approximately 68% of the data values will be within 1 standard deviation of the mean.
- Approximately 95% of the data values will be within 2 standard deviations of the mean.
- Almost all of the items (99.7%) will be within 3 standard deviations of the mean.

Detecting Outliers
- An outlier is an unusually small or unusually large value in a data set.
- A data value with a z-score less than -3 or more than +3 might be considered an outlier.
- An outlier might be an incorrectly recorded data value, a data value that was incorrectly included in the data set, or a correctly recorded data value that belongs in the data set.

Exploratory Data Analysis

Five-Number Summary
- The five numbers used to summarize the data are: smallest value, first quartile, median, third quartile, and largest value.

Box Plot
- A box is drawn with its ends located at the first and third quartiles.
- A vertical line is drawn in the box at the location of the median.
- Limits are located (not drawn) using the interquartile range (IQR).
  - The lower limit is located 1.5(IQR) below Q1.
  - The upper limit is located 1.5(IQR) above Q3.
- Data outside these limits are considered outliers and are shown with the symbol * .
- Dashed lines are drawn from the ends of the box to the smallest and largest data values inside the limits.

Measures of Association Between Two Variables

Covariance
- The covariance is a measure of the linear association between two variables.
- Positive values indicate a positive relationship.
- Negative values indicate a negative relationship.
- If the data set is a sample, the covariance is denoted by s_{xy}.

$$s_{xy} = \frac{\sum (x_i - \bar{x})(y_i - \bar{y})}{n-1}$$

- If the data set is a population, the covariance is denoted by σ_{xy}.

$$\sigma_{xy} = \frac{\sum (x_i - \mu_x)(y_i - \mu_y)}{N}$$

Correlation Coefficient
- The coefficient can take on values between -1 and +1.
- Values near -1 indicate a strong negative linear relationship.
- Values near +1 indicate a strong positive linear relationship.
- If the data sets are samples, the coefficient is r_{xy}.

$$r_{xy} = \frac{s_{xy}}{s_x s_y}$$

- If the data sets are populations, the coefficient is ρ_{xy}.

$$\rho_{xy} = \frac{\sigma_{xy}}{\sigma_x \sigma_y}$$

Weighted Mean
- When the mean is computed by giving each data value a weight that reflects its importance, it is referred to as a weighted mean, $\bar{x}$.

$$x_{wt} = (\Sigma w_i x_i)/\Sigma w_i$$

where: x_i = value of observation i and w_i = weight for observation i

- In the computation of a grade point average (GPA), the weights are the number of credit hours earned for each grade.
- When data values vary in importance, the analyst must choose the weight that best reflects the importance of each value.
- The weighted mean computation can be used to obtain approximations of the mean, variance, and standard deviation for grouped data.

Working with Grouped Data

Mean for Grouped Data
- To compute the weighted mean, we treat the midpoint (M_i) of each class i as though it were the mean of all items in the class.
- We compute a weighted mean of the class midpoints using the class frequencies (f_i) as weights.
- If the data set is a sample, the approximated mean is:

$$\bar{x} = \frac{\sum f_i M_i}{n}$$

- If the data set is a population, the approximated mean is:

$$\mu = \frac{\sum f_i M_i}{N}$$

Variance for Grouped Data
- If the data set is a sample, the approximated variance is:

$$s^2 = \frac{\sum f_i (M_i - \bar{x})^2}{n-1}$$

- If the data set is a population, the approximated variance is:

$$\sigma^2 = \frac{\sum f_i (M_i - \mu)^2}{N}$$

Standard Deviation for Grouped Data
- If the data set is a sample, the approximated standard deviation is:

$$s = \sqrt{s^2}$$

- If the data set is a population, the approximated standard deviation is:

$$\sigma = \sqrt{\sigma^2}$$

KEY CONCEPTS

CONCEPT	EXAMPLES	EXERCISES
Measures of Location		
Mean	①⑤	1,5
Median	①⑤	1,5
Mode	①⑤	1,5
Percentiles	②	2
Quartiles	②	2
Measures of Variability		
Range	③⑤	3,5
Interquartile Range	③	3
Variance	④⑤	4,5
Standard Deviation	④⑤	4,5
Coefficient of Variation	④	4
Measures of Relative Location		
z-Scores	⑥	6
Chebyshev's Theorem	⑥	6
Empirical Rule	⑥	6
Detecting Outliers	⑥	6
Exploratory Data Analysis		
Five-Number Summary	7	7
Box Plot	7	7
Measures of Assoc. Between Two Variables		
Covariance	⑧	8
Correlation Coefficient	⑧	8
Weighted Mean	9	9
Grouped Data		
Mean	⑩	10
Variance	⑩	10
Standard Deviation	⑩	10

◯ Excel Used

EXAMPLES

EXAMPLE 1

Mean, Median, and Mode

A sample of monthly rent values ($) for efficiency apartments in a particular city was taken. The data collected from the 70-apartment sample is listed below in ascending order. Determine the mean, median, and mode for this data set.

```
525  440  450  615  480  510  575  430  440  450
470  485  515  575  430  440  450  470  490  525
580  435  445  450  472  490  425  590  435  445
450  475  490  525  600  435  445  460  475  500
535  600  435  445  460  475  500  549  600  435
445  460  480  500  550  600  440  450  465  480
500  570  615  440  450  465  480  510  570  465
```

SOLUTION 1

Using a Calculator

Sample Mean:

$$\bar{x} = \frac{\sum x_i}{n} = \frac{34,356}{70} = 490.8$$

Sample Median:
- First, arrange the data in ascending order.

```
425  430  430  435  435  435  435  435  440  440
440  440  440  445  445  445  445  445  450  450
450  450  450  450  450  460  460  460  465  465
465  470  470  472  475  475  475  480  480  480
480  485  490  490  490  500  500  500  500  510
510  515  525  525  525  535  549  550  570  570
575  575  580  590  600  600  600  600  615  615
```

- Compute index i, the position of the median (or 50th percentile).

$$i = (p/100)n = (50/100)70 = 35$$

- Because the value of i is an integer (35), the median (or 50th percentile) is the average of the values in the 35th and 36th positions.

$$\text{Median (or } 50^{th} \text{ Percentile)} = (475 + 475)/2 = 475$$

Sample Mode:
   Mode = 450 because it is the value with the greatest frequency (7).

Using Excel's AVERAGE, MEDIAN, and MODE Functions

Enter Data: Labels and the rent amounts are entered in cells A1:B71 of the worksheet.

Enter Functions and Formulas: Excel's AVERAGE function can be used to compute the mean. Similarly, Excel's MEDIAN and MODE functions can be used to compute the median and mode. The labels Mean, Median, and Mode are entered into cells D2:D4.

Formula Worksheet:

	A	B	C	D	E
1	Apart-ment	Monthly Rent ($)			
2	1	525		Mean	=AVERAGE(B2:B71)
3	2	440		Median	=MEDIAN(B2:B71)
4	3	450		Mode	=MODE(B2:B71)

Note: Rows 5-71 are not shown.

Value Worksheet:

	A	B	C	D	E
1	Apart-ment	Monthly Rent ($)			
2	1	525		Mean	490.4
3	2	440		Median	475.0
4	3	450		Mode	450.0

Note: Rows 5-71 are not shown.

EXAMPLE 2

Percentiles and Quartiles

Refer again to the apartment rent data presented in Example 1. What is the 80th percentile? What is the third quartile?

SOLUTION 2

Using a Calculator

80th Percentile:
- First, arrange the data in ascending order.

    (See Solution 1 above for the ordered data.)

- Compute index i, the position of the 80th percentile.

    $i = (p/100)n = (80/100)70 = 56$

- Because the value of i is an integer (56), the 80th percentile is the average of the values in the 56th and 57th positions.

$$80^{th} \text{ Percentile} = (535 + 549)/2 = 542$$

3rd Quartile:
- First, arrange the data in ascending order.

    (See Solution 1 above for the ordered data.)

- Compute index i, the position of the 3rd Quartile (or 75th percentile).

    $$i = (p/100)n = (75/100)70 = 52.5$$

- Because the value of i is not an integer (52.5), it is rounded up to the nearest integer. Hence, the 3rd Quartile (or 75th percentile) is the value in the 53rd position.

    $$3^{rd} \text{ Quartile} = 525$$

Using Excel's PERCENTILE and QUARTILE Functions

Keep in mind that for small data sets, Excel's PERCENTILE and QUARTILE functions do not always provide results that satisfy the true definition of percentiles and quartiles.

Enter Data: The rent data are already entered (see solution to Example 1).

Enter Functions and Formulas: The label "80th Percentile" is entered into cell D1. The PERCENTILE function is entered into cell D2.

Formula Worksheet:

	A	B	C	D	E
1	Apart-ment	Monthly Rent ($)		80th Percentile	
2	1	525		=PERCENTILE(B2:B71,.8)	
3	2	440			
4	3	450			

Note: Rows 5-71 are not shown.

We see in the worksheet below that Excel returns a value of 537.8 for the 80th percentile. This differs slightly from the value of 542 that we determined using a calculator and the method outlined in the textbook.

Value Worksheet:

	A	B	C	D	E
1	Apart-ment	Monthly Rent ($)		80th Percentile	
2	1	525		537.8	
3	2	440			
4	3	450			

Note: Rows 5-71 are not shown.

Enter Functions and Formulas: The label "3rd Quartile" is entered into cell D1. The QUARTILE function is entered into cell D2.

Formula Worksheet:

	A	B	C	D	E
1	Apart-ment	Monthly Rent ($)		3rd Quartile	
2	1	525		=QUARTILE(B2:B71,3)	
3	2	440			
4	3	450			

Note: Rows 5-71 are not shown.

We see in the worksheet below that Excel returns a value of 522.5 for the 3rd Quartile. This differs slightly from the value of 525 that we determined using a calculator and the method outlined in the textbook.

Value Worksheet:

	A	B	C	D	E
1	Apart-ment	Monthly Rent ($)		3rd Quartile	
2	1	525		522.5	
3	2	440			
4	3	450			

Note: Rows 5-71 are not shown.

Using Excel's RANK AND PERCENTILE Tool

Excel's Rank and Percentile tool computes the rank and percentile for each observation in the data set.

Enter Data: The rent data and labels are already entered (see solution to Example 1).

Enter Functions and Formulas: No functions or formulas are needed.

Apply Tools: The following steps describe how to use Excel's Rank and Percentile tool.

Step 1 Select the **Tools** menu
Step 2 Choose **Data Analysis**
Step 3 Choose **Rank and Percentile** from the list of Analysis Tools
Step 4 When the Rank and Percentile dialog box appears:

Rank and Percentile Dialog Box

Value Worksheet

	B	C	D	E	F	G
1	**Rent**		*Point*	*Rent*	*Rank*	*Percent*
2	525		4	615	1	98.50%
3	440		63	615	1	98.50%
4	450		35	600	3	92.70%
5	615		42	600	3	92.70%
6	480		49	600	3	92.70%
7	510		56	600	3	92.70%
8	575		28	590	7	91.30%
9	430		21	580	8	89.80%
10	440		7	575	9	86.90%
11	450		14	575	9	86.90%
12	470		62	570	11	84.00%
13	485		69	570	11	84.00%
14	515		55	550	13	82.60%
15	575		48	549	14	81.10%
16	430		41	535	15	79.70%

EXAMPLE 3

Range and Interquartile Range

Refer again to the apartment rent data presented in Example 1. Compute the range and interquartile range for the data set.

SOLUTION 3

Using a Calculator

Range:

The range equals the largest data value minus the smallest data value. We can see from Solution 1 that the largest value is 615 and the smallest value is 425.

$$Range = 615 - 425 = 190$$

Interquartile Range:

The interquartile range equals the 3rd quartile minus the 1st quartile (or 75th percentile minus the 25th percentile). We must determine the 75th percentile and 25th percentile using the steps outlined in Solution 2. Executing those steps, we find that the 75th percentile is 525, and the 25th percentile is 445.

$$Interquartile\ Range = Q3 - Q1 = 525 - 445 = 80$$

Using Excel's MIN, MAX and QUARTILE Functions

Keep in mind that for small data sets, Excel's QUARTILE function does not always provide results that satisfy the true definition of quartiles.

Enter Data: The rent data and labels are already entered (see solution to Example 1).

Enter Functions and Formulas: See the formula worksheet below.

Formula Worksheet:

	A	B	C	D	E
1	**Apart-ment**	**Monthly Rent ($)**			
2	1	525		**Maximum**	=MAX(B2:B71)
3	2	440		**Minimum**	=MIN(B2:B71)
4	3	450		**Range**	=E2-E3
5	4	615			
6	5	480		**3rd Quartile**	=QUARTILE(B2:B71,3)
7	6	435		**1st Quartile**	=QUARTILE(B2:B71,1)
8	7	435		**Interquartile Range**	=E6-E7

Note: Rows 9-71 are not shown.

We see in the worksheet below that Excel returns a value of 76.25 for the interquartile range. This differs slightly from the value of 80 that we determined using a calculator and the method outlined in the textbook.

Value Worksheet:

	A	B	C	D	E
1	**Apart-ment**	**Monthly Rent ($)**			
2	1	525		**Maximum**	615
3	2	440		**Minimum**	425
4	3	450		**Range**	190
5	4	615			
6	5	480		**3rd Quartile**	522.50
7	6	435		**1st Quartile**	446.25
8	7	435		**Interquartile Range**	76.25

Note: Rows 9-71 are not shown.

EXAMPLE 4

Variance, Standard Deviation, and Coefficient of Variation

Refer again to the apartment rent data presented in Example 1. Compute the sample variance, sample standard deviation, and the coefficient of variation.

SOLUTION 4

Using Excel's VAR and STDEV Functions

We will use Excel functions to compute the sample variance and standard deviation. There is no function in Excel for solely computing the coefficient of variation, so we will use a formula.

Enter Data: The rent data and labels are already entered (see solution to Example 1).

Enter Functions and Formulas: In order to compute the coefficient of variation, we need the value of the mean that was found in the solution to Example 1. The sample variance is computed by entering the following formula into cell E5:

$$=VAR(B2:B71)$$

The sample standard deviation is computed by entering the following formula into cell E6:

$$=STDEV(B2:B71)$$

The formula for the coefficient of variation (CV) is:

$$\frac{Standard\ Deviation}{Mean} \times 100$$

To compute the CV we enter the formula =E6/E2*100 into cell E7. Last, we enter labels to identify the output.

Formula Worksheet:

	A	B	C	D	E
1	Apart-ment	Monthly Rent ($)			
2	1	525		Mean	=AVERAGE(B2:B71)
3	2	440		Median	=MEDIAN(B2:B71)
4	3	450		Mode	=MODE(B2:B71)
5	4	615		Variance	=VAR(B2:B71)
6	5	480		Std. Dev.	=STDEV(B2:B71)
7	6	510		C.V.	=E6/E2*100

Note: Rows 8-71 are not shown.

Value Worksheet:

	A	B	C	D	E
1	Apart-ment	Monthly Rent ($)			
2	1	525		Mean	490.80
3	2	440		Median	475.00
4	3	450		Mode	450.00
5	4	615		Variance	2996.16
6	5	480		Std. Dev.	54.74
7	6	510		C.V.	11.15

Note: Rows 8-71 are not shown.

EXAMPLE 5

Descriptive Statistics

Refer again to the apartment rent data presented in Example 1. Use Excel's Descriptive Statistics tool to compute a variety of descriptive statistics at once rather than one by one using individual functions such as AVERAGE, MEDIAN, and STDEV.

SOLUTION 5

Using Excel's DESCRIPTIVE STATISTICS Tool

Enter Data: The rent data and labels are already entered (see solution to Example 1).

Enter Functions and Formulas: No functions or formulas are needed.

Apply Tools: The following steps describe how to use Excel's Descriptive Statistics tool.

Step 1 Select the **Tools** pull-down menu
Step 2 Choose the **Data Analysis** option
Step 3 Choose **Descriptive Statistics** from the list of Analysis Tools

Descriptive Statistics Dialog Box:

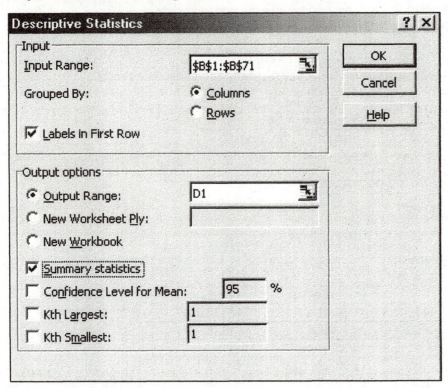

Value Worksheet:

	A	B	C	D	E
1	Apart-ment	Monthly Rent ($)		*Monthly Rent ($)*	
2	1	525		Mean	490.8
3	2	440		Standard Error	6.542348114
4	3	450		Median	475
5	4	615		Mode	450
6	5	480		Standard Deviation	54.73721146
7	6	510		Sample Variance	2996.162319
8	7	575		Kurtosis	-0.334093298
9	8	430		Skewness	0.924330473
10	9	440		Range	190
11	10	450		Minimum	425
12	11	470		Maximum	615
13	12	485		Sum	34356
14	13	515		Count	70

EXAMPLE 6

z-Scores, Chebyshev's Theorem, Empirical Rule, and Outliers

Refer again to the apartment rent data presented in Example 1. Compute the z-score for every value in the data set and then answer the following questions.

a) What is the z-score for the minimum value in the data set? What is the z-score for the maximum value in the data set?

b) Based on Chebyshev's Theorem, what percentage of the data values must be within 1.5 standard deviations of the mean. What percentage of the data values <u>actually</u> falls within +/- 1.5 standard deviations?

c) Apply the empirical rule to the data set. How close are the actually percentages to the percentages dictated by the empirical rule?

d) Using +/- 3 standard deviations as the criterion, identify any outliers in the data set.

SOLUTION 6

Using Excel

Enter Data: The rent data and labels are already entered (see solution to Example 1).

Enter Functions and Formulas: We need the mean and standard deviation in order to compute z-scores, so we will use the worksheet we developed in Example 4. First, sort the data in cells B2:B71 in ascending order. Next, expand column C and enter the label **z-Score** into cell C1. The formula for computing a z-score is:

$$z_i = \frac{x_i - \bar{x}}{s}$$

Formula Worksheet:

	A	B	C	D	E
1	Apart-ment	Monthly Rent ($)	z-Score		
2	1	425	=(B2-$E$2)/$E$6	Mean	=AVERAGE(B2:B71)
3	2	430	=(B3-$E$2)/$E$6	Median	=MEDIAN(B2:B71)
4	3	430	=(B4-$E$2)/$E$6	Mode	=MODE(B2:B71)
5	4	435	=(B5-$E$2)/$E$6	Variance	=VAR(B2:B71)
6	5	435	=(B6-$E$2)/$E$6	Std. Dev.	=STDEV(B2:B71)
7	6	435	=(B7-$E$2)/$E$6	C.V.	=E6/E2*100

Note: Rows 8-71 are not shown.

Value Worksheet:

	A	B	C	D	E
1	Apart-ment	Monthly Rent ($)	z-Score		
2	1	425	-1.20	Mean	490.80
3	2	430	-1.11	Median	475.00
4	3	430	-1.11	Mode	450.00
5	4	435	-1.02	Variance	2996.16
6	5	435	-1.02	Std. Dev.	54.74
7	6	435	-1.02	C.V.	11.15

Note: Rows 8-71 are not shown.

a) From the resulting worksheet we see that the z-scores for the minimum and maximum data values are −1.20 and 2.27, respectively. (Scroll down to the last data value in your worksheet to see the last z-score of 2.27.)

b) Let $z = 1.5$ with $\bar{x} = 490.80$ and $s = 54.74$. At least $(1 - 1/(1.5)^2) = 1 - 0.44 = 0.56$ or 56% of the rent values must be between:

$$\bar{x} - z(s) = 490.80 - 1.5(54.74) = \underline{409}$$
$$\text{and}$$
$$\bar{x} + z(s) = 490.80 + 1.5(54.74) = \underline{573}$$

Actually, 86% of the data values are between 409 and 573.

c)

	Interval	Actual % in Interval	Empir.Rule % in Interval
Within +/- 1s	436.06 to 545.54	48/70 = 69%	approx. 68%
Within +/- 2s	381.32 to 600.28	68/70 = 97%	approx. 95%
Within +/- 3s	326.58 to 655.02	70/70 = 100%	almost 100%

d) The most extreme z-scores are -1.20 and 2.27. Using $|z| \geq 3$ as the criterion for an outlier, there are no outliers in this data set.

EXAMPLE 7

Five-Number Summary and Box Plot

Refer again to the apartment rent data presented in Example 1. Provide a five-number summary of the data set and graph your results using a box plot.

SOLUTION 7

The five-number summary includes the minimum data value, first quartile, median, third quartile, and maximum data value. We solved for all of these values in previous examples.

Five-Number Summary:

Minimum	= 425	(computed in Example 5)
First Quartile	= 445	(computed in Example 3)
Median	= 475	(computed in Example 5)
Third Quartile	= 525	(computed in Example 3)
Maximum	= 615	(computed in Example 5)

Box Plot:

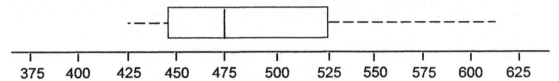

EXAMPLE 8

Covariance and Correlation Coefficient

Angela Lopez, a golf instructor, is interested in investigating the relationship between a golfer's average driving distance and 18-hole score. She recently observed the performance of six golfers during one round of a tournament and measured, as accurately as possible, the distances (yards) of their drives and noted their final scores. She then computed each golfer's average drive distance for 18 holes. The results of her sample are shown below.

Golfer	Avg. Drive (yards)	18-Hole Score
1	277.6	69
2	259.5	71
3	269.1	70
4	267.0	70
5	255.6	71
6	272.9	69

Compute and interpret both the sample covariance and the sample correlation coefficient.

SOLUTION 8

Using Excel's COVAR and CORREL Functions

Excel provides functions for computing the covariance and correlation coefficient. However, the covariance function treats the data as if it were a population, while the correlation coefficient function treats the data as if it were a sample.

Enter Data: Labels and data on the six golfers are entered into cells A1:C7 of a new worksheet. The rent data and labels are already entered (see solution to Example 1).

Enter Functions and Formulas: Excel's covariance function, COVAR, can be used to compute the <u>population</u> covariance. To convert the population covariance to the sample covariance we multiply the former by $n/(n-1)$. In this example, the sample size is 6, so the conversion factor is $6/(6-1) = 6/5$.

Excel's correlation function, CORREL, can be used to compute the sample correlation coefficient.

Formula Worksheet:

	A	B	C	D	E
1	Golfer	Avg. Drive Distance	18-Hole Score		
2	1	277.6	69	Popul. Covariance	=COVAR(B2:B7,C2:C7)
3	2	259.5	71	Sample Covariance	=6/5*E2
4	3	269.1	70		
5	4	267.0	70	Samp. Correlation	=CORREL(B2:B7,C2:C7)
6	5	255.6	71		
7	6	272.9	69		

The value worksheet below shows a sample covariance value of –7.08 that indicates a negative relationship between driving distance and final score. This is not surprising. Unless a golfer's putting performance is relatively poor, we would expect longer driving distances to lead to lower final scores. To judge the strength of the relationship between the two variables we turn to interpreting the correlation coefficient. Its value is -.96 that indicates (because it is so close to −1.00) an exceptionally strong negative correlation between driving distance and final score.

Value Worksheet:

	A	B	C	D	E
1	Golfer	Avg. Drive Distance	18-Hole Score		
2	1	277.6	69	Popul. Covariance	-5.90
3	2	259.5	71	Sample Covariance	-7.08
4	3	269.1	70		
5	4	267.0	70	Samp. Correlation	-0.96
6	5	255.6	71		
7	6	272.9	69		

EXAMPLE 9

Weighted Mean

Del Michaels had a successful morning, or so he thinks, selling 1300 surplus notebook computers over the telephone to three commercial customers. The three customers were not equally skillful at negotiating a low unit price. Customer A bought 600 computers for $1252 each, B bought 300 units at $1310 each, and C bought 400 at $1375 each.

Del's manager told him he expected Del to sell, by the end of the day, the 2500 surplus computers at an average price of $1312 each. How is Del doing so far? What should be Del's strategy in the afternoon, considering his morning results?

SOLUTION 9

Using a Calculator

To determine the average price he got for the 1300 computers Del sold we must compute a weighted average of the three prices he charged, not a simple average (because he did not sell the same number of computers at each price).
The formula for computing a weighted mean is:

$$x_{wt} = (\Sigma w_i x_i)/\Sigma w_i$$

where: x_i = value of observation i
w_i = weight for observation i

The weight we place on each price, in computing the average price, is the number of computers sold at that price. Essentially, the steps to computing a weighted mean in this example are: 1) multiply each price by its respective weight, 2) sum the products from step 1, and 3) divide the sum from step 2 by the sum of the weights.

$$(600(1252) + 300(1310) + 400(1375))/1300 = 1303.23$$

Del is not meeting his manager's expectation of an average selling price of $1312. He under priced the computers he sold by an average of $8.77. He needs to sell the remaining 1200 computers at an average price of $1321.50 in order to meet expectations.

EXAMPLE 10

Grouped Data

Given below is a sample of 70 monthly rents for one-bedroom apartments presented as grouped data in the form of a frequency distribution. Compute the sample mean, variance, and standard deviation.

Rent ($)	Frequency	Rent ($)	Frequency
420-439	8	520-539	4
440-459	17	540-559	2
460-479	12	560-579	4
480-499	8	580-599	2
500-519	7	600-619	6

SOLUTION 10

Using Excel for Grouped Data

Computing the Sample Mean:

Enter Data: Labels, rent classes and frequencies are entered into a new worksheet.

Enter Functions and Formulas: First, we compute the midpoint of each rent class. Midpoint of a Class = (Lower Limit + Upper Limit)/2. For example, the midpoint of the first class is (420 + 439)/2 = 429.5. Next, we multiply the midpoint of each class by the class' frequency. Next, we sum the class frequencies. Then, we sum the products of the frequencies and the class midpoints. Finally, we compute the sample mean.

Formula Worksheet:

	A	B	C	D
		Frequency	Class Midpt.	
1	Rent ($)	f_i	M_i	$f_i M_i$
2	420-439	8	429.5	=B2*C2
3	440-459	17	449.5	=B3*C3
4	460-479	12	469.5	=B4*C4
5	480-499	8	489.5	=B5*C5
6	500-519	7	509.5	=B6*C6
7	520-539	4	529.5	=B7*C7
8	540-559	2	549.5	=B8*C8
9	560-579	4	569.5	=B9*C9
10	580-599	2	589.5	=B10*C10
11	600-619	6	609.5	=B11*C11
12	Totals	=SUM(B2:B11)		=SUM(D2:D11)
13	Sample Mean	=D12/B12		

Value Worksheet:

	A	B	C	D
		Frequency	Class Midpt.	
1	Rent ($)	f_i	M_i	$f_i M_i$
2	420-439	8	429.5	3436.0
3	440-459	17	449.5	7641.5
4	460-479	12	469.5	5634.0
5	480-499	8	489.5	3916.0
6	500-519	7	509.5	3566.5
7	520-539	4	529.5	2118.0
8	540-559	2	549.5	1099.0
9	560-579	4	569.5	2278.0
10	580-599	2	589.5	1179.0
11	600-619	6	609.5	3657.0
12	Totals	70		34525.0
13	Sample Mean	493.21		

Computing the Sample Variance and Standard Deviation:

Enter Data: We will continue with the above worksheet. We will erase the contents of column D and use the column for new calculations.

Enter Functions and Formulas: We begin by subtracting the sample mean from the midpoint of each of the rent classes to get the deviations. Next, we square the deviations. Next, we multiply the squared deviations by their respective class frequencies. And then we sum these products.

Now we are ready to compute the sample variance. The sample standard deviation is the square root of the sample variance.

Formula Worksheet:

	A	B	C	D	E	F
1	Rent ($)	Frequency f_i	Class Midpt. M_i	Deviation M_i - Mean	Sq. Dev.	f_i(Sq.Dev.)
2	420-439	8	429.5	=C2-$B$13	=D2^2	=B2*E2
3	440-459	17	449.5	=C3-$B$13	=D3^2	=B3*E3
4	460-479	12	469.5	=C4-$B$13	=D4^2	=B4*E4
5	480-499	8	489.5	=C5-$B$13	=D5^2	=B5*E5
6	500-519	7	509.5	=C6-$B$13	=D6^2	=B6*E6
7	520-539	4	529.5	=C7-$B$13	=D7^2	=B7*E7
8	540-559	2	549.5	=C8-$B$13	=D8^2	=B8*E8
9	560-579	4	569.5	=C9-$B$13	=D9^2	=B9*E9
10	580-599	2	589.5	=C10-$B$13	=D10^2	=B10*E10
11	600-619	6	609.5	=C11-$B$13	=D11^2	=B11*E11
12	Totals	=SUM(B2:B11)				=SUM(F2:F11)
13	Sample Mean	493.21				
14	Sample Var.	=F12/(B12-1)				
15	Sample S.D.	=SQRT(B14)				

Value Worksheet:

	A	B	C	D	E	F
1	Rent ($)	Frequency f_i	Class Midpt. M_i	Deviation M_i - Mean	Sq. Dev.	f_i(Sq.Dev.)
2	420-439	8	429.5	-63.7	4058.96	32471.71
3	440-459	17	449.5	-43.7	1910.56	32479.59
4	460-479	12	469.5	-23.7	562.16	6745.97
5	480-499	8	489.5	-3.7	13.76	110.11
6	500-519	7	509.5	16.3	265.36	1857.55
7	520-539	4	529.5	36.3	1316.96	5267.86
8	540-559	2	549.5	56.3	3168.56	6337.13
9	560-579	4	569.5	76.3	5820.16	23280.66
10	580-599	2	589.5	96.3	9271.76	18543.53
11	600-619	6	609.5	116.3	13523.36	81140.18
12	Totals	70				208234.29
13	Sample Mean	493.21				
14	Sample Var.	3017.89				
15	Sample S.D.	54.94				

EXERCISES

EXERCISE 1

Mean, Median, and Mode

Missy Walters owns a mail-order business specializing in clothing, linens, and furniture for children. She is considering offering her customers a discount on shipping charges for furniture based on the dollar-amount of the furniture order. Before Missy decides the discount policy, she needs a better understanding of the dollar-amount distribution of the furniture orders she receives.

Missy had an assistant randomly select 50 recent orders that included furniture. The assistant recorded the value, to the nearest dollar, of the furniture portion of each order. The data collected is listed below.

136	281	226	123	178	445	231	389	196	175
211	162	212	241	182	290	434	167	246	340
194	242	368	258	323	196	183	209	198	210
277	348	173	409	264	237	490	222	472	248
231	154	166	214	311	141	159	362	189	260

Determine the mean, median, and mode for this data set.

EXERCISE 2

Percentiles and Quartiles

Refer again to the furniture data presented in Exercise 1. What is the 80th percentile? What is the first quartile?

EXERCISE 3

Range and Interquartile Range

Refer again to the furniture data presented in Exercise 1. Compute the range and interquartile range for the data set.

EXERCISE 4

Variance, Standard Deviation, and Coefficient of Variation

Refer again to the furniture data presented in Exercise 1. Compute the sample variance, sample standard deviation, and the coefficient of variation.

EXERCISE 5

Descriptive Statistics

Refer again to the furniture data presented in Exercise 1. Use Excel's Descriptive Statistics tool to compute a variety of descriptive statistics at once rather than one by one using individual functions such as AVERAGE, MEDIAN, and STDEV.

EXERCISE 6

z-Scores, Chebyshev's Theorem, Empirical Rule, and Outliers

Refer again to the furniture data presented in Exercise 1. Compute the z-score for every value in the data set and then answer the following questions.

a) What is the z-score for the minimum value in the data set? What is the z-score for the maximum value in the data set?

b) Based on Chebyshev's Theorem, what percentage of the data values must be within 1.5 standard deviations of the mean. What percentage of the data values <u>actually</u> falls within +/- 1.5 standard deviations?

c) Apply the empirical rule to the data set. How close are the actually percentages to the percentages dictated by the empirical rule?

d) Using +/- 3 standard deviations as the criterion, identify any outliers in the data set.

EXERCISE 7

Five-Number Summary and Box Plot

Refer again to the furniture data presented in Exercise 1. Provide a five-number summary of the data set and graph your results using a box plot.

EXERCISE 8

Covariance and Correlation Coefficient

Reed Auto periodically has a special week-long sale. As part of the advertising campaign Reed runs one or more television commercials during the weekend preceding the sale. Data from a sample of 5 previous sales are shown below.

Week	TV Ads	Cars Sold
1	1	14
2	3	24
3	2	18
4	1	17
5	3	27

Compute and interpret both the sample covariance and the sample correlation coefficient.

EXERCISE 9

Weighted Mean

Ron Butler, a custom home builder, is looking over the expenses he incurred for a house he just completed constructing. For the purpose of pricing future construction projects, he would like to know the average wage ($/hour) he paid the workers he employed. (The cost of materials is estimated in advance by the architect.) Listed below are the categories of worker he employed, along with their respective wage and total hours worked.

Worker	Wage ($/hr)	Total Hours
Carpenter	21.60	520
Electrician	28.72	230
Laborer	11.80	410
Painter	19.75	270
Plumber	24.16	160

What is the average wage ($/hour) he paid the workers?

EXERCISE 10

Grouped Data

The manager of Hudson Auto Repair has recorded the following frequency distribution for the cost of new parts used in doing an engine tune-up in a sample of 50 tune-ups.

Parts Cost ($)	Frequency
50-59	2
60-69	13
70-79	17
80-89	7
90-99	6
100-109	5

Compute the sample mean, variance, and standard deviation.

SELF-TEST

TRUE/FALSE

_____ 1. The interquartile range is the difference between the third and second quartiles.

_____ 2. The absolute value of the correlation coefficient is equal to the value of the coefficient of determination.

_____ 3. The descriptive statistics for grouped data are only approximations of the descriptive statistics that would result from using the original data directly.

_____ 4. The steps for computing percentiles can be directly applied in the computation of quartiles.

_____ 5. When a data set contains an even number of data values, there can be two median values for the data set.

FILL-IN-THE-BLANK

1. When observations vary in importance, the analyst must choose the _____ that best reflects the importance of each observation in the determination of the mean.

2. In computing descriptive statistics for grouped data, the _____ are used to approximate the data values in each class.

3. It is better to use the median than the mean as a measure of central location when the data set contains _____.

4. The _____ is an important measure of location for qualitative data.

5. Although the _____ is the easiest of the measures of variability to compute, it is seldom used as the only measure.

MULTIPLE CHOICE

_____ 1. Which one of the following is not a measure of variability of a single variable?
   a) range
   b) covariance
   c) standard deviation
   d) coefficient of variation

_____ 2. The empirical rule states that, for data having a bell-shaped distribution, the percentage of data values being within one standard deviation of the mean is approximately
   a) 34
   b) 50
   c) 68
   d) 95

_____ 3. A box plot is a graphical representation of data that is based on
   a) the empirical rule
   b) z-scores
   c) a histogram
   d) a five-number summary

_____ 4. The coefficient of variation indicates how large the standard deviation is relative to the
   a) mean
   b) median
   c) range
   d) variance

_____ 5. Which one of the following descriptive statistics is not measured in the same units as the data?
   a) 35th percentile
   b) standard deviation
   c) variance
   d) interquartile range

ANSWERS

EXERCISES

1) mean = 251.46; median = 228.5; modes are 196 and 231 (data set is bimodal)

2) 80th percentile = 331.5; first quartile = 183

3) range = 367 ; interquartile range = 107

4) variance = 8398.50; standard deviation = 91.64; coefficient of variation = 36.44

5)

Furniture Orders ($)	
Mean	251.46
Standard Error	12.96032
Median	228.5
Mode	231
Standard Deviation	91.64332
Sample Variance	8398.498
Kurtosis	0.326096
Skewness	1.032534
Range	367
Minimum	123
Maximum	490
Sum	12573
Count	50

6) a) min. $z = -1.40$; max. $z = 2.60$
   b) 55.5%; 44/50 = 88%
   c) 72% are +/- 1σ; 94% are +/- 2σ; 100% are +/- 3σ; all are relatively close
   d) no outliers

7) 123, 183, 228.5, 290, 490

8) sample covariance = 5.0 ; sample correlation coefficient = 0.937

9) $20.05

10) sample mean = 77.9; sample variance = 186.16; sample standard deviation = 13.64

TRUE/FALSE

1) False
2) False
3) True
4) True
5) False

FILL-IN-THE-BLANK

1) weight
2) class midpoints
3) extreme values
4) mode
5) range

MULTIPLE CHOICE

1) b
2) c
3) d
4) a
5) c

CHAPTER 4

Introduction to Probability

Experiments, Counting Rules,
and Assigning Probabilities

Events and Their Probabilities

Some Basic Relationships of Probability

Conditional Probability

Bayes' Theorem

LEARNING OBJECTIVES

1. Obtain an appreciation of the role probability information plays in the decision making process.

2. Understand probability as a numerical measure of the likelihood of occurrence.

3. Know the three methods commonly used for assigning probabilities and understand when they should be used.

4. Know how to use the laws that are available for computing the probabilities of events.

5. Understand how new information can be used to revise initial (prior) probability estimates using Bayes' theorem.

REVIEW

Probability
- Probability is a numerical measure of the likelihood that an event will occur.
- Probability values are always assigned on a scale from 0 to 1.
- A probability near 0 indicates an event is very unlikely to occur.
- A probability near 1 indicates an event is almost certain to occur.
- A probability of 0.5 indicates the occurrence of the event is just as likely as it is unlikely.

An Experiment and Its Sample Space
- An experiment is any process that generates well-defined outcomes.
- The sample space for an experiment is the set of all experimental outcomes.
- A sample point is an element of the sample space, any one particular experimental outcome.
- The sum of the probabilities of all the sample points in the sample space must equal 1.

Counting Rules

Counting Rule for Multiple-Step Experiments
- If an experiment consists of a sequence of k steps in which there are n_1 possible results for the first step, n_2 possible results for the second step, and so on, then the total number of experimental outcomes is given by $(n_1)(n_2) \ldots (n_k)$.
- A helpful graphical representation of a multiple-step experiment is a tree diagram.

Counting Rule for Combinations
- Another useful counting rule enables us to count the number of experimental outcomes when n objects are to be selected from a set of N objects.
- The number of combinations of N objects taken n at a time is

$$C_n^N = \binom{N}{n} = \frac{N!}{n!(N-n)!}$$

where $N! = N(N-1)(N-2) \ldots (2)(1)$
$n! = n(n-1)(n-2) \ldots (2)(1)$
$0! = 1$

Counting Rule for Permutations

- A third useful counting rule enables us to count the number of experimental outcomes when n objects are to be selected from a set of N objects where the order of selection is important.
- An experiment will have more permutations than combinations for the same number of objects because every selection of n objects has $n!$ different ways to order them.
- The number of permutations of N objects taken n at a time is

$$P_n^N = n! \binom{N}{n} = \frac{N!}{(N-n)!}$$

Assigning Probabilities

Classical Method

- Assigning probabilities based on the assumption of equally likely outcomes.
- If an experiment has n possible outcomes, this method would assign a probability of $1/n$ to each outcome.

Relative Frequency Method

- Assigning probabilities based on experimentation or historical data.
- The probability assigned to an outcome is found by dividing the frequency of the outcome by the total frequency for all of the outcomes.

Subjective Method

- Assigning probabilities based on the assignor's judgment.
- When economic conditions and a company's circumstances change rapidly it might be inappropriate to assign probabilities based solely on historical data.
- We can use any data available as well as our experience and intuition, but ultimately a probability value should express our degree of belief that the experimental outcome will occur.
- The best probability estimates often are obtained by combining the estimates from the classical or relative frequency approach with the subjective estimates.

Events and Their Probability

- An event is a collection of sample points.
- The probability of any event is equal to the sum of the probabilities of the sample points in the event.
- If we can identify all the sample points of an experiment and assign a probability to each, we can compute the probability of an event.

Some Basic Relationships of Probability

- There are some basic probability relationships that can be used to compute the probability of an event without knowledge of all the sample point probabilities.
- One method frequently used for visualizing relationships between event sets is the Venn diagram. This is a picture with a rectangle representing the entire sample space, S, and event sets represented by circles within the rectangle.

Complement of an Event
- The complement of event *A* is defined to be the event consisting of all sample points that are not in *A*.
- The complement of *A* is denoted by A^c.
- The probability of the complement of the event *A* is $P(A^c) = 1 - P(A)$.
- The Venn diagram below illustrates the concept of a complement.

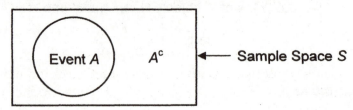

Union of Two Events
- The union of events *A* and *B* is the event containing all sample points that are in *A* or *B* or both.
- The union is denoted by $A \cup B$.
- The union of *A* and *B* is illustrated below.

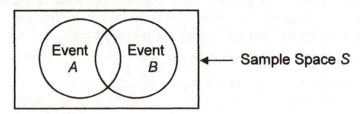

Intersection of Two Events
- The intersection of events *A* and *B* is the set of all sample points that are in both *A* and *B*.
- The intersection is denoted by $A \cap B$.
- The intersection of *A* and *B* is the area of overlap in the illustration below.

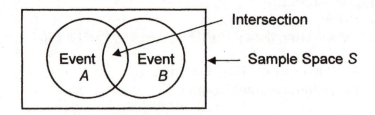

Addition Law
- The addition law provides a way to compute the probability of event *A*, or *B*, or both *A* and *B* occurring.
- The addition law is written as:
$$P(A \cup B) = P(A) + P(B) - P(A \cap B)$$

Mutually Exclusive Events

- Two events are said to be mutually exclusive if the events have no sample points in common. (*A* and *A^c* are mutually exclusive.)

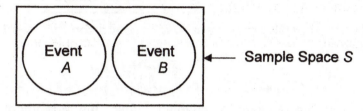

- Two events are mutually exclusive if, when one event occurs, the other cannot occur.
- For mutually exclusive events P(*A*|*B*) = P(*B*|*A*) = 0, (e.g. the probability a coin comes up heads given it comes up tails is 0.)

Addition Law for Mutually Exclusive Events

- Addition Law for Mutually Exclusive Events is written as:

$$P(A \cup B) = P(A) + P(B)$$

Conditional Probability

- The probability of an event given that another event has occurred is called a conditional probability.
- The conditional probability of *A* given *B* is denoted by P(*A*|*B*).
- A conditional probability is computed as follows:

$$P(A \mid B) = \frac{P(A \cap B)}{P(B)}$$

Multiplication Law

- The multiplication law provides a way to compute the probability of an intersection of two events.
- The law is written as:

$$P(A \cap B) = P(B)P(A|B)$$

- P(*A*∩*B*) is the joint probability of events *A* and *B*.

Independent Events

- Events *A* and *B* are independent if P(*A*|*B*) = P(*A*) or P(*B*|*A*) = P(*B*).

Multiplication Law for Independent Events

- Multiplication Law for Independent Events:

$$P(A \cap B) = P(A)P(B)$$

- The multiplication law also can be used as a test to see if two events are independent.

Bayes' Theorem

- Often we begin probability analysis with initial or prior probabilities.
- Then, from a sample, special report, or a product test we obtain some additional information.
- Given this information, we calculate revised or posterior probabilities.

- Bayes' theorem provides the means for revising the prior probabilities.

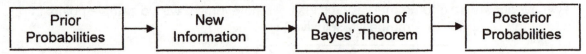

- To find the posterior probability that event A_i will occur given that event B has occurred we apply Bayes' theorem.

$$P(A_i \mid B) = \frac{P(A_i)P(B \mid A_i)}{P(A_1)P(B \mid A_1) + P(A_2)P(B \mid A_2) + \ldots + P(A_n)P(B \mid A_n)}$$

- Bayes' theorem is applicable when the events for which we want to compute posterior probabilities are mutually exclusive and their union is the entire sample space.

Tabular Approach to Bayes' Theorem Calculations

- Step 1   Prepare the following three columns:
    - Column 1 - The mutually exclusive events for which posterior probabilities are desired.
    - Column 2 - The prior probabilities for the events.
    - Column 3 - The conditional probabilities of the new information *given* each event.
- Step 2   In Column 4, compute the joint probabilities for each event and the new information B by using the multiplication law. Multiply the prior probabilities in column 2 by the corresponding conditional probabilities in column 3. That is, $P(A_i \cap B) = P(A_i)$ $P(B \mid A_i)$.
- Step 3   Sum the joint probabilities in column 4. The sum is the probability of the new information $P(B)$.
- Step 4   In Column 5, compute the posterior probabilities using the basic relationship of conditional probability.

$$P(A_i \mid B) = \frac{P(A_i \cap B)}{P(B)}$$

CONCEPTS

CONCEPT	EXAMPLES	EXERCISES
Experiments, Sample Spaces, and Counting Rule	1	1
Assignment of Probabilities	2,4	5

Probability Relationships:
    Complement
    Union
    Intersection
    Mutually Exclusive
    Addition Law
    Conditional Probability
    Independence
    Multiplication Law
	2,3,4,5	1,2,3,6,7,8

Tree Diagram	6	10
Bayes' Theorem	⑥,7	4,9,10

◯ Excel Used

EXAMPLES

EXAMPLE 1

Experiments, Sample Spaces, and Counting Rule

Mini Car Motors offers its luxury car in three colors: gold, silver and blue. The vice president of advertising is interested in the order of popularity of the color choices by customers during the first month of sales.

a) How many sample points are there in this experiment?

b) If the event A = gold is the most popular color, list the outcome(s) in event A.

c) If the event B = blue is the least popular color, list the outcome(s) in $A \cap B$.

d) List the outcome(s) in $A \cap B^C$.

SOLUTION 1

a) Sample space = {(GSB),(GBS),(SGB),(SBG),(BGS),BSG)} = 6 sample points

b) Event A = {(GSB),(GBS)} = 2 sample points

c) $A \cap B$ = sample points common to both Event A and Event B = {(GSB)}

d) $A \cap B^C$ = sample points in Event A that are not in Event B = {(GBS)}

EXAMPLE 2

Assignment of Probabilities and Probability Relationships

A market study taken at a local sporting goods store showed that of 20 people questioned, 6 owned tents, 10 owned sleeping bags, 8 owned camping stoves, 4 owned both tents and camping stoves, and 4 owned both sleeping bags and camping stoves.

Let: Event A = owns a tent
Event B = owns a sleeping bag
Event C = owns a camping stove

and let the sample space be the 20 people questioned.

a) Find $P(A)$, $P(B)$, $P(C)$, $P(A \cap C)$, $P(B \cap C)$.

b) Are the events A and C mutually exclusive? Explain briefly.

c) Are the events B and C independent events? Explain briefly.

d) If a person questioned owns a tent, what is the probability he also owns a camping stove?

e) If two people questioned own a tent, a sleeping bag, and a camping stove, how many own only a camping stove? In this case is it possible for 3 people to own both a tent and a sleeping bag, but not a camping stove?

SOLUTION 2

a) Using the relative frequency method, the probability equals the number of sample points in the event divided by the number of sample points in the sample space. Thus,

$$P(A) = \ 6/20 = .3$$
$$P(B) = 10/20 = .5$$
$$P(C) = \ 8/20 = .4$$

$$P(A \cap B) = P(\text{owns a tent and owns a camping stove}) = 4/20 = .2$$
$$P(B \cap C) = P(\text{owns a sleeping bag and owns a camping stove}) = 4/20 = .2$$

b) Events B and C are not mutually exclusive because there are people (4 people) who both own a tent and a camping stove.

c) To see whether events B and C are independent, check to see if $P(B \cap C) = P(B)P(C)$. Since $P(B \cap C) = .2$ and $P(B)P(C) = (.5)(.4) = .2$, then <u>these events are independent</u>.

d) Here the probability that a person owns a camping stove <u>given</u> he owns a tent or $P(C|A)$ must be determined. Using conditional probability,

$$P(C|A) = P(A \cap C)/P(A) = .2/.3 = .667$$

e) Using a Venn diagram gives the following:

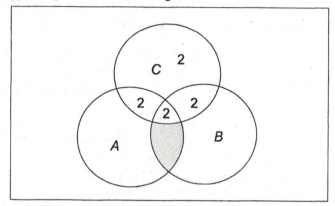

Note that <u>two</u> people own only a camping stove. To determine whether it is possible for three people to own both a tent and a sleeping bag, but not a camping stove, note that the total size of event A is 6. Thus, the shaded area above could not have a value of 3.

EXAMPLE 3

Probability Relationships

The Bidwell Valve Company requires all prospective employees to be interviewed by a three-person committee. Each member of the committee votes individually for or against a recommendation of employment. Upon examining the company's records over the past year, the personnel director has noted the following probabilities for eight possible outcomes:

	Vote of Member			
Outcome	1	2	3	Probability
E_1	for	for	for	.20
E_2	for	for	against	.14
E_3	for	against	for	.12
E_4	for	against	against	.07
E_5	against	for	for	.08
E_6	against	for	against	.11
E_7	against	against	for	.06
E_8	against	against	against	.22

Denote the following events: A = Member 1 votes for employment
                                      B = Member 2 votes for employment
                                      C = Member 3 votes for employment

a) Find P(A), P(B), and P(C).

b) Which sample outcomes correspond to the event $D = A \cup B$ (Member 1 <u>or</u> Member 2 votes for employment)? Find P(D).

c) Which sample outcomes correspond to the event $G = A \cap B$ (Member 1 <u>and</u> Member 2 vote for employment)? Use the addition law of probability to find P(G).

d) Let the event $F = B^c \cap C$ (Member 2 votes against employment and Member 3 votes for employment). Draw a Venn diagram to represent the event $G \cup F$.

e) If a new employee is hired only if a majority of the committee members vote for employment, what is the probability that a prospective employee is hired? Does a job applicant stand a better or worse chance of being employed going before the committee than one of the individuals?

SOLUTION 3

a) Find the outcomes corresponding to events A, B, and C.

$A = \{E_1, E_2, E_3, E_4\}$. Thus P($A$) = P($E_1$) + P($E_2$) + P($E_3$) + P($E_4$)
          = .20 + .14 + .12 + .07 = .53

$B = \{E_1, E_2, E_5, E_6\}$. Thus P($B$) = P($E_1$) + P($E_2$) + P($E_5$) + P($E_6$)
          = .20 + .14 + .08 + .11 = .53

$C = \{E_1, E_3, E_5, E_7\}$. Thus P($C$) = P($E_1$) + P($E_3$) + P($E_5$) + P($E_7$)
          = .20 + .12 + .08 + .06 = .46

b) The event D corresponds to all sample points that are either in event A or event B or both. Thus $D = \{E_1, E_2, E_3, E_4, E_5, E_6\}$.

     P(D) = P(E_1) + P(E_2) + P(E_3) + P(E_4) + P(E_5) + P(E_6)
            = .20 + .14 + .12 + .07 + .08 + .11 = .72

c) The event G corresponds to sample points in both event A and event B. Thus $G = \{E_1, E_2\}$.

       The addition law states: P($A \cup B$) = P(A) + P(B) - P($A \cap B$)
       or in this case: P(G) = P(A) + P(B) - P(D) = .53 + .53 - .72 = .34
       Note that this checks with P(G) = P(E_1) + P(E_2) = .20 + .14 = .34

d) Event $B^c = \{E_3, E_4, E_7, E_8\}$. $F = B^c \cap C$ = the events common to both B^c and $C = \{E_3, E_7\}$. The Venn diagram for $G \cup F$ is:

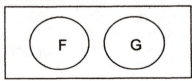

e) Let event L = the event that the majority of the committee members vote for employment, i.e. two or three vote for employment. Thus, $L = \{E_1, E_2, E_3, E_5\}$. $P(L) = P(E_1) + P(E_2) + P(E_3) + P(E_5)$. Thus $P(L) = .20 + .14 + .12 + .08 = .54$. Since this is higher than $P(A)$, $P(B)$, and $P(C)$, the job applicant has a better chance of being employed by going before the committee.

EXAMPLE 4

Assignment of Probabilities and Probability Relationships

Harry owns shares of stock in both Bidwell Valve Company and Mini Car Motors, Inc. Harry has recorded the performance of these shares on each day for a 200-day period as to whether the price has risen, fallen or remained unchanged. Harry's data is as follows:

Event	Bidwell	Mini Car	# of Days
E_1	Rise	Rise	40
E_2	Rise	Unchanged	14
E_3	Rise	Fall	20
E_4	Unchanged	Rise	18
E_5	Unchanged	Unchanged	12
E_6	Unchanged	Fall	14
E_7	Fall	Rise	28
E_8	Fall	Unchanged	16
E_9	Fall	Fall	38

a) Using this data and the relative frequency approach, find the following probabilities:
   (1) a rise in the price of Bidwell stock
   (2) a fall in the price of Mini Car stock
   (3) a rise in Bidwell and a fall in Mini Car stock
   (4) a rise in Bidwell or a fall in Mini Car stock (Use the addition law.)

b) Suppose Harry is told that Bidwell stock has risen. What is the probability that Mini Car stock has fallen?

c) Suppose Harry is told that Mini Car stock has fallen. What is the probability that Bidwell stock has risen?

d) Are the events "a rise in Bidwell stock" and "a fall in Mini Car stock" independent?

SOLUTION 4

a) Let: event A = "rise in Bidwell stock" = $\{E_1, E_2, E_3\}$
        event B = "fall in Mini Car stock" = $\{E_3, E_6, E_9\}$

Using the relative frequency approach,

$$P(E_1) = 40/200 = .20 \qquad P(E_6) = 14/200 = .07$$
$$P(E_2) = 14/200 = .07 \qquad P(E_7) = 28/200 = .14$$
$$P(E_3) = 20/200 = .10 \qquad P(E_8) = 16/200 = .08$$
$$P(E_4) = 18/200 = .09 \qquad P(E_9) = 38/200 = .19$$
$$P(E_5) = 12/200 = .06$$

(1) $P(A) = P(E_1) + P(E_2) + P(E_3) = .20 + .07 + .10 = .37$
(2) $P(B) = P(E_3) + P(E_6) + P(E_9) = .10 + .07 + .19 = .36$
(3) $P(A \cap B) = P(E_3) = .10$
(4) $P(A \cup B) = P(A) + P(B) - P(A \cap B) = .37 + .36 - .10 = .63$

b) $P(B|A) = P(A \cup B)/P(A) = .10/.37 = .27$

c) $P(A|B) = P(A \cup B)/P(B) = .10/.36 = .28$

d) There are several ways to check if events A and B are independent. One method is to see if $P(A|B) = P(A)$. Since $P(A|B) = .28$ and $P(A) = .37$, these events are dependent.

EXAMPLE 5

Probability Relationships

The Board of Directors of Bidwell Valve Company has made the following estimates for the upcoming year's annual earnings:

$$P(\text{earnings lower than this year}) \qquad = .30$$
$$P(\text{earnings about the same as this year}) = .50$$
$$P(\text{earnings higher than this year}) \qquad = .20$$

After talking with union leaders, the human resource department has drawn the following conclusions:

$$P(\text{Union will request wage increase|lower earnings next year}) = .25$$
$$P(\text{Union will request wage increase|same earnings next year}) = .40$$
$$P(\text{Union will request wage increase|higher earnings next year}) = .90$$

a) Are the probabilities developed by the directors and personnel manager based on the classical, relative frequency, or subjective method?

b) Calculate the following probabilities:
   (1) The company earns the same as this year and the union requests a wage increase
   (2) The company has higher earnings next year and the union does not request a wage increase
   (3) The union requests a wage increase

SOLUTION 5

a) Since the predicted outcomes of earnings and wage increase requests have unequal probabilities, they are not based on the classical method. Similarly, since the outcomes arise from a unique situation, the relative frequency method is not applicable. Instead, the probabilities stated reflect the judgment of the individuals involved, and hence are developed by the <u>subjective method</u>.

b) Define the following events: L = lower earnings next year; S = about the same earnings next year; H = higher earnings next year. Further define R = union requests a pay increase next year, so R^c = union does not request a pay increase next year.

   (1) This is $P(S \cap R)$. Now, $P(S) = .50$ and $P(R|S) = .40$.
       Thus, $P(S \cap R) = P(S)P(R|S) = (.50)(.40) = .20$
   (2) This is $P(H \cap R^c)$. Now, $P(H) = .20$ and $P(R^c|H) = 1 - P(R|H) = .10$
       Thus, $P(H \cap R^c) = P(H)P(R^c|H) = (.20)(.10) = .02$
   (3) This is $P(R)$. $P(R) = P(R|H)P(H) + P(R|S)P(S) + P(R|L)P(L)$
                    $= (.25)(.30) + (.40)(.50) + (.90)(.20) = .455$

EXAMPLE 6

Tree Diagram and Bayes' Theorem

    A proposed shopping center will provide strong competition for downtown businesses like L. S. Clothiers. If the shopping center is built, the owner of L. S. Clothiers feels it would be best to relocate. The shopping center cannot be built unless the town council approves a zoning change. The planning board must first make a recommendation, for or against the zoning change, to the council.

   Let: A_1 = town council approves the zoning change
         A_2 = town council disapproves the change

   Prior to the planning board making a recommendation, the probabilities of A_1 and A_2 were subjective judged to be: $P(A_1) = .7$ and $P(A_2) = .3$
   New information is now available! The planning board has recommended <u>against</u> the zoning change. Let B denote the event of a negative recommendation by the board.
   Given that B has occurred, L. S. Clothiers can revise the probabilities that the town council will approve or disapprove the zoning change. Past history with the planning board and the town council indicates the following: $P(B|A_1) = .2$ and $P(B|A_2) = .9$

a) Draw a tree diagram to represent, and better understand, this multiple-step experiment.

b) Using Excel, compute the posterior (revised) probability of the town council approving the zoning change.

SOLUTION 6

a) Tree diagram:

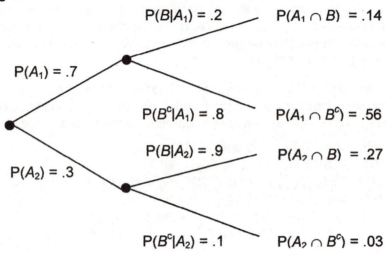

$$P(B|A_1) = .2 \qquad P(A_1 \cap B) = .14$$

$$P(A_1) = .7$$

$$P(B^c|A_1) = .8 \qquad P(A_1 \cap B^c) = .56$$

$$P(B|A_2) = .9 \qquad P(A_2 \cap B) = .27$$

$$P(A_2) = .3$$

$$P(B^c|A_2) = .1 \qquad P(A_2 \cap B^c) = .03$$

b) To find the posterior probability that event A_1 will occur given that event B has occurred we apply Bayes' theorem. The steps for using Excel in this problem are as follows:

Excel Steps

1. Open a new worksheet and enter the following labels and data.

	A	B	C	D	E
1	CHAPTER 4 - EXAMPLE 5 - BAYES' THEOREM				
2					
3		Prior	Conditional	Joint	Posterior
4	Events	Probabilities	Probabilities	Probabilities	Probabilities
5	A_1	0.7	0.2		
6	A_2	0.3	0.9		
7			P(B) =		
8					

Col. A - The mutually exclusive events for which posterior probabilities are desired.
Col. B - The prior probabilities for the events.
Col. C - The conditional probabilities of the new information *given* each event.

2. In column D, enter the formulas for computing the joint probabilities for each event and the new information B using the multiplication law. Multiply the prior probabilities in column B by the corresponding conditional probabilities in column C. That is, $P(A_i \cap B) = P(A_i) P(B|A_i)$.

3. Enter the formula for summing the joint probabilities in column D. The sum is the probability of the new information $P(B)$.

4. In column E, enter the formulas for computing the posterior probabilities using the basic relationship of conditional probability.

$$P(A_i \mid B) = \frac{P(A_i \cap B)}{P(B)}$$

Note that the joint probabilities $P(A_i \mid B)$ are in column D and the probability $P(B)$ is the sum of column D.

Formula Worksheet:

	A	B	C	D	E
1	CHAPTER 4 - EXAMPLE 5 - BAYES' THEOREM				
2					
3		Prior	Conditional	Joint	Posterior
4	Events	Probabilities	Probabilities	Probabilities	Probabilities
5	A_1	0.7	0.2	=B5*C5	=D5/$D$7
6	A_2	0.3	0.9	=B6*C6	=D6/$D$7
7			P(*B*)	=SUM(D5:D6)	=SUM(E5:E6)
8					

We see in the resulting worksheet below, in column D, that there is a .14 probability of the town council approving the zoning change and a negative recommendation by the planning board. There is a .27 probability of the town council disapproving the zoning change and a negative recommendation by the planning board. The sum .14 + .27 shows an overall probability of .41 of a negative recommendation by the planning board.

Value Worksheet:

	A	B	C	D	E
1	CHAPTER 4 - EXAMPLE 5 - BAYES' THEOREM				
2					
3		Prior	Conditional	Joint	Posterior
4	Events	Probabilities	Probabilities	Probabilities	Probabilities
5	A_1	0.7	0.2	0.14	0.34
6	A_2	0.3	0.9	0.27	0.66
7			P(*B*)	0.41	1.00
8					

Conclusion - The planning board's recommendation is good news for L. S. Clothiers. The posterior probability of the town council approving the zoning change is .34 (compared to a prior probability of .70).

EXAMPLE 7

Bayes' Theorem

An accounting firm has noticed that of the companies it audits, 85% show no inventory shortages, 10% show small inventory shortages and 5% show large inventory shortages. The firm has devised a new accounting test for which it believes the following probabilities hold:

$$P(\text{company will pass test}|\text{no shortage}) = .90$$
$$P(\text{company will pass test}|\text{small shortage}) = .50$$
$$P(\text{company will pass test}|\text{large shortage}) = .20$$

a) If a company being audited fails this test, what is the probability of a large or small inventory shortage?

b) If a company being audited passes this test, what is the probability of no inventory shortage?

SOLUTION 7

a) Let: A_1 = no inventory shortage P = company passes test
A_2 = small inventory shortage F = company fails test
A_3 = large inventory shortage

Event	Prior Probabilities $P(A_i)$	Conditional Probabilities $P(F|A_i)$	Joint Probabilities $P(A_i \cap F)$	Posterior Probabilities $P(A_i|F)$
A_1	.85	.10	.085	.486
A_2	.10	.50	.050	.286
A_3	.05	.80	.040	.229
			$P(F) = .175$	

Here, $P(F|A_i) = 1 - P(P|A_i)$; the joint probabilities are the multiples of the prior and conditional probabilities and the posterior probabilities are the joint probabilities divided by $P(F)$. The probability of a large or small shortage = $.286 + .229 = .515$

b)

Event	Prior Probabilities $P(A_i)$	Conditional Probabilities $P(P|A_i)$	Joint Probabilities $P(A_i \cap P)$	Posterior Probabilities $P(A_i|P)$
A_1	.85	.90	.765	.927
A_2	.10	.50	.050	.061
A_3	.05	.20	.010	.012
			$P(P) = .825$	

The solution is $P(A_1|P) = .927$

EXERCISES

EXERCISE 1

Experiments, Sample Spaces, and Counting Rule

Providence Land Development Company has just hired four new salespersons. After six months on the job each salesperson will be rated as either poor, average or excellent and will be compensated accordingly. Assume that Providence is concerned with the number of salespersons in each category.

a) List the outcomes of this experiment.

b) Let event A = at least two salespersons are rated average and let event B = exactly one salesperson is rated poor. List the outcomes in $A \cap B$.

c) Let event C = exactly two salespersons are rated excellent. List the outcomes in $D = B \cap C$.

d) Are events D and A mutually exclusive?

e) Are events D and A collectively exhaustive?

f) Let the event E = at most one salesperson is rated average. Are events A and E mutually exclusive and collectively exhaustive?

EXERCISE 2

Probability Relationships

Global Airlines operates two types of jet planes: jumbo and ordinary. On jumbo jets, 25% of the passengers are on business while on ordinary jets 30% of the passengers are on business. Of Global's air fleet, 40% of its capacity is provided on jumbo jets. (Hint: You have been given two conditional probabilities.)

a) What is the probability a randomly chosen business customer flying with Global is on a jumbo jet?

b) What is the probability a randomly chosen non-business customer flying with Global is on an ordinary jet?

EXERCISE 3

Probability Relationships

The following probability model describes the number of snowstorms for Washington, D. C. for a given year:

# of Snowstorms	0	1	2	3	4	5	6
Probability	.25	.33	.24	.11	.04	.02	.01

The probability of 7 or more snowstorms in a year is 0.

a) What is the probability of more than 2 but less than 5 snowstorms?

b) Given this a particularly cold year (in which 2 snowstorms have already been observed), what is the conditional probability that 4 or more snowstorms will be observed?

c) If at the beginning of winter there is a snowfall, what is the probability of at least one more snowstorm before winter is over?

EXERCISE 4

Bayes' Theorem

Safety Insurance Company has compiled the following statistics. For any one year period:

P(accident | male driver under 25)   = .22
P(accident | male driver over 25)   = .15
P(accident | female driver under 25) = .16
P(accident | female driver over 25) = .14

The percentage of Safety's policyholders in each category is:

Male Under 25	20%
Male Over 25	40%
Female Under 25	10%
Female Over 25	30%

a) What is the probability that a randomly selected policyholder will have an accident within the next year?

b) Given that a driver has an accident, what is the probability the driver is a male over 25?

c) Given that a driver has no accident, what is the probability the driver is a female?

d) Does knowing the fact that a driver has had no accidents give us a great deal of information regarding the driver's sex?

EXERCISE 5

Assignment of Probabilities

Sales of the first 500 luxury Mini Cars were as follows: 250 gold, 150 silver, and 100 blue. Assume the relative frequency method is used to assign probabilities for color choice and the color of each car sold is independent of that of any other car sold.

a) What is the probability that the next two cars sold will both be gold?

b) What is the probability that neither of the next two cars sold will be silver?

c) What is the probability that of the next two cars sold, one will be silver and the other will be blue?

EXERCISE 6

Probability Relationships

The sales manager for Widco Distributing Company has estimated demand for a new combination microwave oven and color television will be between 0 and 2 units per day. He believes the probability of selling no units is .65, of one unit is .25, and two units is .10. The company is interested in sales over a two-day period.

a) What is the probability of selling no units during the two days?

b) What is the probability of selling one unit during the two days?

c) What is the probability of selling three or more units during the two days?

d) What is the probability of selling two units during the two days?

EXERCISE 7

Probability Relationships

Super Cola sales breakdown as 80% regular soda and 20% diet soda. Men purchase 60% of the regular soda, but only 30% of the diet soda. If a woman purchases Super Cola, what is the probability that it is a diet soda?

EXERCISE 8

Probability Relationships

Stanton Marketing conducted a taste preference test among married and single persons for the Super Cola Company. Among single people, 11% of the population questioned preferred Super Cola to all other brands. For married people the data was:

	Wife Prefers	Wife Does Not Prefer
Husband Prefers	.08	.06
Does Not Prefer	.07	.79

a) Using this study as a basis for a probability measure, find the probability that if two single people are questioned: (1) they both prefer Super Cola; (2) they both do not prefer Super Cola; and (3) one prefers Super Cola and the other does not.

b) What is the probability that a married female prefers Super Cola?

c) Given that a husband prefers Super Cola, what is the probability his wife also prefers it?

d) Is the event "husband prefers Super Cola" independent of the event "wife prefers Super Cola"?

e) Do married people prefer Super Cola more than single people?

EXERCISE 9

Bayes' Theorem

Higbee Manufacturing Corp. has recently received 5 cases of a certain part from one of its suppliers. The defect rate for the parts is normally 5%, but the supplier has just notified Higbee that one of the cases shipped to them has been made on a misaligned machine that has a defect rate of 97%. So Higbee selects a case at random and tests a part.

a) What is the probability that the part is defective?

b) Suppose the part is defective, what is the probability that this is from the case made on the misaligned machine?

c) After finding that the first part was defective, suppose a second part from the case is tested. However, this part is found to be good. Using the revised probabilities from part (b) compute the new probability of these parts being from the defective case.

d) Do you think you would obtain the same posterior probabilities as in part (c) if the first part was not found to be defective but the second part was?

e) Suppose, because of other evidence, the plant manager was 80% certain this case was the one made on the misaligned machine. How would your answer to part (b) change?

EXERCISE 10

Tree Diagram and Bayes' Theorem

An investment advisor recommends the purchase of shares in Probaballistics, Inc. He has made the following predictions:

P(Stock goes up 20% | Rise in GDP) = .6
P(Stock goes up 20% | Level GDP) = .5
P(Stock goes up 20% | Fall in GDP) = .4

An economist has predicted that the probability of a rise in the GDP is 30%, whereas the probability of a fall in the GDP is 40%.

a) Draw a tree diagram to represent, and better understand, this multiple-step experiment.

b) What is the probability that the stock will go up 20%?

c) We have been informed that the stock has gone up 20%. What is the probability of a rise or fall in the GDP?

████████████████ **SELF-TEST** ████████████████

TRUE/FALSE

_____ 1. $P(A|B) = 1 - P(B|A)$ for all events A and B.

_____ 2. If A and B are mutually exclusive, $P(A \cap B) = 0$.

_____ 3. $P(A|B) + P(A|B^C) = 1$ for all A and B.

_____ 4. A joint probability can have a value greater than 1.

_____ 5. Posterior probabilities are conditional probabilities.

FILL-IN-THE-BLANK

1. A method of assigning probabilities that assumes the experimental outcomes are equally likely is the _____ method.

2. Events that have no sample points in common are _____.

3. An element of the sample space is a _____.

4. _____ is a numerical measure of the likelihood that an event will occur.

5. The _____ law is used to compute the probability of an intersection of two events.

MULTIPLE CHOICE

_____ 1. A graphical representation helpful in defining sample points of an experiment involving multiple steps is a
a) Venn diagram
b) Bayes' table
c) Scatter diagram
d) Tree diagram

_____ 2. The probability of at least one head in two flips of a coin is
a) 0.33
b) 0.50
c) 0.75
d) 1.00

_____ 3. Revised probabilities of events based on additional information are
a) joint probabilities
b) posterior probabilities
c) marginal probabilities
d) complementary probabilities

___ 4. Posterior probabilities are computed using
   a) the classical method
   b) the subjective method
   c) the relative frequency method
   d) Bayes' theorem

___ 5. The complement of $P(A|B)$ is
   a) $P(A^C|B)$
   b) $P(A|B^C)$
   c) $P(B|A)$
   d) $P(A \cap B)$

ANSWERS

EXERCISES

1) a) Let E_j = (# poor, # average, # excellent).
   E_1 = (4,0,0), E_2 = (3,1,0), E_3 = (3,0,1), E_4 = (2,2,0), E_5 = (2,1,1),
   E_6 = (2,0,2), E_7 = (1,3,0), E_8 = (1,2,1), E_9 = (1,1,2), E_{10} = (1,0,3),
   E_{11} = (0,4,0), E_{12} = (0,3,1), E_{13} = (0,2,2), E_{14} = (0,1,3), E_{15} = (0,0,4).
   b) $\{E_7, E_8\}$
   c) $\{E_9\}$
   d) yes
   e) no
   f) yes

2) a) .357
   b) .583

3) a) .15
   b) .167
   c) .56

4) a) .162
   b) .370
   c) .408
   d) no

5) a) .25
   b) .49
   c) .12

6) a) .4225
   b) .325
   c) .06
   d) .1925

7) .304

8) a) (1) .0121; (2) .7921 (3) .1958
   b) .15
   c) .571
   d) No
   e) .145; more

9) a) .234
   b) .829
   c) .133
   d) yes
   e) .987

10) a) see below
    b) .490
    c) .694

10) a)

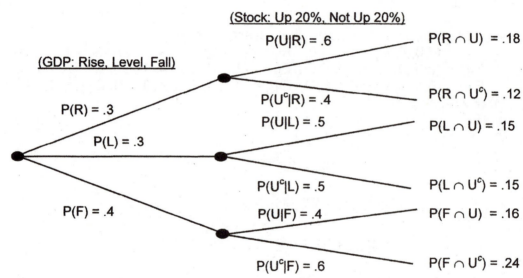

TRUE/FALSE	FILL-IN-THE-BLANK	MULTIPLE CHOICE
1) False	1) classical method	1) d
2) True	2) mutually exclusive	2) c
3) False	3) sample point	3) b
4) False	4) Probability	4) d
5) True	5) multiplication	5) a

CHAPTER 5

Discrete
Probability Distributions

Random Variables

Discrete Probability Distributions

Expected Value and Variance

Binomial Probability Distribution

Poisson Probability Distribution

Hypergeometric Probability Distribution

LEARNING OBJECTIVES

1. Understand the concepts of a random variable and a probability distribution.

2. Be able to distinguish between discrete and continuous random variables.

3. Be able to compute and interpret the expected value, variance, and standard deviation for a discrete random variable and understand how an Excel worksheet can be used to ease the burden of the calculations.

4. Be able to compute probabilities using a binomial probability distribution and be able to compute these probabilities using Excel's BINOMDIST function.

5. Be able to compute probabilities using a Poisson probability distribution and be able to compute these probabilities using Excel's POISSON function.

6. Know when and how to use the hypergeometric probability distribution and be able to compute these probabilities using Excel's HYPGEOMDIST function.

REVIEW

Random Variables
*   A random variable is a numerical description of the outcome of an experiment.
*   A random variable can be classified as being either discrete or continuous depending on the numerical values it assumes.
*   A discrete random variable may assume either a finite number of values or an infinite sequence of values.
*   A continuous random variable may assume any numerical value in an interval or collection of intervals.

Discrete Probability Distributions
*   The probability distribution for a random variable describes how probabilities are distributed over the values of the random variable.
*   The probability distribution is defined by a probability function, denoted by $f(x)$, which provides the probability for each value of the random variable.
*   The required conditions for a discrete probability function are:
$$f(x) \geq 0$$
$$\Sigma f(x) = 1$$
*   We can describe a discrete probability distribution with a table, graph, or equation.

Discrete Uniform Probability Distribution
*   The discrete uniform probability distribution is the simplest example of a discrete probability distribution given by a formula.
*   The discrete uniform probability function is
    $f(x) = 1/n$ where: n = the number of values the random variable may assume
*   Note that the values of the random variable are equally likely.

Expected Value and Variance

- The expected value, or mean, of a random variable is a measure of its central location.
- Expected value of a discrete random variable:

$$E(x) = \mu = \Sigma x f(x)$$

- The variance summarizes the variability in the values of a random variable.
- Variance of a discrete random variable:

$$Var(x) = \sigma^2 = \Sigma(x - \mu)^2 f(x)$$

- The standard deviation, σ, is defined as the positive square root of the variance.
- The standard deviation is measured in the same units as the random variable and therefore is often preferred in describing variability.

Binomial Probability Distribution

- The binomial probability distribution is associated with a multiple-step experiment that we call the binomial experiment
- A binomial experiment has the following four properties:
  - The experiment consists of a sequence of n identical trials.
  - Two outcomes, success and failure, are possible on each trial.
  - The probability of a success, denoted by p, does not change from trial to trial (this property is called the stationarity assumption).
  - The trials are independent.
- A special mathematical formula, called the binomial probability function, can be used to compute the probability of x successes in n trials.

Binomial Probability Function

- The function can be viewed as consisting of two parts.
- Part 1: Number of experiments; outcomes providing exactly x successes in n trials is:

$$\frac{n!}{x!(n-x)!}$$

- Part 2: Probability of a particular sequence of trial outcomes with x successes in n trials is:

$$p^x (1-p)^{(n-x)}$$

- Putting the two parts together, we get the binomial probability function:

$$f(x) = \frac{n!}{x!(n-x)!} p^x (1-p)^{(n-x)}$$

where: $f(x)$ = probability of x successes in n trials
   n = number of trials
   p = probability of a success on any one trial
   $(1 - p)$ = probability of a failure on any one trial

Expected Value and Variance for the Binomial Distribution

- The expected value is:

$$E(x) = \mu = np$$

- The variance is:

$$Var(x) = \sigma^2 = np(1 - p)$$

Poisson Probability Distribution

- The Poisson probability distribution is often useful in estimating the number of occurrences over a specified interval of time or space.
- A Poisson experiment has the following two properties:
  - The probability of an occurrence is the same for any two intervals of equal length.
  - The occurrence or nonoccurrence in any interval is independent of the occurrence or nonoccurrence in any other interval.
- The Poisson probability function is:

$$f(x) = \frac{\mu^x e^{-\mu}}{x!}$$

where: $f(x)$ = probability of x occurrences in an interval

μ = mean number of occurrences in an interval

e = 2.71828

Hypergeometric Probability Distribution

- The hypergeometric distribution is closely related to the binomial distribution.
- With the hypergeometric distribution, the trials are not independent, and the probability of success changes from trial to trial.
- The hypergeometric probability function is used to compute the probability that in a random sample of n elements, selected without replacement, we will obtain x elements labeled success and $n - x$ elements labeled failure.
- The hypergeometric probability function is:

$$f(x) = \frac{\binom{r}{x}\binom{N-r}{n-x}}{\binom{N}{n}} \quad \text{for } 0 \le x \le r$$

where: $f(x)$ = probability of x successes in n trials

n = number of trials

N = number of elements in the population

r = number of elements in the population labeled success

- The function can be viewed as consisting of three parts.
- Part 1: Number of ways a sample of size n can be selected from a population of size N:

$$\binom{N}{n} = \frac{N!}{n!(N-n)!}$$

- Part 2: Number of ways that x successes can be selected from a total of r successes in the population:

$$\binom{r}{x} = \frac{r!}{x!(r-x)!}$$

- Part 3: Number of ways that $n - x$ failures can be selected from a total of $N - r$ failures in the population:

$$\binom{N-r}{n-x} = \frac{(N-r)!}{(n-x)!(N-r-n+x)!}$$

KEY CONCEPTS

CONCEPT	EXAMPLES	EXERCISES
Random Variables	1	1
Discrete Probability Distribution	2,③	2,3
Expected Value and Variance	④	4,5
Binomial Probability Distribution	⑤	6,7,8
Poisson Probability Distribution	⑥	9,10,11
Hypergeometric Probability Distribution	⑦	12

◯ Excel Used

EXAMPLES

EXAMPLE 1

Random Variables

Dollar Department Stores is planning to open a new store on the corner of Main and Vine Streets. It has asked the Stanton Marketing Company to do a market study of randomly selected families within a five-mile radius of the store. Among the questions it wishes Stanton to ask each homeowner are: (a) family income; (b) family size; (c) distance from home to the store site; and, (d) whether or not the family owns a dog or a cat.

For each of the four questions, develop a random variable of interest to Dollar Department Stores. Denote which of these variables are discrete and which are continuous.

SOLUTION 1

Question	Random Variable	Discrete or Continuous
(a) Family income	x = Annual dollar gross income the family reported on their tax return	Discrete
(b) Family size	x = Number of dependents in the family reported on their tax return	Discrete
(c) Distance from home to store	x = Distance in miles from home to the store site	Continuous
(d) Dog/Cat	x = 1 if own no pet; = 2 if own dog(s) only; = 3 if own cat(s) only; = 4 if own dog(s) and cat(s)	Discrete

EXAMPLE 2

Discrete Probability Distribution

Stanton Marketing reported back to Dollar Department Stores the following information. Out of 400 families surveyed, 260 owned no pet, 120 owned dogs and 50 owned cats.

a) On the basis of this information, find the probability distribution for the random variable x, defined in (d) in Example 1.

b) Dollar Department Stores is considering opening a pet department if the expected number of families owning pets shopping at its store exceeds 4,000. If Dollar expects to serve 12,000 families, should it open a pet department?

SOLUTION 2

Since 260 owned no pets, 140 owned pets. Since 120 owned dogs and 50 owned cats (total = 170), then 30 must own both dogs and cats.

a) Since 120 owned dogs and 30 owned dogs and cats, 120 - 30 = 90 own dogs only. Similarly, 50 - 30 = 20 own cats only. Using the relative frequency method to calculate $f(x)$:

$$f(1) = 260/400 = .65 \qquad f(3) = 20/400 = .05$$
$$f(2) = 90/400 = .225 \qquad f(4) = 30/400 = .075$$

b) The probability of owning a pet = 1 - the probability of not owning a pet = $1 - f(1) =$ 1 - .65 = .35. Multiply this probability by the total number of families Dollar expects to serve to obtain the expected number of families owning pets = (.35)(12,000) = 4,200. Since this is greater than 4,000, Dollar should open a pet department.

EXAMPLE 3

Discrete Probability Distribution

Abbey Grant is a part-time salesperson at McNair's Appliances. For the last 200 days she has kept a record of the number of televisions she sold each day.

Units Sold	Number of Days
0	80
1	50
2	40
3	10
4	20
	200

a) Develop a probability distribution for the number of televisions sold in a day.

b) What is the most probable number of televisions Abbey will sell in a day?

c) What is Abbey's expected number of televisions sold per day?

d) What is the probability that Abbey will sell more than one television in a day?

e) Draw a graph of the probability distribution.

SOLUTION 3

Using Excel

Enter Data: The data needed are the values for the random variable and their corresponding frequencies.

Enter Functions and Formulas: To develop the probability distribution we compute the probability of each value of the random variable using the relative frequency approach. That is, the probability is equal to the frequency of the value relative to the total frequency for all values of the random variable.

Formula Worksheet:

	A	B	C
1	Sales	Frequency	Probability
2	0	80	=B2/$B$7
3	1	50	=B3/$B$7
4	2	40	=B4/$B$7
5	3	10	=B5/$B$7
6	4	20	=B6/$B$7
7	Total	=SUM(B2:B6)	

Value Worksheet:

	A	B	C
1	Sales	Frequency	Probability
2	0	80	0.40
3	1	50	0.25
4	2	40	0.20
5	3	10	0.05
6	4	20	0.10
7	Total	200	

b) Abbey is most likely to sell 0 televisions in a day.

c) E(x) = .40(0) + .25(1) + .20(2) + .05(3) + .10(4) = 1.2 televisions

d) P(x ≥ 2) = P(x = 2) + P(x = 3) + P(x = 4) = .20 + .05 + .10 = .35

e)

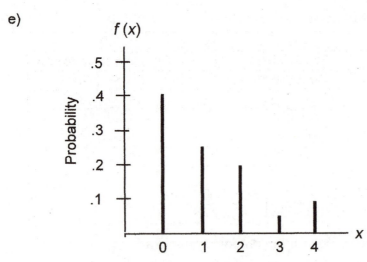

Number of Televisions Sold During a Day

EXAMPLE 4

Expected Value and Variance

Refer to the probability distribution for daily television sales developed in Example 3. Compute the expected value, variance, and standard deviation for the distribution.

SOLUTION 4

Using Excel's SUMPRODUCT Function

Excel's SUMPRODUCT function can be used to compute the expected value and variance for daily television sales. We will continue with the worksheet we developed in Solution 3.

Enter Data: The data is already entered (see Solution 3).

Enter Functions and Formulas: To compute the expected value for the distribution, we do the following. The SUMPRODUCT function multiplies each value in one range by the corresponding value in another range, and sums the products.

To compute the variance for the distribution, we first compute the squared deviation from the mean value for each value of the random variable. The variance is the sum of the products of the squared deviations and the corresponding probabilities.

To compute the standard deviation for the distribution, we take the square root of the variance.

Formula Worksheet:

	A	B	C	D
1	Sales	Frequency	Probability	Sq. Dev. from Mean
2	0	80	=B2/$B$7	=(A2-$C$8)^2
3	1	50	=B3/$B$7	=(A3-$C$8)^2
4	2	40	=B4/$B$7	=(A4-$C$8)^2
5	3	10	=B5/$B$7	=(A5-$C$8)^2
6	4	20	=B6/$B$7	=(A6-$C$8)^2
7	Total	=SUM(B2:B6)		
8		Exp. Value	=SUMPRODUCT(A2:A6,C2:C6)	
9		Variance	=SUMPRODUCT(D2:D6,C2:C6)	
10		Std. Dev.	=SQRT(C9)	

Value Worksheet:

	A	B	C	D
1	Sales	Frequency	Probability	Sq. Dev. from Mean
2	0	80	0.40	1.44
3	1	50	0.25	0.04
4	2	40	0.20	0.64
5	3	10	0.05	3.24
6	4	20	0.10	7.84
7	Total	200		
8		Exp. Value	1.20	
9		Variance	1.66	
10		Std. Dev.	1.29	

EXAMPLE 5

Binomial Distribution

Evans Electric is concerned about a low retention rate for employees. On the basis of past experience, management has seen an annual turnover of 10% of the hourly employees. Thus, for any hourly employee chosen at random, management estimates a probability of 0.1 that the person will not be with the company next year.

a) Choosing 3 hourly employees at random, what is the probability that exactly 1 of them will leave the company this year?

b) What is the probability that <u>at least</u> one of the three chosen workers stays?

SOLUTION 5

a)

Using a Tree Diagram

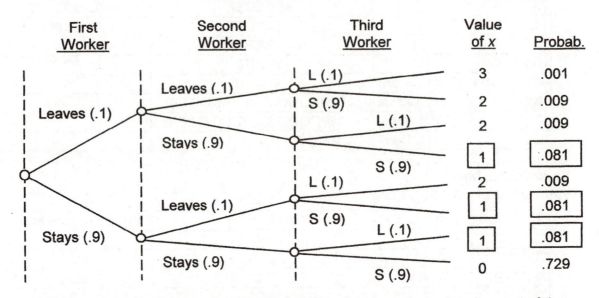

First Worker	Second Worker	Third Worker	Value of x	Probab.

We see in the tree diagram that the probability of one employee leaving, out of the sample of three, is .081 + .081 + .081 = .243.

Using the Binomial Probability Function

In order to compute a binomial probability we must know the number of trials (n), the probability of success (p), and the value of the random variable (x). For Evans Electric, the number of trials is 3, the probability of success (leaving) is .1, and the value of x is 1.

$$f(x) = \frac{n!}{x!(n-x)!} p^x (1-p)^{(n-x)}$$

$$f(1) = \frac{3!}{1!(3-1)!} (.1)^1 (1-.1)^{(3-1)} = 3(.1)(.81) = 3(.081) = .243$$

Using Excel's BINOMDIST Function

Enter Data: We enter the value 3 for n and the value .1 for p. We are specifically interested in the probability of $x = 1$, however we can find the probabilities for all possible values of x quite easily using Excel.

Enter Functions and Formulas: The BINOMDIST function has four arguments: the first is the value of x, the second is the value of n, the third is the value of p, and the fourth is FALSE or TRUE. We choose FALSE because we want a probability, not a cumulative probability.

Formula Worksheet:

	A	B
1	3	**= Number of Trials (*n*)**
2	0.1	**= Probability of Success (*p*)**
3		
4	*x*	*f(x)*
5	0	=BINOMDIST(A5,$A$1,$A$2,FALSE)
6	1	=BINOMDIST(A6,$A$1,$A$2,FALSE)
7	2	=BINOMDIST(A7,$A$1,$A$2,FALSE)
8	3	=BINOMDIST(A8,$A$1,$A$2,FALSE)

We see below in the resulting worksheet that the probability of one of the three chosen workers leaving is .243, which agrees with our result using the tree diagram.

Value Worksheet:

	A	B
1	3	**= Number of Trials (*n*)**
2	0.1	**= Probability of Success (*p*)**
3		
4	*x*	*f(x)*
5	0	0.729
6	1	0.243
7	2	0.027
8	3	0.001

b) "What is the probability that at least one of the three chosen workers stays?" is equivalent to asking "what is the probability that the number of workers leaving is two or less?" The answer can be computed by again using the BINOMDIST function, but this time we will enter TRUE for the fourth argument in the function.

Formula Worksheet:

	A	B
1	3	**= Number of Trials (*n*)**
2	0.1	**= Probability of Success (*p*)**
3		
4	*x*	**Cumulative Probability**
5	0	=BINOMDIST(A5,$A$1,$A$2,TRUE)
6	1	=BINOMDIST(A6,$A$1,$A$2,TRUE)
7	2	=BINOMDIST(A7,$A$1,$A$2,TRUE)
8	3	=BINOMDIST(A8,$A$1,$A$2,TRUE)
9		

We see in the resulting worksheet below that the probability of two or less of the three chosen workers leaving is .999.

Value Worksheet:

	A	B
1	3	= Number of Trials (n)
2	0.1	= Probability of Success (p)
3		
4	x	Cumulative Probability
5	0	0.729
6	1	0.972
7	2	0.999
8	3	1.000
9		

EXAMPLE 6

Poisson Probability Distribution

Patients arrive at the emergency room of Mercy Hospital at the average rate of 6 per hour on weekend evenings. What is the probability of 4 arrivals in 30 minutes on a weekend evening? What is the probability of 6 or fewer arrivals in one hour?

SOLUTION 6

Using the Poisson Probability Function

In order to compute a Poisson probability we must know the mean number of occurrences (μ) per time period and the number of occurrences (x) for which we want to compute the probability. For this problem, x equals 4.

For our purposes, μ does not equal 6. The average number of arrivals in <u>one hour</u> is 6, but we are interested in a 30-minute time period. For this reason we convert the hourly average to a half-hour average by dividing 6 by 2. Thus $\mu = 3$.

$$f(x) = \frac{\mu^x e^{-\mu}}{x!} \qquad f(4) = \frac{3^4 (2.71828)^{-3}}{4!} = \frac{81(.0497872)}{24} = .1680$$

Using Excel's POISSON Function

Enter Data: We enter the value 3 for the mean number of arrivals. We are specifically interested in the probability of $x = 4$, but we can find the probabilities for a wide range of all possible values of x quite easily using Excel.

Enter Functions and Formulas: The POISSON function has three arguments: the first is the value of μ, the second is the value of x, and the third is TRUE or FALSE. We choose FALSE because we want a probability, not a cumulative probability.

Formula Worksheet:

	A	B
1	3	= Mean No. of Occurrences (μ)
2		
3	Number of Arrivals (x)	Probability $f(x)$
4	0	=POISSON(A4,$A$1,FALSE)
5	1	=POISSON(A5,$A$1,FALSE)
6	2	=POISSON(A6,$A$1,FALSE)
7	3	=POISSON(A7,$A$1,FALSE)
8	4	=POISSON(A8,$A$1,FALSE)
9	5	=POISSON(A9,$A$1,FALSE)
10	6	=POISSON(A10,$A$1,FALSE)
11	7	=POISSON(A11,$A$1,FALSE)
12	8	=POISSON(A12,$A$1,FALSE)

We see in the resulting worksheet below that the probability of four arrivals in 30 minutes is .168.

Value Worksheet:

	A	B
1	3	= Mean No. of Occurrences (H)
2		
3	Number of Arrivals (x)	Probability $f(x)$
4	0	0.0498
5	1	0.1494
6	2	0.2240
7	3	0.2240
8	4	0.1680
9	5	0.1008
10	6	0.0504
11	7	0.0216
12	8	0.0081

The second part of the problem we are solving asks "What is the probability of 6 or fewer arrivals in one hour? Now we use $\mu = 6$ because we are examining a one-hour time period. Also, this time we enter TRUE as the third argument in the POISSON function because we want a cumulative probability.

Formula Worksheet:

	A	B
1	6	**= Mean No. of Occurrences (μ)**
2		
3	**Number of Arrivals (x)**	**Cumulative Probability**
4	0	=POISSON(A4,$A$1,TRUE)
5	1	=POISSON(A5,$A$1,TRUE)
6	2	=POISSON(A6,$A$1,TRUE)
7	3	=POISSON(A7,$A$1,TRUE)
8	4	=POISSON(A8,$A$1,TRUE)
9	5	=POISSON(A9,$A$1,TRUE)
10	6	=POISSON(A10,$A$1,TRUE)
11	7	=POISSON(A11,$A$1,TRUE)
12	8	=POISSON(A12,$A$1,TRUE)

We see in the resulting worksheet below that the probability of six or fewer arrivals in one hour is .6063.

Value Worksheet:

	A	B
1	6	**= Mean No. of Occurrences (μ)**
2		
3	**Number of Arrivals (x)**	**Cumulative Probability**
4	0	0.0025
5	1	0.0174
6	2	0.0620
7	3	0.1512
8	4	0.2851
9	5	0.4457
10	6	0.6063
11	7	0.7440
12	8	0.8472

EXAMPLE 7

Hypergeometric Distribution

Bob Neveready has removed two dead batteries from a flashlight and inadvertently mingled them with the two good batteries he intended as replacements. The four batteries look identical.

Bob now randomly selects two of the four batteries. What is the probability he selects the two good batteries?

SOLUTION 7

Using the Hypergeometric Probability Function

We can use the hypergeometric probability function to compute the probability we are solving for. The computation is as follows:

$$f(x) = \frac{\binom{r}{x}\binom{N-r}{n-x}}{\binom{N}{n}} = \frac{\binom{2}{2}\binom{2}{0}}{\binom{4}{2}} = \frac{\left(\frac{2!}{2!0!}\right)\left(\frac{2!}{0!2!}\right)}{\left(\frac{4!}{2!2!}\right)} = \frac{1}{6} = .167$$

where: $x = 2$ = number of <u>good</u> batteries selected
$n = 2$ = number of batteries selected
$N = 4$ = number of batteries in total
$r = 2$ = number of <u>good</u> batteries in total

Using Excel's HYPGEOMDIST Function

Enter Data: We enter the value 2, for the number of successes and the value 2, for the number of trials. We enter the value 2, for the number of elements in the population labeled success (good batteries). We enter the value 4 for the total number of elements (batteries).

Enter Functions and Formulas: The Excel function for computing hypergeometric probabilities, HYPERGEOMDIST, only computes probabilities, not cumulative probabilities. The function has four arguments: x for the number of successes, n for the number of trials, r for the number of elements in the population labeled success, and N for the total number of elements in the population. In this problem, $x = 2$, $n = 2$, $r = 2$, and $N = 4$.

Formula Worksheet:

	A	B
1	2	**= Number of Successes (*x*)**
2	2	**= Number of Trials (*n*)**
3	2	**= Number of Elements in the Population Labeled Success (*r*)**
4	4	**= Number of Elements in the Population (*N*)**
5		
6	*f(x)* =	=HYPGEOMDIST(A1,A2,A3,A4)
7		

We see in the resulting worksheet below that the probability of selecting two good batteries from a group of four batteries containing only two good batteries is .167.

Value Worksheet:

	A	B
1	2	= **Number of Successes (*x*)**
2	2	= **Number of Trials (*n*)**
3	2	= **Number of Elements in the Population Labeled Success (*r*)**
4	4	= **Number of Elements in the Population (*N*)**
5		
6	*f*(*x*) =	0.167
7		

EXERCISES

EXERCISE 1

Random Variables

Waters' Edge is a clothing retailer that promotes its products via catalog and accepts customer orders by all of the conventional ways including the Internet. Waters' Edge has an excellent reputation as a result of the superior service, speed of delivery, and product value it provides its customers. The company has gained these competitive advantages in part by collecting data about its operations and the customer each time an order is processed.

Among the data collected with each order are: (a) order quantity, (b) shipping weight of order, (c) inventory status of items ordered, (d) customer's prior orders, (e) method of payment, and (f) gender of orderer. For each of the six categories of data, develop a random variable of interest to the managers of Waters' Edge. Denote which of the variables are discrete and which are continuous.

EXERCISE 2

Discrete Probability Distribution

June's Specialty Shop sells designer original dresses. On 10% of her dresses, June makes a profit of $10, on 20% of her dresses she makes a profit of $20, on 30% of her dresses she makes a profit of $30, and on 40% of her dresses she makes a profit of $40.

a) What is the expected profit June earns on the sale of a dress?

b) On a given day, the probability of June having no customers is .05, of one customer is .10, of two customers is .20, of three customers is .35, of four customers is .20, and of five customers is .10. June's daily operating cost is $40 per day. Using your answer to (a), find the expected net profit June earns per day. (Hint: To find the expected daily gross profit, multiply the expected profit per dress by the expected number of customers per day.)

c) June is considering moving to a larger store. She estimates that doing so will double the expected number of customers. If the larger store will increase her operating costs to $100 per day, should she make the move?

EXERCISE 3

Discrete Probability Distribution

Ace Mopeds sells mopeds with a one-month warranty. Over a one-year period the following data were compiled.

Month	Number Sold in Month	Number Returned for Warranty Service	Month	Number Sold in Month	Number Returned for Warranty Service
Jan	4	1	Jul	20	4
Feb	6	2	Aug	20	4
Mar	3	0	Sep	20	4
Apr	20	1	Oct	16	3
May	10	2	Nov	16	3
Jun	16	4	Dec	10	3

a) Based on this data, determine the probability distribution for: (1) the number of mopeds sold in a month; (2) the number of mopeds returned for warranty in a given month; (3) the percentage of mopeds returned for warranty in a given month.

b) Which of these distributions are for discrete and which are for continuous random variables.

c) Which distribution would be of concern to (1) the quality control engineer at the moped factory; (2) the sales department at Ace; and, (3) the service department at Ace.

d) What is the probability that the percentage of Mopeds returned for service in a randomly selected month is between 10% and 21%?

e) What is the probability that the number of mopeds returned for service in a randomly selected month is greater than 1 and less than 4?

f) What is the expected number of mopeds Ace sells in a month?

g) What is the expected number of mopeds returned for service in a month?

h) What is the expected percentage of mopeds returned for service in a month?

i) Is the answer to part (h) equal to the answer in part (g) divided by the answer to part (f)?

EXERCISE 4

Expected Value and Variance

Two headache remedies, <u>Relief</u> and <u>Comfort</u> are waging an advertising campaign. Each claims it eliminates a headache faster. The data compiled by an independent testing agency is as follows:

Time (in minutes) after taking remedy	Percentage of headaches cured at that time using	
	Relief	Comfort
5	.60	0
10	0	.10
15	0	.75
20	0	.15
25	0	0
30	.40	0

a) What are the means and variances of the time until headache cure (1) using Relief; (2) using Comfort?

b) Which remedy has the maximum probability of relieving a headache within 10 minutes?

c) Which remedy has the maximum probability of relieving a headache within 20 minutes?

EXERCISE 5

Expected Value and Variance

The salespeople at Gold Key Realty sell up to 9 houses per month. The probability distribution of a salesperson selling x houses in a month is as follows:

Sales (x)	0	1	2	3	4	5	6	7	8	9
Probability f (x)	.05	.10	.15	.20	.15	.10	.10	.05	.05	.05

130   *CHAPTER 5*

a) What are the mean and standard deviation for the number of houses sold by a salesperson per month?

b) Any salesperson selling more houses than the amount equal to the mean plus two standard deviations receives a bonus. How many houses per month must a salesperson sell to receive a bonus?

EXERCISE 6

Binomial Probability Distribution

Sandy's Pet Center grooms large and small dogs. It takes Sandy 40 minutes to groom a small dog and 70 minutes to groom a large dog. Large dogs account for 20% of Sandy's business. Sandy has 5 appointments on August 15.

a) What is the probability that all 5 dogs are small?

b) What is the probability that two of the dogs are large?

c) What is the expected amount of time to finish all five dogs?

EXERCISE 7

Binomial Probability Distribution

Ralph's Gas Station is running a giveaway promotion. With every fill-up of gasoline, Ralph gives out a lottery ticket that has a 25% chance of being a winning ticket. Customers who collect four winning lottery tickets are eligible for the "BIG SPIN" for large payoffs.

What is the probability of qualifying for the big spin if a customer fills up: (a) 3 times; (b) 4 times; (c) 7 times?

EXERCISE 8

Binomial Probability Distribution

Chez Paul is an exclusive French restaurant that seats only 10 couples for dinner. Paul is famous for his "truffle salad for two" which must be prepared one day in advance. The probability of any couple ordering the salad is .4 and each couple orders independently of other couples.

a) What is the expected number of "truffle salads for two" that Paul serves per dinner? What is the variance?

b) What is the probability that on a given evening, at most three couples want a "truffle salad for two"?

c) How many salads should Paul prepare if he wants the probability of not having enough salads for all customers who desire one to be no greater than .10?

d) There is a 70% chance a couple will order coffee after dinner. What is the probability that on a given evening, exactly eight of the ten couples will order coffee? (Again assume that couples order independently of each other.)

EXERCISE 9

Poisson Probability Distribution

The number of customers at Winkies Donuts between 8:00a.m. and 9:00a.m. is believed to follow a Poisson distribution with a mean of 2 customers per minute.

a) During a randomly selected one-minute interval during this time period, what is the probability of 6 customers arriving to Winkies?

b) What is the probability that at least 2 minutes elapse between customer arrivals?

EXERCISE 10

Poisson Probability Distribution

During lunchtime, customers arrive at Bob's Drugs according to a Poisson distribution with $\lambda = 4$ per minute.

a) During a one minute interval, determine the following probabilities: (1) no arrivals; (2) one arrival; (3) two arrivals; and, (4) three or more arrivals.

b) What is the probability of two arrivals in a two-minute period?

EXERCISE 11

Poisson Probability Distribution

Telephone calls arrive at the Global Airline reservation office in Lemonville according to a Poisson distribution with a mean of 1.2 calls per minute.

a) What is the probability of receiving exactly one call during a one-minute interval?

b) What is the probability of receiving at most 2 calls during a one-minute interval?

c) What is the probability of receiving at least two calls during a one-minute interval?

d) What is the probability of receiving exactly 4 calls during a <u>five</u>-minute interval?

e) What is the probability that at most 2 minutes elapse between one call and the next?

EXERCISE 12

Hypergeometric Probability Distribution

Before dawn Josh hurriedly packed some clothes for a job-interview trip while his roommate was still sleeping. He reached in his disorganized sock drawer where there were five black socks and five navy blue socks, although they appeared to be the same color in the dimly lighted room. Josh grabbed six socks, hoping that at least two, and preferably four, of them were black to match the gray suit he had packed. With no time to spare, he then raced to the airport to catch his plane.

a) What is the probability that Josh packed at least two black socks so that he will be dressed appropriately the day of his interview?

b) What is the probability that Josh packed at least four black socks so that he will be dressed appropriately the latter day of his trip as well?

SELF-TEST

TRUE/FALSE

____ 1. The binomial probability distribution is most symmetric when p equals 0.5.

____ 2. A discrete random variable may assume an infinite sequence of values.

____ 3. If one wanted to find the probability of ten customer arrivals in an hour at a service station, one would generally use the Poisson distribution.

____ 4. The binomial probability function cannot be applied to all binomial experiments.

____ 5. There is an upper limit on the value of x, the number of occurrences in an interval, when x is a random variable described by the Poisson probability function.

FILL-IN-THE-BLANK

1. A _____ is a numerical description of the outcome of an experiment.

2. To compute the probability that in a random sample of *n* elements, selected without replacement, we will obtain *x* successes, we would use the _____ probability function.

3. The _____ probability function is based in part on the counting rule for combinations.

4. A _____ probability distribution shows the probability of *x* occurrences of an event over a specified interval of time or space.

5. Experimental outcomes that are based on measurement scales such as time, weight, and distance can be described by _____ random variables.

MULTIPLE CHOICE

____ 1. Which one of the following properties of a binomial experiment is called the stationarity assumption?
   a) The experiment consists of *n* identical trials.
   b) Two outcomes are possible on each trial.
   c) The probability of success is the same for each trial.
   d) The trials are independent.

____ 2. The function used to compute the probability of *x* successes in *n* trials, when the trials are dependent, is the
   a) binomial probability function
   b) hypergeometric probability function
   c) Poisson probability function
   d) discrete uniform probability function

____ 3. The expected value of a random variable is the
   a) most probable value
   b) simple average of all the possible values
   c) median value
   d) mean value

____ 4. In a binomial experiment consisting of five trials, the number of different values that *x* (the number of successes) can assume is
   a) 2
   b) 5
   c) 6
   d) 10

____ 5. A binomial probability distribution with $p = .3$ is
   a) negatively skewed
   b) symmetrical
   c) positively skewed
   d) bimodal

ANSWERS

EXERCISES

1) (a) Order quantity x = Number of items ordered   Discrete
   (b) Shipping weight x = Weight (lbs) of packages shipped   Continuous
   (c) Inventory status x = 0 if any items unavailable   Discrete
                             1 if all items available
   (d) Order fill time x = Time (hrs) from order   Continuous
                             receipt until shipped
   (d) Prior orders x = Number of orders in last 12 months Discrete
   (e) Payment method x = 0 if gift certificate   Discrete
                             1 if personal check
                             2 if credit card
                             3 if debit card

2) a) $30   b) $45.50   c) Yes, new daily profit = $71

3) a) (1) P(3) = 1/12, P(4) = 1/12, P(6) = 1/12, P(10) = 1/6, P(16) = 1/4, P(20) = 1/3,
             all other P(x) = 0.
        (2) P(0) = 1/12, P(1) =1/6, P(2) = 1/6, P(3) = 1/6, P(4) = 1/3, all other P(y) = 0
        (3) P(0) = 1/12, P(.05) = 1/12, P(.1875) = 1/6, P(.20) = 1/3, P(.25) = 1/6,
             P(.3) = 1/12, P(.333) = 1/12, all other P(z) = 0
    b) all distributions are for discrete random variables
    c) (1) the third; (2) the first; (3) the second.
    d) 1/2   e) 5/12   f) 13.417   g) 2.583   h) 17.15%   i) No

4) a) Relief μ = 15, σ^2 = 150; Comfort μ = 15.25, σ^2 = 6.19   b) Relief   c) Comfort

5) a) mean = 3.9, standard deviation = 2.34   6) a) .3277   c) 230 mins.
   b) 8.58 or 9 houses   b) .2048

7) a) 0   8) a) μ = 4, σ^2 = 2.4   c) 6
   b) .0039   b) .3822   d) .2335
   c) .0705

9) a) .0120   b) .0183

10) a) .0183, .0733, .1465, .7619   b) .0107

11) a) .36   b) .88   c) .34   d) .135   e) .9093

12) a) .976   b) .262

TRUE/FALSE

1) True
2) True
3) True
4) False
5) False

FILL-IN-THE-BLANK

1) random variable
2) hypergeometric
3) binomial
4) Poisson
5) continuous

MULTIPLE CHOICE

1) c
2) b
3) d
4) c
5) c

CHAPTER 6

Continuous
Probability Distributions

Uniform Probability Distribution

Normal Probability Distribution

Exponential Probability Distribution

LEARNING OBJECTIVES

1. Understand the difference between how probabilities are computed for discrete and continuous random variables.

2. Know how to compute probability values for a continuous uniform probability distribution and be able to compute the expected value and variance for such a distribution.

3. Be able to compute probabilities using a normal probability distribution. Understand the role of the standard normal distribution in this process.

4. Be able to use tables for the standard normal probability distribution to compute both standard normal probabilities and probabilities for any normal distribution.

5. Given a cumulative probability be able to compute the z-value and x-value that cuts off the corresponding area in the left tail of a normal distribution.

6. Be able to use Excel's NORMSDIST and NORMDIST functions to compute probabilities for the standard normal distribution and any normal distribution.

7. Be able to use Excel's NORMSINV and NORMINV function to find z and x values corresponding to given cumulative probabilities.

8. Be able to compute probabilities using an exponential probability distribution and using Excel's EXPONDIST function.

9. Understand the relationship between the Poisson and exponential probability distributions.

REVIEW

Continuous Probability Distributions
- A continuous random variable can assume any value in an interval on the real line or in a collection of intervals.
- It is not possible to talk about the probability of the random variable assuming a particular value.
- Instead, we talk about the probability of the random variable assuming a value within a given interval.
- The probability of the random variable assuming a value within some given interval from x_1 to x_2 is defined to be the area under the graph of the probability density function between x_1 and x_2.
- The total area under the graph $f(x)$ is equal to 1.

Area as a Measure of Probability
- The area under the graph of $f(x)$ and probability are the same.
- The probability that x takes a value between some lower value x_1 and some higher value x_2 can be found by computing the area under the graph of $f(x)$ over the interval x_1 and x_2.

Uniform Probability Distribution
- If a random variable is restricted to be within some interval and the probability density function is constant over the interval, (a,b), the continuous random variable is said to have a uniform distribution between a and b.
- Its density function is given by:
$$f(x) = 1/(b\text{-}a) \text{ for } a \leq x \leq b, \text{ and } = 0 \text{ outside this interval.}$$
- The formula for the expected value of x is:
$$E(x) = (a + b)/2$$
- The formula for the variance of x is:
$$Var(x) = (b - a)^2/12$$

Normal Probability Distribution
- The normal distribution is perhaps the most widely used distribution for describing a continuous random variable.
- The normal probability density function is:
$$f(x) = \frac{1}{\sigma\sqrt{2\pi}} e^{-(x-\mu)^2/2\sigma^2}$$
where: μ = mean
σ = standard deviation
π = 3.14159
e = 2.71828

Characteristics of the Normal Probability Distribution
- The shape of the normal curve is often illustrated as a bell-shaped curve.
- Two parameters, μ (mean) and σ (standard deviation), determine the location and shape of the distribution.
- The highest point on the normal curve is at the mean, which is also the median and mode.
- The mean can be any numerical value: negative, zero, or positive.
- The normal curve is symmetric (left and right halves are mirror images).
- The standard deviation determines the width of the curve: larger values result in wider, flatter curves.
- The total area under the curve is 1 (0.5 to the left of the mean and 0.5 to the right).
- Areas under the curve give probabilities for the normal random variable.
- Unlike the uniform distribution, the height of the normal distribution's curve varies and calculus is required to compute the areas that represent probability.
- Areas under the normal curve have been computed and are available in tables that can be used in computing probabilities.
- The percentage of values in some commonly used intervals are:
  - 68.26% of values of a normal random variable are within +/- 1 standard deviation of its mean.
  - 95.44% of values of a normal random variable are within +/- 2 standard deviations of its mean.
  - 99.72% of values of a normal random variable are within +/- 3 standard deviations of its mean.

Standard Normal Probability Distribution
- A random variable that has a normal distribution with a mean of zero and a standard deviation of one is said to have a standard normal probability distribution.
- The letter z is commonly used to designate this normal random variable.
- We can think of z as a measure of the number of standard deviations x is from μ..
- The formula used to convert any normal random variable x, with mean μ and standard deviation σ, to the standard normal distribution is:
$$z = (x - \mu)/\sigma$$

Exponential Probability Distribution
- A continuous probability distribution frequently used for computing the probability of the time to complete a task is the exponential distribution.
- If the average time to complete a task is denote by μ, then the probability density function for the amount of time, x, to complete the task is given by:
$$f(x) = (1/\mu)e^{-(x/\mu)} \text{ for } x \geq 0 \text{ and } \mu > 0.$$
- From this distribution, the probability a task is completed within a specified time, x_0, is:
$$P(x < x_0) = 1 - e^{-(x_0/\mu)}.$$

Relationship Between the Poisson and Exponential Distributions
- If the Poisson distribution provides an appropriate description of the number of occurrences per interval, the exponential distribution provides a description of the length of the interval between occurrences.
- As an example: If customers arrive according to a Poisson distribution with a mean of λ customers, then the interarrival times of customers follows an exponential distribution with $\mu = 1/\lambda$.

KEY CONCEPTS

CONCEPT	EXAMPLES	EXERCISES
Uniform Probability Distribution	1,2	1,2
Normal Probability Distribution	③	3,4,5,6
Exponential Probability Distribution	④	7

◯ Excel Used

EXAMPLES

EXAMPLE 1

Uniform Probability Distribution

Customers of Slater's Buffet are charged for the amount of salad they take. Sampling suggests that the amount of salad taken is uniformly distributed between 5 ounces and 15 ounces.

a) Compute the expected value and variance for the distribution.

b) What is the probability that a customer will take between 12 and 15 ounces of salad?

c) Graph the probability density function.

SOLUTION 1

a) Expected Value of x = E(x) = (a + b)/2 = (5 + 15)/2 = 10

Variance of x = Var(x) = (b - a)^2/12 = (15 – 5)^2/12 = 8.33

b) P(12 $\leq$ x $\leq$ 15) = 1/10(3) = .3

c)

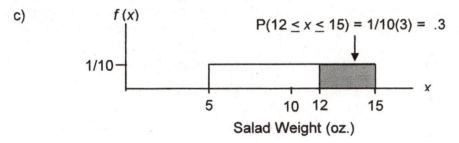

EXAMPLE 2

Uniform Probability Distribution

Suppose a random variable x has a continuous uniform distribution with values ranging from 5 to 15.

a) What is the probability that x has a value between 8 and 10?

b) What is the probability that the value for x is less than 7 or greater than 12?

c) What is the probability that x has a value less than 20?

d) What is the probability that x equals 11?

SOLUTION 2

Since x has a uniform distribution between 5 and 15, $f(x) = 1/10$ for $5 \leq x \leq 15$
$= 0$ elsewhere.

a) To find the probability x has a value between 8 and 10, multiply the interval width (2) by $f(x)$. This equals $(2)(.1) = .2$.

b) The event "7 or less" is the interval between 5 and 7 = 2, and "greater than 12" is between 12 and 15 = 3. The total interval width of the event is 3+2 = 5. Hence its probability is 5(.1) = .50

c) Since x can only be 15 or less, the probability $x \leq 20$ is 1.

d) The probability that x exactly equals 11 is 0 by definition.

EXAMPLE 3

Normal Probability Distribution

Pep Zone sells auto parts and supplies including a popular multi-grade motor oil. When the stock of this oil drops to 20 gallons, a replenishment order is placed.
The store manager is concerned that sales are being lost due to stockouts while waiting for a replenishment order. It has been determined that lead-time demand is normally distributed with a mean of 15 gallons and a standard deviation of 6 gallons.

a) The manager would like to know the probability of a stockout, $P(x > 20)$.

b) If the manager of Pep Zone wants the probability of a stockout to be no more than .05, what should the reorder point be?

SOLUTION 3

a) We are solving for the (tail) area to the right of the 20-gallon line in the graph below. The <u>Cumulative Probabilities for the Standard Normal Distribution</u> table in the textbook does not directly provide the area for the upper tail region of the distribution. So, we will first determine the area under the curve to the left of the reorder point.

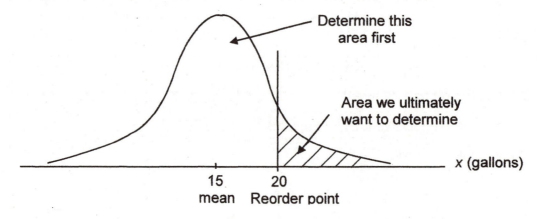

We begin by converting our normal distribution (measured in gallons here) to the standard normal distribution so that we can use the Standard Normal table of areas. Essentially, we must compute how many standard deviations lie between the mean demand value μ (15) and the reorder point value x (20).

$$z = (x - \mu)/\sigma = (20 - 15)/6 = .83$$

The Cumulative Probabilities for the Standard Normal Distribution table shows an area of .7967 for the region to the left of the reorder point (where $z = .83$).

z	.00	.01	.02	.03	.04	.05	.06	.07	.08	.09
.5	.6915	.6950	.6985	.7019	.7054	.7088	.7123	.7157	.7190	.7224
.6	.7257	.7291	.7324	.7357	.7389	.7422	.7454	.7486	.7518	.7549
.7	.7580	.7612	.7642	.7673	.7704	.7734	.7764	.7794	.7823	.7852
.8	.7881	.7910	.7939	.7967	.7995	.8023	.8051	.8078	.8106	.8133
.9	.8159	.8186	.8212	.8238	.8264	.8289	.8315	.8340	.8365	.8389

The upper tail area is 1.0 - .7967 = .2033. The probability of a stock-out is .2033.

Using Excel's NORMSDIST Function

Excel's NORMSDIST function can be used to solve this portion of the problem. The NORMSDIST function is used to compute the cumulative probability for the standard normal distribution. Essentially, we are converting a normal distribution to the standard normal distribution by computing and using a z value rather than an x value.

Enter Data: We enter the mean value of 15, the standard deviation value of 6, and the x value of 20 (for which we want a cumulative probability).

Enter Functions and Formulas: The NORMSDIST function requires one argument (input), a z value, so we compute the z value for $x = 20$. To compute the probability of the random variable assuming a value less than the x value, we use the function =NORMSDIST.

To compute the probability of the random variable assuming a value greater than the x value, we enter the formula =1-NORMSDIST.

Formula Worksheet:

	A	B
1	FINDING A PROBABILITY, USING A z VALUE	
2	Mean	15
3	Standard Deviation	6
4	x Value	20
5	z Value	=(B4-B2)/B3
6	Probability of a Lesser x Value	=NORMSDIST(B5)
7	Probability of a Greater x Value	=1-NORMSDIST(B5)

We see in the resulting worksheet below that the probability of demand during replenishment lead time exceeding 20 gallons is .2023. This probability differs slightly from the one we earlier computed manually (.2033) because in our manual calculation we rounded the z value to .83.

Value Worksheet:

	A	B
1	FINDING A PROBABILITY, USING A z VALUE	
2	Mean	15
3	Standard Deviation	6
4	x Value	20
5	z Value	0.8333
6	Probability of a Lesser x Value	0.7977
7	Probability of a Greater x Value	0.2023

Using Excel's NORMDIST Function

Excel's NORMDIST function can also be used to solve this portion of the problem The NORMDIST function computes the cumulative probability for <u>any normal distribution</u>. We do not need to convert an x value to a z value.

Enter Data: We enter the mean value, 15, into cell B2, the standard deviation value, 6, into cell B3, and the x value (for which we want a cumulative probability) into cell B4.

Enter Functions and Formulas: The NORMSDIST function requires four arguments: (1) the x value for which we want to compute the cumulative probability, (2) the mean, (3) the standard deviation, and (4) a value of TRUE or FALSE. We want a cumulative probability, so we enter TRUE.
   To compute the probability of the random variable assuming a value <u>less</u> than the x value entered into cell B4, we enter the formula =NORMDIST(B4,B2,B3,TRUE) into cell B6. To compute the probability of the random variable assuming a value <u>greater</u> than the x value specified, we enter the formula =1-B6 into cell B7. (We could also enter the formula =1- NORMSDIST(B4,B2,B3,TRUE) into cell B7.)

Formula Worksheet:

	A	B
1	FINDING A PROBABILITY, USING AN x VALUE	
2	Mean	15
3	Standard Deviation	6
4	x Value	20
5		
6	Probability of a Lesser x Value	=NORMDIST(B4,B2,B3,TRUE)
7	Probability of a Greater x Value	=1-B6

   The result of using the NORMDIST function is identical to that of the NORMSDIST function as evidenced below.

Value Worksheet:

	A	B
1	FINDING A PROBABILITY, USING AN *x* VALUE	
2	Mean	15
3	Standard Deviation	6
4	*x* Value	20
5		
6	Probability of a Lesser *x* Value	0.7977
7	Probability of a Greater *x* Value	0.2023

b) Rather than having an *x* value and solving for the cumulative probability, we now have a cumulative probability and we are solving for the *x* value. We are solving for the reorder point (*x*) value that corresponds to an upper (right) tail area of .05.

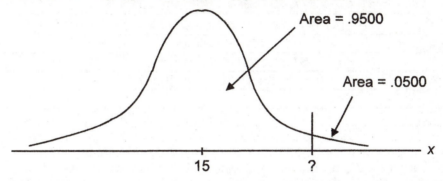

Let $z_{.05}$ represent the *z* value cutting the .05 tail area. We now look up the .9500 area in the <u>Cumulative Probabilities for the Standard Normal Distribution</u> table to find the corresponding $z_{.05}$ value.

z	.00	.01	.02	.03	.04	.05	.06	.07	.08	.09
1.5	.9332	.9345	.9357	.9370	.9382	.9394	.9406	.9418	.9429	.9441
1.6	.9452	.9463	.9474	.9484	.9495	.9505	.9515	.9525	.9535	.9545
1.7	.9554	.9564	.9573	.9582	.9591	.9599	.9608	.9616	.9625	.9633
1.8	.9641	.9649	.9656	.9664	.9671	.9678	.9686	.9693	.9699	.9706
1.9	.9713	.9719	.9726	.9732	.9738	.9744	.9750	.9756	.9761	.9767

$z_{.05}$ = 1.645 is a reasonable estimate. The corresponding value of *x* is given by

$$x = \mu + z_{.05}\sigma$$
$$= 15 + 1.645(6)$$
$$= 24.87$$

A reorder point of 24.87 gallons will place the probability of a stockout during lead time at .05. Perhaps Pep Zone should set the reorder point at 25 gallons to keep the probability under .05.

Using Excel's NORMINV Function

Excel's NORMINV function can be used to solve this portion of the problem. The NORMINV function is used to compute the *x* value for a given cumulative probability.

Enter Data: We enter the mean value, 15, into cell B2, the standard deviation value, 6, into cell B3, and the cumulative probability, .95, into cell B4. (Note: the tail area is .05, but the cumulative probability or area up to the tail is .95.)

Enter Functions and Formulas: The NORMINV function requires three arguments (inputs): the cumulative probability, the mean, and the standard deviation. To compute the *x* value we enter the formula =NORMINV(B4,B2,B3) into cell B6.

Formula Worksheet:

	A	B
1	FINDING AN x VALUE, GIVEN A PROBABILITY	
2	Mean	15
3	Standard Deviation	6
4	Cumulative Probability	0.95
5		
6	x Value	=NORMINV(B4,B2,B3)

The result, shown below, agrees with our manual calculation. The reorder point necessary for a .05 probability of a stockout during lead time is 24.87.

Value Worksheet:

	A	B
1	FINDING AN x VALUE, GIVEN A PROBABILITY	
2	Mean	15
3	Standard Deviation	6
4	Cumulative Probability	0.95
5		
6	x Value	24.87

EXAMPLE 4

Exponential Probability Distribution

The time between arrivals of cars at Al's Carwash follows an exponential probability distribution with a mean time between arrivals of 3 minutes. Al would like to know the probability that the time between two successive arrivals will be 2 minutes or less.

SOLUTION 4

Using the Exponential Distribution: Cumulative Probability Formula

To compute the exponential probability asked for here we use the formula:

$$P(x \le x_0) = 1 - e^{-x_0/\mu}$$

It provides the cumulative probability of obtaining a value for the exponential random variable of less than or equal to some specific value of x, denoted by x_0.

In this problem, $\mu = 3$ and $x_0 = 2$. The result is:

$$P(x \le 2) = 1 - 2.71828^{-2/3} = 1 - .5134 = .4866$$

There is a .4866 probability that the time between two successive arrivals at the car wash will be two minutes or less.

The exponential probability distribution in this problem can be graphed as follows:

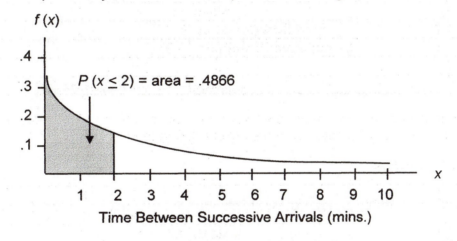

Time Between Successive Arrivals (mins.)

Using Excel's EXPONDIST Function

Excel's EXPONDIST function can be used to compute exponential probabilities.

Enter Data: No data are entered in the worksheet. We simply enter the appropriate values for the exponential random variable (time between successive arrivals) directly into the formula as needed.

Enter Functions and Formulas: The EXPONDIST function has three arguments: the first is the value of x_0, the second is $1/\mu$, and the third is TRUE or FALSE. We will always select TRUE because we are seeking a cumulative probability. Hence, we enter the formula =EXPONDIST(2,1/3,TRUE) into cell B3 and enter labels to identify the output.

Formula Worksheet:

	A	B
1	Probabilities: Exponential Distribution	
2		
3	$P(x \le 2) =$	=EXPONDIST(2,1/3,TRUE)
4		

Value Worksheet:

	A	B
1	Probabilities: Exponential Distribution	
2		
3	$P(x \leq 2) =$	0.4866
4		

EXERCISES

EXERCISE 1

Uniform Probability Distribution

The Harbour Island Ferry leaves on the hour and at 15-minute intervals. The time, x, it takes John to drive from his house to the ferry has a uniform distribution with x between 10 and 20 minutes. One morning John leaves his house at precisely 8:00a.m.

a) What is the probability John will wait less than 5 minutes for the ferry?

b) What is the probability John will wait less than 10 minutes for the ferry?

c) What is the probability John will wait less than 15 minutes for the ferry?

d) What is the probability John will not have to wait for the ferry?

e) Suppose John leaves at 8:05a.m. What is the probability John will wait (1) less than 5 minutes for the ferry; (2) less than 10 minutes for the ferry?

f) Suppose John leaves at 8:10a.m. What is the probability John will wait (1) less than 5 minutes for the ferry; (2) less than 10 minutes for the ferry?

g) What appears to be the best time for John to leave home if he wishes to maximize the probability of waiting less than 10 minutes for the ferry?

EXERCISE 2

Uniform Probability Distribution

Delicious Candy markets a two-pound box of assorted chocolates. Because of imperfections in the candy making equipment, the actual weight of the chocolate has a continuous uniform distribution ranging from 31.8 and 32.6 ounces.

a) Define a probability density function for the weight of the box of chocolate.

b) What is the probability that a box weighs (1) exactly 32 ounces; (2) more than 32.3 ounces; (3) less than 31.8 ounces?

c) The government requires that at least 60% of all products sold weigh at least as much as the stated weight. Is Delicious violating government regulations?

EXERCISE 3

Normal Probability Distribution

The time at which the mailman delivers the mail to Ace Bike Shop follows a normal distribution with mean 2:00 PM and standard deviation of 15 minutes.

a) What is the probability the mail will arrive after 2:30 PM?

b) What is the probability the mail will arrive before 1:36 PM?

c) What is the probability the mail will arrive between 1:48 PM and 2:09 PM?

EXERCISE 4

Normal Probability Distribution

Dollar Department Stores has compiled the following data concerning its daily sales. The sales for each day of the week are normally distributed with the following parameters:

Day	Mean = μ	Standard Deviation = σ
Monday	$120,000	$20,000
Tuesday	$100,000	$25,000
Wednesday	$100,000	$10,000
Thursday	$120,000	$40,000
Friday	$140,000	$20,000
Saturday	$160,000	$50,000

For each day of the week, find the probability that the store sales are between $110,000 and $150,000.

EXERCISE 5

Normal Probability Distribution

The township of Middleton sets the speed limit on its roads by conducting a traffic study and determining the speed (to the nearest 5 miles per hour) at which 80% of the drivers travel at or below. A study was done on Brown's Dock Road that indicated driver's speeds follow a normal distribution with a mean of 36.25 miles per hour and a variance of 6.25.

a) What should the speed limit be?

b) What percent of the drivers travel below that speed?

EXERCISE 6

Normal Probability Distribution

Joe's Record World has two stores. The sales at each store follow a normal distribution. For store 1, $\mu = \$2,000$ and $\sigma = \$200$ per day. For store 2, $\mu = \$1,900$ and $\sigma = \$400$ per day.

a) Which store has the higher average daily sales?

b) What is the probability that daily sales are greater than $2,200 for store 1? for store 2?

c) Is there a contradiction between parts (a) and (b)? Explain.

PROBLEM 7

Exponential Probability Distribution

A light bulb manufacturer claims its light bulbs will last 500 hours on the average. The lifetime of a light bulb is assumed to follow an exponential distribution.

a) What is the probability that the light bulb will have to be replaced within 500 hours?

b) What is the probability that the light bulb will last more than 1000 hours?

c) What is the probability that the light bulb will last between 200 and 800 hours.

SELF-TEST

TRUE/FALSE

____ 1. The height of a probability density function is a probability.

____ 2. If x is a continuous random variable, then $P(a \leq x \leq b) = P(a < x < b)$.

____ 3. For the normal probability distribution, larger values of the standard deviation result in taller probability density curves.

____ 4. If arrivals follow a Poisson distribution, the time between arrivals must follow an exponential distribution.

____ 5. For the uniform, normal, and exponential probability distributions, the area to the left of the mean is .5.

FILL-IN-THE-BLANK

1. A fundamental difference separates discrete and continuous random variables in terms of how _____ are computed.

2. Whenever the probability is proportional to the length of the interval, the random variable is _____ distributed.

3. A continuous probability distribution that is useful in computing probabilities for the time or space between occurrences of an event is the _____ distribution.

4. Given a z value, we use the _____ to find the appropriate probability (an area under the curve).

5. The probability of any particular value for a continuous random variable is _____.

MULTIPLE CHOICE

____ 1. There is a lower limit but no upper limit for a random variable that follows the
   a) uniform probability distribution
   b) normal probability distribution
   c) exponential probability distribution
   d) none of the above

____ 2. The form of the continuous uniform probability distribution is
   a) triangular
   b) rectangular
   c) bell-shaped
   d) a series of vertical lines

___ 3. The mean, median, and mode have the same value for which one of the following probability distributions?
    a) uniform
    b) normal
    c) exponential
    d) none of the above

___ 4. The probability distribution that can be described by just one parameter is the
    a) uniform
    b) normal
    c) exponential
    d) none of the above

___ 5. The values of the mean and standard deviation for the standard normal probability distribution are, respectively,
    a) 0, 1
    b) .5, .5
    c) 1, .5
    d) 1, 1

ANSWERS

EXERCISES

1) a) 1/2
  b) 1/2
  c) 1
  d) 0
  e) (1) 0   (2) 1/2
  f) (1) 1/2 (2) 1
  g) 8:10

2) a) f(x) = 1.25 for 31.8 < x < 32.6, 3)   a) .0228
         = 0 otherwise   b) .0548
  b) 0, .375, 0   c) .5138
  c) No. 75% are 32 oz. or more

4) M- .6247
  T- .3218
  W- .1587
  R- .3721
  F- .6247
  S- .2620

5) a) 40 mph
  b) 93.32%

6) a) Store 1   7) a) .632
  b) Store 1 - .1587, Store 2 - .2266   b) .135
  c) No - Store has larger std. deviation   c) .468

TRUE/FALSE

1) False
2) True
3) False
4) True
5) False

FILL-IN-THE-BLANK

1) probabilities
2) uniformly
3) exponential
4) standard normal table
5) zero

MULTIPLE CHOICE

1) c
2) b
3) b
4) c
5) a

CHAPTER 7

Sampling and Sampling Distributions

Simple Random Sampling

Point Estimation

Introduction to Sampling Distributions

Sampling Distribution of $\bar{x}$

Sampling Distribution of $\bar{p}$

Sampling Methods

LEARNING OBJECTIVES

1. Understand the importance of sampling and how results from samples can be used to provide estimates of population parameters such as the population mean, the population standard deviation and/or the population proportion.

2. Know what simple random sampling is and how simple random samples are selected.

3. Be able to select a simple random sample using Excel.

4. Understand the concept of a sampling distribution.

5. Know the central limit theorem and the important role it plays in sampling.

6. Know the characteristics of the sampling distribution of the sample mean ($\bar{x}$) and the sampling distribution of the sample proportion ($\bar{p}$).

7. Learn about a variety of sampling methods including stratified random sampling, cluster sampling, systematic sampling, convenience sampling and judgment sampling.

8. Know the definition of the following terms:

simple random sampling	finite population correction factor
sampling with replacement	standard error
sampling without replacement	point estimator
sampling distribution	

REVIEW

Purpose of Sampling
*   A population is the set of all the elements of interest.
*   A parameter is a numerical characteristic of a population.
*   Often times we cannot examine the entire population (conduct a census) in order to learn the value of a parameter.
*   Examining the entire population might be time and/or cost prohibitive or simply not feasible.
*   Instead, we examine a sample taken from the population.
*   A sample is a subset of the population.
*   The sample results provide estimates of the values of the population characteristics.
*   With proper sampling methods, the sample results will provide "good" estimates of the population characteristics.
*   Several methods can be used to select a sample from a population.
*   One of the most common methods is simple random sampling.

Simple Random Sampling

Finite Population

- A simple random sample from a finite population of size N is a sample selected such that each possible sample of size n has the same probability of being selected.
- Replacing each sampled element before selecting subsequent elements is called sampling with replacement.
- Sampling without replacement is the procedure used most often.
- One approach to sampling without replacement is to choose the element for the sample one at a time in such a way that each of the elements remaining in the population has the same probability of being selected.
- In large sampling projects, computer-generated random numbers are often used to automate the sample selection process.

Infinite Population

- A simple random sample from an infinite population is a sample selected such that the following conditions are satisfied.
  - Each element selected comes from the same population.
  - Each element is selected independently.
- The population is usually considered infinite if it involves an ongoing process that makes listing or counting every element impossible.
- The random number selection procedure cannot be used for infinite populations because a listing of the population is impossible.

Point Estimation

- In point estimation we use the data from the sample to compute a value of a sample statistic that serves as an estimate of a population parameter.
- We refer to $\bar{x}$ as the point estimator of the population mean μ.
- s is the point estimator of the population standard deviation σ.
- $\bar{p}$ is the point estimator of the population proportion p.

Sampling Error

- The absolute difference between an unbiased point estimate and the corresponding population parameter is called the sampling error.
- Sampling error is the result of using a subset of the population (the sample), and not the entire population to develop estimates.
- The sampling errors are:
  - $|\bar{x} - \mu|$ for sample mean
  - $|s - \sigma|$ for sample standard deviation
  - $|\bar{p} - p|$ for sample proportion

Sampling Distribution of $\bar{x}$

- The sampling distribution of $\bar{x}$ is the probability distribution of all possible values of the sample mean $\bar{x}$.
- The expected value of $\bar{x}$ is

$$E(\bar{x}) = \mu$$

where μ is the population mean.

- The standard deviation of $\bar{x}$ for a finite population is

$$\sigma_{\bar{x}} = (\frac{\sigma}{\sqrt{n}})\sqrt{\frac{N-n}{N-1}}$$

  where $\sqrt{(N-n)/(N-1)}$ is the finite correction factor.

- The standard deviation of $\bar{x}$ for a infinite population is

$$\sigma_{\bar{x}} = \frac{\sigma}{\sqrt{n}}$$

- A finite population is treated as being infinite if $n/N \leq .05$.
- $\sigma_{\bar{x}}$ is referred to as the standard error of the mean.
- If we use a large ($n > 30$) simple random sample, the central limit theorem enables us to conclude that the sampling distribution of $\bar{x}$ can be approximated by a normal probability distribution.
- When the simple random sample is small ($n < 30$), the sampling distribution of $\bar{x}$ can be considered normal only if we assume the population has a normal probability distribution.

Sampling Distribution of $\bar{p}$

- The sampling distribution of $\bar{p}$ is the probability distribution of all possible values of the sample proportion $\bar{p}$.
- The expected value of $\bar{p}$ is

$$E(\bar{p}) = p$$

  where p = the population proportion
- The standard deviation of $\bar{p}$ for a finite population is

$$\sigma_{\bar{p}} = \sqrt{\frac{p(1-p)}{n}}\sqrt{\frac{N-n}{N-1}}$$

- The standard deviation of $\bar{p}$ for a infinite population is

$$\sigma_{\bar{p}} = \sqrt{\frac{p(1-p)}{n}}$$

- $\bar{p}$ is referred to as the standard error of the proportion.

Sampling Methods

Stratified Random Sampling
- The population is first divided into groups of elements called strata.
- Each element in the population belongs to one and only one stratum.
- Best results are obtained when the elements within each stratum are as much alike as possible (i.e. homogeneous group).
- A simple random sample is taken from each stratum.
- Formulas are available for combining the stratum sample results into one population parameter estimate.
- Advantage: If strata are homogeneous, this method is as "precise" as simple random sampling but with a smaller total sample size.
- Example: The basis for forming the strata might be department, location, age, etc.

Cluster Sampling

- The population is first divided into separate groups of elements called clusters.
- Ideally, each cluster is a representative small-scale version of the population (i.e. heterogeneous group).
- A simple random sample of the clusters is then taken.
- All elements within each sampled (chosen) cluster form the sample.
- Advantage: The close proximity of elements can be cost effective (I.e. many sample observations can be obtained in a short time).
- Disadvantage: This method generally requires a larger total sample size than simple or stratified random sampling.
- Example: A primary application is area sampling, where clusters are city blocks or other well-defined areas.

Systematic Sampling

- If a sample size of n is desired from a population containing N elements, we might sample one element for every n/N elements in the population.
- We randomly select one of the first n/N elements from the population list.
- We then select every n/Nth element that follows in the population list.
- This method has the properties of a simple random sample, especially if the list of the population elements is a random ordering.
- Advantage: The sample usually will be easier to identify than it would be if simple random sampling were used.
- Example: Select every 100th listing in a telephone book after the first randomly selected listing.

Convenience Sampling

- It is a nonprobability sampling technique. Items are included in the sample without known probabilities of being selected.
- The sample is identified primarily by convenience.
- Advantage: Sample selection and data collection are relatively easy.
- Disadvantage: It is impossible to determine how representative of the population the sample is.
- Example: A professor conducting research uses student volunteers to constitute a sample.

Judgment Sampling

- The person most knowledgeable on the subject of the study selects elements of the population that he or she feels are most representative of the population.
- It is a nonprobability sampling technique.
- Advantage: It is a relatively easy way of selecting a sample.
- Disadvantage: The quality of the sample results depends on the judgment of the person selecting the sample.
- Example: A reporter might sample three or four senators, judging them as reflecting the general opinion of the senate.

KEY CONCEPTS

CONCEPT	EXAMPLES	EXERCISES
Simple Random Sampling		
Using a Random Number Generator	①	1
Point Estimation		
Population Mean and Standard Deviation	②	2
Population Proportion	②	6
Sampling Distribution of $\bar{x}$		
Expected Value and Standard Deviation of $\bar{x}$	③	3
Probability Information about the Size of the Sampling Error	④	4
Sample Size and Sampling Distribution of $\bar{x}$	⑤	5
Sampling Distribution of $\bar{p}$		
Expected Value and Standard Deviation of $\bar{p}$	⑥	7
Probability Information about the Size of the Sampling Error	⑦	8

◯ Excel Used

EXAMPLES

EXAMPLE 1

Simple Random Sampling from a Finite Population

St. Andrew's College receives 900 applications annually from prospective students. A completed application contains a variety of information including the individual's scholastic aptitude test (SAT) score and whether or not the individual desires on-campus housing.

The director of admissions would like to know the average SAT score for the applicants and the proportion of applicants that want to live on campus. The director decides, for the sake of expedience, to take a simple random sample of 30 applicants and tally their SAT scores and housing preferences.

We will assume that the SAT scores and housing preferences of the 900 applicants are already entered into an Excel worksheet. Use Excel's RAND function to select a simple random sample of 30 applicants without replacement.

SOLUTION 1

Using Excel's RAND Function

We begin by generating 900 random numbers, one for each applicant in the population. Then we choose the 30 applicants corresponding to the 30 smallest random numbers as our sample. Each of the 900 applicants has the same probability of being included.

Enter Data: We will assume that the following data were already entered into columns A, B, and C. The applicant numbers 1-900 are shown in Column A. The SAT score and housing preference are shown in columns B and C, respectively.

Enter Functions and Formulas: The formula =RAND() is entered into cells D2:D901 to generate a random number between 0 and 1 for each of the 900 applicants.

Formula Worksheet:

	A	B	C	D
1	**Applicant Number**	**SAT Score**	**On-Campus Housing**	**Random Number**
2	1	1008	Yes	=RAND()
3	2	1025	No	=RAND()
4	3	952	Yes	=RAND()
5	4	1090	Yes	=RAND()
6	5	1127	Yes	=RAND()
7	6	1015	No	=RAND()
8	7	965	Yes	=RAND()

Note: Rows 9-901 are not shown.

We see that the random number generated for the first applicant is .34194, the random number generated for the second applicant is .07560, and so on.

Value Worksheet:

	A	B	C	D
1	**Applicant Number**	**SAT Score**	**On-Campus Housing**	**Random Number**
2	1	1008	Yes	0.34194
3	2	1025	No	0.07560
4	3	952	Yes	0.42331
5	4	1090	Yes	0.06674
6	5	1127	Yes	0.27756
7	6	1015	No	0.62837
8	7	965	Yes	0.21312

Note: Rows 9-901 are not shown.

Apply Tools: All that remains is to find the applicants associated with the 30 smallest random numbers. To do so, we sort the data in columns A through D into ascending order by random numbers in column D.

Note: Prior to sorting turn off the automatic recalculation option for the worksheet. With the option turned on, any change made to the worksheet will trigger a recalculation of the random numbers. To turn the recalculation option off, select **Tools**, choose **Options**, select the **Calculation** tab, and in the calculation section select **Manual**.

Putting Random Numbers in Ascending Order

Step 1   Select cells A2:A901
Step 2   Select the **Data** pull-down menu
Step 3   Choose the **Sort** option
Step 4   When the **Sort** dialog box appears:
              Choose **Random Numbers** in the **Sort by** text box
              Choose **Ascending**
              Click **OK**

After completing these steps we obtain the worksheet shown below. The applicants listed in rows 2-31 are the ones corresponding to the smallest 30 random numbers that were generated. Hence, this group of 30 applicants is our simple random sample.

Sorted Worksheet:

	A	B	C	D
1	Applicant Number	SAT Score	On-Campus Housing	Random Number
2	12	1107	No	0.00027
3	773	1043	Yes	0.00192
4	408	991	Yes	0.00303
5	58	1008	No	0.00481
6	116	1127	Yes	0.00538
7	185	982	Yes	0.00683
8	510	1163	Yes	0.00749

Note: Rows 9-901 are not shown.

EXAMPLE 2

Point Estimation

Refer to the St. Andrew's sampling problem in Example 1. What is the point estimate of the mean SAT score for the 900 applicants? What is the point estimate of the standard deviation of the 900 SAT scores? What is the point estimate of the proportion of the 900 applicants who want on-campus housing?

SOLUTION 2

Using a Calculator

We will first compute the point estimates manually to demonstrate the mathematical operations. If you could (you cannot) see here all of the data for the sample of 30 applicants in the exhibits above, you would make the following computations.

$\bar{x}$ as Point Estimator of μ

$$\bar{x} = \frac{\sum x_i}{30} = \frac{29,910}{30} = 997$$

s as Point Estimator of σ

$$s = \sqrt{\frac{\sum(x_i - \bar{x})^2}{n-1}} = \sqrt{\frac{163,996}{29}} = 75.20$$

$\bar{p}$ as Point Estimator of p

$$\bar{p} = 20/30 = .667$$

Using Excel

Now we will demonstrate how Excel can be used to compute the point estimate. We will continue with the worksheet developed in Example 1.

Enter Data: The data for the simple random sample of 30 applicants are already entered into cells A2:C31 (See Solution 1).

Enter Functions and Formulas: We are using the mean SAT score in the sample as the point estimate of the population's average SAT score. To compute the sample mean we use the AVERAGE function.

We are using the standard deviation of the SAT scores in the sample as the point estimate of the standard deviation of the population's SAT scores. To compute the sample standard deviation we use the STDEV function.

We are using the proportion of the sample that wants on-campus housing as the point estimate of the proportion of the population that wants on-campus housing. To compute the sample proportion we count the number of Yes responses in the sample using the COUNTIF function and divide the number by 30.

Formula Worksheet:

	A	B	C	D	E	F
1	Applicant Number	SAT Score	On-Campus Housing	Random Number		Point Estimates
2	12	1107	No	0.00027		
3	773	1043	Yes	0.00192	Estimate μ	=AVERAGE(B2:B31)
4	408	991	Yes	0.00303	Estimate σ	=STDEV(B2:B31)
5	58	1008	No	0.00481	Estimate p	=COUNTIF(C2:C31,"Yes")/30
6	116	1127	Yes	0.00538		

Note: Rows 7-31 are not shown.

The results are shown in the worksheet below. Keep in mind that different random numbers would have identified a different sample, resulting in different point estimates.

Value Worksheet:

	A	B	C	D	E	F
1	Applicant Number	SAT Score	On-Campus Housing	Random Number		Point Estimates
2	12	1107	No	0.00027		
3	773	1043	Yes	0.00192	Estimate μ	997
4	408	991	Yes	0.00303	Estimate σ	75.20
5	58	1008	No	0.00481	Estimate p	0.667
6	116	1127	Yes	0.00538		

EXAMPLE 3

Sampling Distribution of $\bar{x}$

Refer to the St. Andrew's sampling problem in Example 1. Assume we know the mean and standard deviation are 990 and 80, respectively, for the 900 applicants' SAT scores. Show the sampling distribution of $\bar{x}$ where $\bar{x}$ is the mean SAT score for the 30 applicants.

SOLUTION 3

Using a Calculator

If we use a large ($n \geq 30$) simple random sample, the <u>central limit theorem</u> enables us to conclude that the sampling distribution of $\bar{x}$ can be approximated by a normal distribution.

Expected Value of $\bar{x}$

$$E(\bar{x}) = \mu = 990$$
where: μ = the population mean

Standard Deviation of $\bar{x}$

$$\sigma_{\bar{x}} = \frac{\sigma}{\sqrt{n}} = \frac{80}{\sqrt{30}} = 14.61$$

where: σ = the population standard deviation
n = the sample size

Sampling Distribution of $\bar{x}$

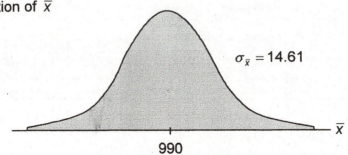

$\sigma_{\bar{x}} = 14.61$

$\bar{x}$

990

Using Excel

Now we will demonstrate how Excel can be used to compute the expected value and standard deviation of $\bar{x}$.

Enter Data: We enter the values of the population mean and standard deviation into cells B2 and B3, respectively. The sample size is entered into cell B6.

Enter Functions and Formulas: The expected value of $\bar{x}$ is simply the value of the population mean, so we enter the formula =B2 into cell B7. We compute the standard error of the mean by entering the formula =B3/SQRT(B6) into cell B8.

Formula Worksheet:

	A	B
1	**POPULATION PARAMETERS**	
2	Population Mean (μ) =	990
3	Population Standard Deviation (σ) =	80
4		
5	**SAMPLING DISTRIBUTION OF xbar**	
6	Sample Size (n) =	30
7	Expected x bar =	=B2
8	Standard Error of the Mean =	=B3/SQRT(B6)

Value Worksheet:

	A	B
1	**POPULATION PARAMETERS**	
2	Population Mean (μ) =	990
3	Population Standard Deviation (σ) =	80
4		
5	**SAMPLING DISTRIBUTION OF xbar**	
6	Sample Size (n) =	30
7	Expected x bar =	990
8	Standard Error of the Mean =	14.61

EXAMPLE 4

Probability Information about the Size of the Sampling Error

Refer to the St. Andrew's problem in Example 1. What is the probability that a simple random sample of 30 applicants will provide an estimate of the population mean SAT score that is within plus or minus 10 of the actual population mean μ, assuming μ = 990?
In other words, what is the probability that $\bar{x}$ will be between 980 and 1000?

SOLUTION 4

Using Excel's NORMDIST Function

We will continue with the worksheet we developed in Example 3.

Enter Data: We enter the value of the sampling error into cell B11.

Enter Functions and Formulas: The upper limit for $\bar{x}$ is the expected value of $\bar{x}$ plus the sampling error, so we enter the formula =B2+B11 into cell B12. Similarly, we compute the lower limit for $\bar{x}$ by entering the formula =B2-B11 into cell B13.

The probability of $\bar{x}$ being between the specified lower and upper limits is computed in three steps. 1) We compute the probability of $\bar{x}$ being less than the upper limit using the NORMSDIST function. 2) We compute the probability of $\bar{x}$ being less than the lower limit, also using the NORMSDIST function. 3) Finally, we compute the probability of $\bar{x}$ being between the lower and upper limits by subtracting the lesser probability from the greater probability.

Formula Worksheet:

	A	B
1	POPULATION PARAMETERS	
2	Population Mean (μ) =	990
3	Population Standard Deviation (σ) =	80
4		
5	SAMPLING DISTRIBUTION OF xbar	
6	Sample Size (n) =	30
7	Expected x bar =	=B2
8	Standard Error of the Mean =	=B3/SQRT(B6)
9		
10	PROBABILITY OF GIVEN SAMPLING ERROR	
11	Sampling Error (μ +/-) =	10
12	Upper Limit for x bar =	=B2+B11
13	Lower Limit for x bar =	=B2-B11
14	Probability of xbar <= Upper Limit =	=NORMDIST(B12,B2,B8,TRUE)
15	Probability of xbar < Lower Limit =	=NORMDIST(B13,B2,B8,TRUE)
16	Probability of xbar between Lower and Upper Limits =	=B14-B15

We see in the resulting worksheet below that the probability of the mean SAT score for the sampled applicants being within +/- 10 points of the mean SAT score for the population of applicants is .5064.

Value Worksheet:

	A	B
1	POPULATION PARAMETERS	
2	Population Mean (μ) =	990
3	Population Standard Deviation (σ) =	80
4		
5	SAMPLING DISTRIBUTION OF xbar	
6	Sample Size (n) =	30
7	Expected xbar =	990
8	Standard Error of the Mean =	14.61
9		
10	PROBABILITY OF GIVEN SAMPLING ERROR	
11	Sampling Error (μ +/-) =	10
12	Upper Limit for xbar =	1000
13	Lower Limit for xbar =	980
14	Probability of xbar <= Upper Limit =	0.7532
15	Probability of xbar < Lower Limit =	0.2468
16	Probability of xbar between Lower and Upper Limits =	0.5064

EXAMPLE 5

Sample Size and the Sampling Distribution of $\bar{x}$

Refer to Example 4. What happens to the sampling distribution of $\bar{x}$ when the sample size is increased from 30 to 100? With a sample size of 100, what is the probability that $\bar{x}$ will be between 980 and 1000?

SOLUTION 5

Using Excel's NORMDIST Function

Enter Data: We simply enter the new value, 100, for the sample size into cell B6.

Enter Functions and Formulas: There are no additions or changes necessary.

We can see in the worksheet below the impact of increasing the sample size from 30 to 100 on two values in particular. The standard error of the mean has decreased from 14.61 to 8.00. This means the bell curve representing the sampling distribution of $\bar{x}$ is narrower and more peaked. This results in more area under the curve lying between the lower and upper limits defined by the specified sampling error (μ +/- 10). In other words, the probability of $\bar{x}$ having a value between 980 and 1000 is now greater. Notice that the probability has increased from .5064 to .7887.

Value Worksheet:

	A	B
1	**POPULATION PARAMETERS**	
2	Population Mean (μ) =	990
3	Population Standard Deviation (σ) =	80
4		
5	**SAMPLING DISTRIBUTION OF xbar**	
6	Sample Size (n) =	100
7	Expected x bar =	990
8	Standard Error of the Mean =	8.00
9		
10	**PROBABILITY OF GIVEN SAMPLING ERROR**	
11	Sampling Error $(\mu$ +/-) =	10
12	Upper Limit for x bar =	1000
13	Lower Limit for x bar =	980
14	Probability of xbar <= Upper Limit =	0.8944
15	Probability of xbar < Lower Limit =	0.1056
16	Probability of xbar between Lower and Upper Limits =	0.7887

Sampling Distributions of $\bar{x}$

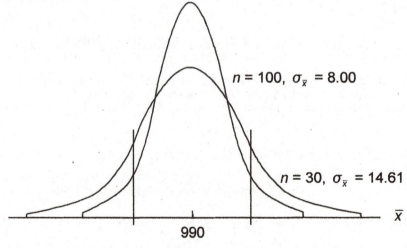

$n = 100, \ \sigma_{\bar{x}} = 8.00$

$n = 30, \ \sigma_{\bar{x}} = 14.61$

$\bar{x}$

990

EXAMPLE 6

Sampling Distribution of $\bar{p}$

Refer to the St. Andrew's sampling problem in Example 1. Describe the sampling distribution of $\bar{p}$ where $\bar{p}$ is the proportion of the 30 applicants who want on-campus housing.

SOLUTION 6

Using a Calculator

We will first manually compute the expected value and standard deviation of $\bar{p}$ to demonstrate the mathematical operations. The sampling distribution of $\bar{p}$ is the probability distribution of all possible values of the sample proportion $\bar{p}$. The normal probability distribution is an acceptable approximation since $np = 30(.72) = 21.6 \geq 5$ and $n(1 - p) = 30(.28) = 8.4 \geq 5$.

Expected Value of $\bar{p}$

$$E(\bar{p}) = p = .72$$

where: p = the population proportion

Standard Deviation of $\bar{p}$

$$\sigma_{\bar{p}} = \sqrt{\frac{p(1-p)}{n}}$$

where: n = the sample size

$$\sigma_{\bar{p}} = \sqrt{\frac{.72(.28)}{30}} = .082$$

Using Excel

Now we will demonstrate how Excel can be used to compute the expected value and standard deviation of $\bar{p}$.

Enter Data: We enter the value of the population proportion into cell B2. The sample size is entered into cell B5.

Enter Functions and Formulas: The expected value of $\bar{p}$ is simply the value of the population proportion, so we enter the formula =B2 into cell B6. We compute the standard error of the proportion by entering the formula =SQRT(B2(1-B2)/B5) into cell B7.

Formula Worksheet:

	A	B
1	POPULATION PARAMETERS	
2	Population Mean (p) =	0.72
3		
4	SAMPLING DISTRIBUTION OF pbar	
5	Sample Size (n) =	30
6	Expected $p$bar =	=B2
7	Standard Error of the Mean =	=SQRT(B2(1-B2)/B5)

Value Worksheet:

	A	B
1	POPULATION PARAMETERS	
2	Population Mean (*p*) =	0.72
3		
4	SAMPLING DISTRIBUTION OF pbar	
5	Sample Size (*n*) =	30
6	Expected *p* bar =	0.72
7	Standard Error of the Mean =	0.0820

EXAMPLE 7

Probability Information about the Size of the Sampling Error

Refer to the St. Andrew's problem in Example 1. What is the probability that a simple random sample of 30 applicants will provide an estimate of the population proportion of applicants desiring on-campus housing that is within plus or minus .05 of the actual population proportion, assuming *p* = .72? In other words, what is the probability that $\bar{p}$ will be between .67 and .77?

SOLUTION 7

Using Excel's NORMDIST Function

We will continue with the worksheet we developed in Example 6.

Enter Data: We enter the value of the sampling error into cell B10.

Enter Functions and Formulas: The upper limit for $\bar{p}$ is the expected value of $\bar{p}$ plus the sampling error. Similarly, the lower limit for $\bar{p}$ is the expected value of $\bar{p}$ minus the sampling error .

The probability of $\bar{p}$ being between the specified lower and upper limits is computed in three steps. 1) We compute the probability of $\bar{p}$ being less than the upper limit by entering the formula =NORMSDIST(B11,B2,B7,TRUE) into cell B13. 2) We compute the probability of $\bar{p}$ being less than the lower limit by entering the formula =NORMSDIST(B12,B2,B7,TRUE) into cell B14. 3) Finally, we compute the probability of $\bar{p}$ being between the lower and upper limits by entering the formula =B13-B14 into cell B15.

Formula Worksheet:

	A	B
1	POPULATION PARAMETERS	
2	Population Mean (*p*) =	0.72
3		
4	SAMPLING DISTRIBUTION OF pbar	
5	Sample Size (*n*) =	30
6	Expected *p* bar =	=B2
7	Standard Error of the Mean =	=SQRT(B2(1-B2)/B5)
8		
9	PROBABILITY OF GIVEN SAMPLING ERROR	
10	Sampling Error (*p* +/-) =	0.05
11	Upper Limit for *p* bar =	=B2+B10
12	Lower Limit for *p* bar =	=B2-B10
13	Probability of *p* bar <= Upper Limit =	=NORMDIST(B11,B2,B7,TRUE)
14	Probability of *p* bar < Lower Limit =	=NORMDIST(B12,B2,B7,TRUE)
15	Probability of *p* bar Between Lower and Upper Limits =	=B13-B14

We see in the resulting worksheet below that the probability of the proportion of the 30 sampled applicants who desire on-campus housing being within +/- .05 of the population proportion is .4581.

Value Worksheet:

	A	B
1	POPULATION PARAMETERS	
2	Population Mean (*p*) =	0.72
3		
4	SAMPLING DISTRIBUTION OF pbar	
5	Sample Size (*n*) =	30
6	Expected *p* bar =	0.72
7	Standard Error of the Mean =	0.0820
8		
9	PROBABILITY OF GIVEN SAMPLING ERROR	
10	Sampling Error (*p* +/-) =	0.05
11	Upper Limit for *p* bar =	0.77
12	Lower Limit for *p* bar =	0.67
13	Probability of *p* bar <= Upper Limit =	0.7290
14	Probability of *p* bar < Lower Limit =	0.2710
15	Probability of *p* bar Between Lower and Upper Limits =	0.4581

EXERCISES

EXERCISE 1

Simple Random Sampling from a Finite Population

Missy Walters owns a mail-order business specializing in clothing, linens, and furniture for children. She is considering offering her customers a discount on shipping charges for furniture based on the dollar-amount of the furniture order. Before Missy decides the discount policy, she needs a better understanding of the average dollar-amount of the furniture orders she receives.

Missy had an assistant identify all of the company's orders in the past month that included furniture. The assistant found 50 furniture orders. The dollar amounts for the furniture orders are listed below.

136	281	226	123	178	445	231	389	196	175
211	162	212	241	182	290	434	167	246	338
194	242	368	258	323	196	183	209	198	212
277	348	173	409	264	237	490	222	472	248
231	154	166	214	311	141	159	362	189	260

Missy needs help in selecting a sample of 10 orders. Use an Excel worksheet and the RAND function to select a simple random sample of 10 orders without replacement.

EXERCISE 2

Point Estimation of μ and σ

Refer to the mail-order problem in Exercise 1 and the sample orders you selected. What is the point estimate of the mean dollar-amount of all furniture orders? What is the point estimate for the standard deviation of the dollar-amount of all furniture orders? (Hint: Base your estimates on the sample statistics you compute using the sample orders you selected.

EXERCISE 3

Sampling Distribution of $\bar{x}$

Refer to the mail-order problem in Exercise 1. Assume we know the mean and standard deviation are $249 and $46, respectively, for all furniture orders Missy receives. Furthermore, Missy is confident the dollar amounts of all her furniture orders are normally distributed (or nearly so).

Describe the sampling distribution of $\bar{x}$, where $\bar{x}$ is the mean dollar-amount of a furniture order for 10 sampled orders.

EXERCISE 4

Probability Information about the Size of the Sampling Error

Refer to the mail-order problem in Exercise 1. What is the probability that a simple random sample of 30 furniture orders will provide an estimate of the population mean dollar-amount of a furniture order that is within plus or minus $10 of the actual population mean, assuming $\mu = \$249$ and $\sigma = \$46.$?

EXERCISE 5

Sample Size and the Sampling Distribution of $\bar{x}$

Refer to the mail-order problem in Exercise 4. What happens to the sampling distribution of $\bar{x}$ when the sample size is increased from 30 to 90? With a sample size of 90, what is the probability that $\bar{x}$ will be between $239 and $259?

EXERCISE 6

Point Estimation of p

It is time for Roger Hall, manager of new car sales at the Maxwell Ford dealership in Los Angeles, to submit his order for new Mustang coupes. These cars will be parked in the lot, available for immediate sale to buyers who are not special-ordering a car. One of the decisions he must make is how many Mustangs of each color he should order. The new color options are very similar to the past year's options.

Roger believes that the colors chosen by customers who special-order their cars best reflect most customers' true color preferences. For that reason, he has tabulated the color preferences specified in a sample of 56 Mustang coupe special orders placed in the past year. The sample data are listed below.

Black	Red	White	Blue	Blue	Green	Red	Black
Red	White	Blue	White	Red	Red	Black	Black
Green	Black	Red	Black	Blue	Black	White	Green
Blue	Red	Black	White	Black	Red	Black	Blue
Blue	Black	Green	White	Black	Red	Red	White
Red	Red	Blue	Black	Red	Black	Green	Black
Green	Red	Black	White	Black	Red	Black	White

What is the point estimate of the proportion of all Mustang coupe special orders that specify a color preference of black?

EXERCISE 7

Sampling Distribution of $\bar{p}$

Refer to the Maxwell Ford problem in Exercise 6. Describe the sampling distribution of $\bar{p}$ where $\bar{p}$ is the proportion of Mustang coupe special orders that specify a color preference of black. Assume that the proportion of all (1200) Mustang coupe special orders having a color preference of black is .36.

EXERCISE 8

Probability Information about the Size of the Sampling Error

Refer to the Maxwell Ford problem in Exercise 6. What is the probability that a simple random sample of 56 special orders will provide an estimate of the population proportion of special orders specifying the color black that is within plus or minus .05 of the actual population proportion, assuming $p = .36$? In other words, what is the probability that $\bar{p}$ will be between .31 and .41?

SELF-TEST

TRUE/FALSE

____ 1. The expected value of $\bar{x}$ equals the mean of the population from which the sample is drawn, regardless of the sample size.

____ 2. An advantage of cluster sampling is that it generally requires a smaller total sample size than simple random sampling.

____ 3. The finite population correction should be used in the computation of the standard error of the mean whenever the population being sampled is finite.

____ 4. Whenever the population has a normal probability distribution, the sampling distribution of $\bar{x}$ has a normal probability distribution, regardless of the sample size.

____ 5. The process of selecting a simple random sample depends on whether the population is finite or infinite.

FILL-IN-THE-BLANK

1. The _____ provides the basis for using a normal probability distribution to approximate the sampling distributions of $\bar{x}$ and $\bar{p}$.

2. The value of the _____ is used to estimate the value of the population parameter.

3. The standard deviation of $\bar{p}$ is referred to as the _____.

4. The _____ can be used to provide probability information about how close the sample mean is to the population mean.

5. The population being studied is usually considered _____ if it involves an ongoing process that makes listing or counting every element in the population impossible.

MULTIPLE CHOICE

____ 1. A probability sampling method in which we randomly select one of the first k elements and then select every k th element thereafter is
   a) stratified random sampling
   b) cluster sampling
   c) systematic sampling
   d) convenience sampling

___ 2. The standard deviation of a point estimator is the
   a) standard error
   b) sample statistic
   c) point estimate
   d) sampling error

___ 3. Which one of the following sampling methods is classified as a nonprobability sampling method?
   a) stratified random sampling
   b) cluster sampling
   c) systematic sampling
   d) convenience sampling

___ 4. The finite population correction factor should be used in the computation of σ_x and $\sigma_{\bar{p}}$ when n/N is greater than
   a) .01
   b) .025
   c) .05
   d) .10

___ 5. The extent of the sampling error may be affected by all of the following factors except
   a) the sampling method used
   b) the sample size
   c) the expected value of the sample statistic being used
   d) the variability of the population

ANSWERS

EXERCISES

1) no <u>one</u> right answer (different random numbers result in different items selected)

2) no <u>one</u> right answer (different items sampled results in different sample statistics)

3) Normally distributed with E(x) = $249 and $\sigma_{\bar{x}}$ = $14.5465

4) .7660   5) .9606   6) .32143

7) Normally distributed with $\bar{p}$ = .36 and $\sigma_{\bar{p}}$ = .064   8) .5646

TRUE/FALSE

1) True
2) False
3) False
4) True
5) True

FILL-IN-THE-BLANK

1) central limit theorem
2) sample statistic
3) standard error of the proportion
4) sampling distribution of $\bar{x}$
5) infinite

MULTIPLE CHOICE

1) c
2) a
3) d
4) c
5) c

CHAPTER 8

Interval Estimation

Population Mean: σ Known

Population Mean: σ Unknown

Determining the Sample Size

Population Proportion

LEARNING OBJECTIVES

1. Be able to construct and interpret an interval estimate of a population mean and/or a population proportion.

2. Understand the concept of a sampling error.

3. Be able to use knowledge of a sampling distribution to make probability statements about the sampling error.

4. Understand and be able to compute the margin of error.

5. Learn about the *t* distribution and when it should be used in constructing an interval estimate for a population mean.

6. Be able to use the worksheets presented in the chapter as templates for constructing interval estimates.

7. Be able to determine the size of a simple random sample necessary to estimate a population mean and a population proportion with a specified margin of error.

8. Know the definition of the following terms:
   confidence interval   degrees of freedom
   confidence coefficient   sampling error
   confidence level   margin of error

REVIEW

Interval Estimation of a Population Mean: σ Known

Sampling Error
- The absolute value of the difference between an unbiased point estimate and the population parameter it estimates is called the sampling error.
- For the case of a sample mean estimating a population mean, the sampling error is:
$$|\bar{x} - \mu|$$
- Knowledge of the sampling distribution of $\bar{x}$ enables us to make confidence statements about the sampling error even though the population mean μ is not known.

Constructing an Interval Estimate
- When the population standard deviation σ is assumed known, the interval is:
$$\bar{x} \pm z_{\alpha/2} \frac{\sigma}{\sqrt{n}}$$

where: $\bar{x}$ is the sample mean

$1 - \alpha$ is the confidence coefficient

$z_{\alpha/2}$ is the z value providing an area of $\alpha/2$ in the upper

tail of the standard normal probability distribution

σ is the population standard deviation

n is the sample size

Determining the Sample Size
- Let E = the desired margin of error.
- E is the amount added to and subtracted from the point estimate to obtain an interval estimate.

$$E = z_{\alpha/2} \frac{\sigma}{\sqrt{n}}$$

- Solving for n we have:

$$n = \frac{(z_{\alpha/2})^2 \sigma^2}{E^2}$$

Interval Estimation of a Population Mean: σ Unknown
- If the population standard deviation σ is unknown, the appropriate interval estimate is based on a probability distribution known as the t distribution.

t Distribution
- The t distribution is a family of similar probability distributions.
- A specific t distribution depends on a parameter known as the degrees of freedom.
- As the number of degrees of freedom increases, the difference between the t distribution and the standard normal probability distribution becomes smaller.
- A t distribution with more degrees of freedom has less dispersion.
- The mean of the t distribution is zero.

Constructing an Interval Estimate
- When the population standard deviation σ is estimated by s, the interval is compute as follows:

$$\bar{x} \pm t_{\alpha/2} \frac{s}{\sqrt{n}}$$

where: $1 - \alpha$ is the confidence coefficient

  $t_{\alpha/2}$ is the t value providing an area of

  $\alpha/2$ in the upper tail of a t distribution
  with $n - 1$ degrees of freedom

  s is the sample standard deviation

  n is the sample size

Interval Estimation of a Population Proportion
- The interval estimate of the population proportion is computed as follows:

$$\bar{p} \pm z_{\alpha/2} \sqrt{\frac{\bar{p}(1-\bar{p})}{n}}$$

where: $1 - \alpha$ is the confidence coefficient

  $z_{\alpha/2}$ is the z value providing an area of $\alpha/2$ in the
  upper tail of the standard normal distribution

  $\bar{p}$ is the sample proportion

  n is the sample size

Determining the Sample Size
- Let E = the desired margin of error.
- We have:

$$E = z_{\alpha/2} \sqrt{\frac{p(1-p)}{n}}$$

- Solving for n we have:

$$n = \frac{(z_{\alpha/2})^2 \, p(1-p)}{E^2}$$

KEY CONCEPTS

CONCEPT	EXAMPLES	EXERCISES
Interval Estimation of a Population Mean		
σ Known Case	①	1
Determining the Sample Size	2	2
σ Unknown Case	③	3
Interval Estimation of a Population Proportion	④	4
Determining the Sample Size	5	5

◯ Excel Used

EXAMPLES

EXAMPLE 1

Interval Estimate of a Population Mean: σ Known

National Discount has 260 retail outlets throughout the United States. National evaluates each potential location for a new retail outlet in part on the mean annual income of the households in the marketing area of the new location. National develops an interval estimate of the mean annual income in a potential marketing area after taking a random sample of households.

For a marketing area being studied, a sample of 36 households was taken and their incomes are listed below. Develop a 95% confidence interval for the mean annual income of households in this marketing area. Based on past experience, National Discount assumes a known value of σ = $4500 for the population standard deviation.

Household	Income	Household	Income	Household	Income
1	25,600	13	19,250	25	26,550
2	19,615	14	27,500	26	15,900
3	20,035	15	23,650	27	18,450
4	21,735	16	30,000	28	14,750
5	17,600	17	19,250	29	20,000
6	26,080	18	24,557	30	19,250
7	28,925	19	19,382	31	27,500
8	25,350	20	20,050	32	23,650
9	15,900	21	21,750	33	18,450
10	17,550	22	17,500	34	14,750
11	14,745	23	19,340	35	20,000
12	20,000	24	30,000	36	15,000

SOLUTION 1

Using a Calculator

Sample Mean:

$$\bar{x} = \frac{\Sigma x_i}{n} = \frac{759,614}{36} = 21,100.39$$

Margin of Error:

$$z_{\alpha/2} \frac{\sigma}{\sqrt{n}} = 1.96 \frac{4,500}{\sqrt{36}} = 1,470$$

95% Confidence Interval:

$$\bar{x} \pm z_{\alpha/2} \frac{\sigma}{\sqrt{n}} = 21,100.39 \pm 1,470$$

Using Excel's CONFIDENCE Function

Enter Data: A label and the income data for the 36 households are entered into column A.

Enter Functions and Formulas: The sample size *n* is determined using the COUNT function. The AVERAGE function is used to compute the sample mean, $\bar{x}$.

The values for the population standard deviation and the confidence coefficient are entered into the worksheet. The level of significance is 1 minus the confidence coefficient.

The margin of error is found by using the CONFIDENCE function, which has three parameters: 1) level of significance, 2) population standard deviation, and 3) sample size.

The point estimate of the population mean is simply the sample mean. The lower limit of the confidence interval is the point estimate minus the margin of error. To find the upper limit of the confidence interval the margin of error is added to the point estimate.

Formula Worksheet:

	A	B	C
1	Income	Sample Size	=COUNT(A2:A37)
2	25,600	Sample Mean	=AVERAGE(A2:A37)
3	19,615		
4	20,035	Popul. Std. Deviation	4500.00
5	21,735	Confidence Coefficient	0.95
6	17,600	Level of Significance	=1-C5
7	26,080		
8	28,925	Margin of Error	=CONFIDENCE(C6,C4,C1)
9	25,350		
10	15,900	Point Estimate	=C2
11	17,550	Lower Limit	=C10-C8
12	14,745	Upper Limit	=C10+C8

Note: Rows 13-37 are not shown.

We see the results of our computations in the value worksheet below. The sample mean is $21,100.39. The margin of error is $1,469.97. Finally, the lower and upper limits of the interval estimate are computed to be $19,630.42 and $22,570.36, respectively. (Note: Excel's results differ slightly from our results using a calculator because Excel uses a more precise z value than we found using a Table of Cumulative Probabilities for the Standard Normal Distribution.)

Value Worksheet:

	A	B	C
1	Income	Sample Size	36
2	25,600	Sample Mean	21,100.39
3	19,615		
4	20,035	Popul. Std. Deviation	4500.00
5	21,735	Confidence Coefficient	0.95
6	17,600	Level of Signif. (alpha)	0.05
7	26,080		
8	28,925	Margin of Error	1469.97
9	25,350		
10	15,900	Point Estimate	21,100.39
11	17,550	Lower Limit	19,630.42
12	14,745	Upper Limit	22,570.36

Note: Rows 13-37 are not shown.

To recap, we are 95% confident that the average annual income for all households in the market area being studied falls in the interval $19,630.42 to $22,570.36.

EXAMPLE 2

Sample Size for an Interval Estimate of a Population Mean

Refer again to the information in Example 1. Suppose that National's management team wants a 95% confidence interval estimate of the population mean with a margin of error of $E = \$500$. How large a sample size is needed?

SOLUTION 2

Using a Calculator

In the σ known case, the margin of error E is computed as follows:

$$E = z_{\alpha/2} \frac{\sigma}{\sqrt{n}}$$

Given values of $z_{\alpha/2}$ and σ, we can determine the sample size n needed to provide any desired margin of error. We arrange the formula above (solving for n) to get:

$$n = \frac{(z_{\alpha/2})^2 \sigma^2}{E^2}$$

$$n = \frac{(1.96)^2 (4500)^2}{(500)^2} = 311.2$$

Thus, we will need to sample 312 households to reach a desired margin of error of $500 at 95% confidence. In other words, in order to <u>reduce</u> the margin of error by a factor of approximately 3, we have to <u>increase</u> the sample size by a factor of nearly 9.

EXAMPLE 3

Interval Estimation of a Population Mean: σ Unknown

A reporter for a student newspaper is writing an article on the cost of off-campus housing. A sample was taken of 10 one-bedroom units within a half-mile of campus and the rents paid are listed below.

Unit	Rent	Unit	Rent
1	600	6	625
2	635	7	570
3	550	8	465
4	535	9	550
5	465	10	505

Provide a 95% confidence interval estimate of the mean rent per month for the population of one-bedroom units within a half-mile of campus. We will assume this population to be normally distributed.

SOLUTION 3

Using a Calculator

Sample Mean:
$$\bar{x} = \frac{\Sigma x_i}{n} = \frac{5,500}{10} = 550.00$$

Sample Standard Deviation:
$$s = \sqrt{\frac{\Sigma(x_i - \bar{x})^2}{n-1}} = \sqrt{\frac{32,450}{9}} = 60.05$$

Appropriate *t* Value:

      At 95% confidence, $1 - \alpha = .95$, $\alpha = .05$, and $\alpha/2 = .025$.

      $t_{.025}$ is based on $n - 1 = 10 - 1 = 9$ degrees of freedom.

      In the partial *t* distribution table below we see that $t_{.025} = 2.262$.

Degrees of Freedom	Area in Upper Tail					
	.02	.10	.05	.025	.01	.005
.	.	.	.	.	.	.
7	.896	1.415	1.895	2.365	2.998	3.499
8	.889	1.397	1.860	2.306	2.896	3.355
9	.883	1.383	1.833	2.262	2.821	3.250
10	.879	1.372	1.812	2.228	2.764	3.169
.	.	.	.	.	.	.

Margin of Error:
$$t_{\alpha/2} \frac{s}{\sqrt{n}} = 2.262 \frac{60.05}{\sqrt{10}} = 42.95$$

95% Confidence Interval:
$$\bar{x} \pm t_{\alpha/2} \frac{s}{\sqrt{n}} = 550.00 \pm 42.95$$

To summarize, we are 95% confident that the mean rent per month for the population of one-bedroom units within a half-mile of campus is between $507.05 and $592.95.

Using Excel's DESCRIPTIVE STATISTICS Tool

Enter Data: A label and the rent data for the 10 households are entered into cells A1:A11.

Apply Analysis Tools: We start by summarizing the data using Excel's Descriptive Statistics tool.

    Step 1. Select the **Tools** menu.

    Step 2. Choose the **Data Analysis** option.

    Step 3. Choose **Descriptive Statistics** from the list of Analysis Tools

Enter Functions and Formulas: We find the point estimate and the lower and upper limits of the confidence interval by using the values of the sample mean and the margin of error (labeled "Confidence Level (95%)") provided by the Descriptive Statistics tool.

Formula Worksheet:

	A	B	C
1	Rent	*Rent*	
2	600	Mean	550
3	635	Standard Error	18.98830049
4	550	Median	550
5	535	Mode	550
6	465	Standard Deviation	60.04627845
7	625	Sample Variance	3605.555556
8	570	Kurtosis	-1.001623843
9	465	Skewness	-0.098633476
10	550	Range	170
11	505	Minimum	465
12		Maximum	635
13		Sum	5500
14		Count	10
15		Confidence Level(95.0%)	42.9545527
16			
17		Point Estimate	=C2
18		Lower Limit	=C2-C15
19		Upper Limit	=C2+C15

Value Worksheet:

	A	B	C
1	Rent	*Rent*	
2	600	Mean	550
3	635	Standard Error	18.99
4	550	Median	550
5	535	Mode	550
6	465	Standard Deviation	60.05
7	625	Sample Variance	3605.56
8	570	Kurtosis	-1.00
9	465	Skewness	-0.10
10	550	Range	170
11	505	Minimum	465
12		Maximum	635
13		Sum	5500
14		Count	10
15		Confidence Level(95.0%)	42.95
16			
17		Point Estimate	550
18		Lower Limit	507.05
19		Upper Limit	592.95

EXAMPLE 4

Interval Estimation of a Population Proportion

Political Science, Inc. (PSI) specializes in voter polls and surveys designed to keep political office seekers informed of their position in a race. Using telephone surveys, interviewers ask registered voters who they would vote for if the election were held that day.

In a recent election campaign, PSI found that 220 registered voters, out of 500 contacted, favored a particular candidate. PSI wants to develop a 95% confidence interval estimate for the proportion of the population of registered voters that favors the candidate.

SOLUTION 4

Using a Calculator

Sample Proportion:
$$\bar{p} = \frac{220}{500} = .44$$

Margin of Error:
$$z_{\alpha/2}\sqrt{\frac{\bar{p}(1-\bar{p})}{n}} = 1.96\sqrt{\frac{.44(1-.44)}{500}} = .0435$$

95% Confidence Interval:
$$\bar{p} \pm z_{\alpha/2}\sqrt{\frac{\bar{p}(1-\bar{p})}{n}} = .44 \pm .0435$$

We are 95% confident that the proportion of the population of registered voters that favors the candidate is between .3965 and .4835.

Using Excel's NORMSINV Function

Assume that the responses to PSI's voter poll had been recorded as a Yes or No for each registered voter polled.

Enter Data: A label and the Yes-No data for the 500 registered voters are entered into cells A1:A501.

Enter Functions and Formulas: The COUNTA function is used to determine the sample size. The COUNTIF function is used to count the number of Yes responses in the data. The sample proportion is computed by dividing the number of Yes responses by the sample size.

The confidence coefficient (0.95) is entered and the level of significance (α) is computed by subtracting the confidence coefficient from 1. The z value corresponding to an upper tail area of $\alpha/2$ is computed using the NORMSINV function.

The estimate of the standard error of the proportion is computed using the sample proportion and the sample size as inputs. Then the margin of error is computed.

The point estimate is the sample proportion. The lower and upper limits are obtained by subtracting and adding the margin of error to the point estimate.

Formula Worksheet:

	A	B	C
1	Favored	Sample Size	=COUNTA(A2:A501)
2	Yes	Response of Interest	Yes
3	Yes	Count for Response	=COUNTIF(A2:A501,C2)
4	No	Sample Proportion	=C2/C1
5	Yes		
6	No	Confid. Coefficient	0.95
7	No	Lev. of Signif. (alpha)	=1-C6
8	No	z Value	=NORMSINV(1-C7/2)
9	No		
10	Yes	Standard Error	=SQRT(C4*(1-C4)/C1)
11	No	Margin of Error	=C8*C10
12	Yes		
13	No	Point Estimate	=C4
14	No	Lower Limit	=C13-C11
15	Yes	Upper Limit	=C13+C11

Note: Rows 16-501 are not shown.

Value Worksheet:

	A	B	C
1	Favored	Sample Size	500
2	Yes	Response of Interest	Yes
3	Yes	Count for Response	220
4	No	Sample Proportion	0.44
5	Yes		
6	No	Confid. Coefficient	0.95
7	No	Lev. of Signif. (alpha)	0.05
8	No	z Value	1.96
9	No		
10	Yes	Standard Error	0.0222
11	No	Margin of Error	0.04350937
12	Yes		
13	No	Point Estimate	0.44
14	No	Lower Limit	0.3965
15	Yes	Upper Limit	0.4835

Note: Rows 16-501 are not shown.

EXAMPLE 5

Sample Size for an Interval Estimate of a Population Proportion

Refer again to Example 4. Suppose that PSI would like 99% confidence that the sample proportion is within +/- .03 of the population proportion. How large a sample size is needed to provide the desired margin of error?

SOLUTION 5

The margin of error, E, associated with an estimate of a population proportion is:

$$E = z_{\alpha/2}\sqrt{p(1-p)/n}$$

We see that the margin of error is based on the values of $z_{\alpha/2}$, p, and n. We can determine the sample size n needed to provide any desired margin of error by rearranging the formula above (solving for n) to get:

$$n = \frac{(z_{\alpha/2})^2 p(1-p)}{E^2}$$

We do not know the population proportion, p, in this problem, so we will use the prior sample proportion, $\bar{p} = .44$, as a suitable substitute. At 99% confidence, $z_{.005} = 2.575$, approximately.

$$n = \frac{(z_{\alpha/2})^2 p^*(1-p^*)}{E^2} = \frac{(2.575)^2(.44)(.56)}{(.03)^2} = 1815.32$$

The required sample size is 1816. Note: If the prior sample of 500 voters had not been taken and no estimate of p was available, then $p = .5$ could be assumed because it provides the largest sample size recommendation. (If we had used $p^* = .5$, the recommended n would have been 1842.)

EXERCISES

EXERCISE 1

Interval Estimate of a Population Mean: σ Known

An apartment complex developer is considering building apartments in College Town, but first wants to do a market study. A sample of monthly rent values ($) for studio apartments in College Town was taken. The data collected from the 70-apartment sample is presented below. Develop a 98% confidence interval for the mean monthly rent for all studio apartments in this city. (Based on past experience, the developer assumes a known value of $\sigma = \$55$ for the population standard deviation.)

```
440  575  580  435  600  435  435  600  615  425
440  515  525  445  525  445  445  550  570  450
450  485  490  450  490  460  460  500  500  465
480  480  480  475  475  475  472  470  470  465
510  500  500  490  480  465  460  450  450  450
510  440  440  525  445  535  549  445  450  615
575  440  435  590  435  600  600  430  430  570
```

EXERCISE 2

Sample Size for an Interval Estimate of a Population Mean

Refer to the apartment rent problem in Exercise 1. Suppose the apartment developer wants a 98% confidence interval estimate of the population mean with a margin of error of $E = \$10$. How large a sample size is needed?

EXERCISE 3

Interval Estimation of a Population Mean: σ Unknown

The manager of Hudson Auto Repair wants to advertise one price for an engine tune-up, with parts included. Before he decides the price to advertise, he needs a good estimate of the average cost of tune-up parts. A sample of 20 customer invoices for tune-ups has been taken and the costs of parts, rounded to the nearest dollar, are listed below.

Provide a 90% confidence interval estimate of the mean cost of parts per tune-up for all of the tune-ups performed at Hudson Auto Repair. We will assume this population to be normally distributed.

91	78	93	57	75	52	99	80	105	62
104	74	62	68	97	73	77	65	80	109

EXERCISE 4

Interval Estimation of a Population Proportion

The manager of University Credit Union (UCU) is concerned about checking account transaction discrepancies. Customers are bringing transaction errors to the attention of the bank's staff several months after they occur. The manager would like to know what proportion of his customers balance their checking accounts within 30 days of receiving a transaction statement from the bank.

Using systematic random sampling, 400 checking account customers are contacted by telephone and asked if they routinely balance their accounts within 30 days of receiving a statement. 271 of the 400 customers respond Yes.

Develop a 95% confidence interval estimate for the proportion of the population of checking account customers at UCU that routinely balance their accounts in a timely manner.

EXERCISE 5

Sample Size for an Interval Estimate of a Population Proportion

Refer again to the University Credit Union problem in Exercise 4. Suppose UCU wants a 95% confidence interval estimate of the population proportion with a margin of error of $E = .025$. How large a sample size is needed?

SELF-TEST

TRUE/FALSE

___ 1. As the degrees of freedom increase, the t distribution approaches the normal distribution.

___ 2. If the margin of error in an interval estimate of μ is 4.6, the interval estimate equals $\bar{x} \pm 2.3$.

___ 3. The level of significance is the probability of correctly concluding that a confidence interval estimate of μ will contain μ.

___ 4. The t distribution is based on the assumption that the population has a normal, or approximately normal, probability distribution.

___ 5. In actual practice, only one sample is selected to develop an interval estimate.

FILL-IN-THE-BLANK

1. The t distribution is a family of similar probability distributions, with each individual distribution depending on a parameter known as the _____.

2. The _____ is the probability that the interval estimation procedure will generate an interval that does not contain the actual value of the population parameter being estimated.

3. The sample mean $\bar{x}$ can be used as a(n) _____ of the population mean μ.

4. To compute the minimum sample size for an interval estimate of μ or p, we must first decide the desired _____.

5. The use of the normal distribution as an approximation of the sampling distribution of $\bar{p}$ is based on the condition that both np and $n(1-p)$ equal _____ or more.

MULTIPLE CHOICE

___ 1. The sample size that guarantees all estimates of proportions will meet the margin of error requirement is computed using a planning value of p equal to
   a) .01
   b) .50
   c) .51
   d) .99

___ 2. We can reduce the margin of error in an interval estimate by doing any one of the following <u>except</u>
  a) increasing the sample size
  b) increasing the level of significance
  c) using the *t* distribution rather than the standard normal distribution
  d) reducing the confidence coefficient

___ 3. In determining an interval estimate of a population mean when σ is unknown, we use a *t* distribution with
  a) $\sqrt{n-1}$ degrees of freedom
  b) $\sqrt{n}$ degrees of freedom
  c) $n-1$ degrees of freedom
  d) n degrees of freedom

___ 4. The expression used to compute an interval estimate of μ may depend on any of the following factors <u>except</u>
  a) the sample size
  b) whether the population standard deviation is known
  c) whether the population has an approximately normal probability distribution
  d) whether there is sampling error

___ 5. The mean of the *t* distribution is
  a) 0
  b) .5
  c) 1
  d) problem specific

ANSWERS

EXERCISES

1) $\bar{x} = 490.8$; $z_{\alpha/2} = 2.33$; 98% confidence interval is 475.48 to 506.12

2) 162

3) 80.05 to 86.59   4) .632 to .723

5) 1343

TRUE/FALSE	FILL-IN-THE-BLANK	MULTIPLE CHOICE
1) True	1) degrees of freedom	1) b
2) False	2) level of significance	2) c
3) False	3) point estimator	3) c
4) True	4) margin of error	4) d
5) True	5) 5	5) a

CHAPTER 9

Hypothesis Testing

Developing Null and Alternative Hypotheses

Type I and Type II Errors

Population Mean: σ Known

Population Mean: σ Unknown

Population Proportion

LEARNING OBJECTIVES

1. Learn how to formulate and test hypotheses about a population mean and a population proportion.

2. Be able to use an Excel worksheet to conduct hypothesis tests about population means and proportions.

3. Understand the types of errors possible when conducting a hypothesis test.

4. Be able to determine the probability of making various errors in hypothesis tests.

5. Know how to compute and interpret p-values.

6. Know the definition of the following terms:

null hypothesis	level of significance
alternative hypothesis	one-tailed test
type I error	two-tailed test
type II error	p-value
critical value	

REVIEW

Developing Null and Alternative Hypotheses
- Hypothesis testing can be used to determine whether a statement about the value of a population parameter should or should not be rejected.
- The null hypothesis, denoted by H_0, is a tentative assumption about a population parameter.
- The alternative hypothesis, denoted by H_a, is the opposite of what is stated in the null.
- Hypothesis testing is similar to a criminal trial. The hypotheses are:
  - H_0: The defendant is innocent
  - H_a: The defendant is guilty

Testing Research Hypotheses
- The research hypothesis should be expressed as the alternative hypothesis.
- The conclusion that the research hypothesis is true comes from sample data that contradict the null hypothesis.

Testing the Validity of a Claim
- Manufacturers' claims are usually given the benefit of the doubt and stated as the null hypothesis.
- The conclusion that the claim is false comes from sample data that contradict the null hypothesis.

Testing in Decision-Making Situations
- A decision maker might have to choose between two courses of action, one associated with the null hypothesis and another associated with the alternative hypothesis.
- Example: Accepting a shipment of goods from a supplier or returning the shipment of goods to the supplier.

Summary of Forms for Null and Alternative Hypotheses: Population Mean
- The equality part of the hypotheses always appears in the null hypothesis.
- In general, a hypothesis test about the value of a population mean μ must take one of the following three forms (where μ_0 is the hypothesized value of the population mean).

$$H_0 : \mu \geq \mu_0 \qquad H_0 : \mu \leq \mu_0 \qquad H_0 : \mu = \mu_0$$
$$H_a : \mu < \mu_0 \qquad H_a : \mu > \mu_0 \qquad H_a : \mu \neq \mu_0$$

Type I and Type II Errors
- Since hypothesis tests are based on sample data, we must allow for the chance of errors.
- A Type I error is rejecting H_0 when it is true.
- A Type II error is accepting H_0 when it is false.
- The person conducting the hypothesis test specifies the maximum allowable probability of making a Type I error, denoted by α and called the level of significance.
- Generally, we cannot control for the probability of making a Type II error, denoted by β.
- Statisticians avoid the risk of making a Type II error by using "do not reject H_0" and not "accept H_a".

One-Tailed Tests About a Population Mean: σ Known

p -Values for One-Tailed Tests
- The p -value is the probability of obtaining a sample result that is at least as unlikely as what is observed.
- The p -value can be used to make the decision in a hypothesis test by noting that if the p -value is less than or equal to the level of significance α, the value of the test statistic is in the rejection region. If the p -value is greater than α, the value of the test statistic is not in the rejection region.
- Reject H_0 if the p-value $\leq \alpha$.

Steps of Hypothesis Testing: One-Tailed Case
- Develop the null and alternative hypotheses.
  - $H_0 : \mu \geq \mu_0$ and $H_a : \mu < \mu_0$ (lower-tail test)
  - $H_0 : \mu \leq \mu_0$ and $H_a : \mu > \mu_0$ (upper-tail test)
- Specify the level of significance α for the test.
- Collect the sample data and compute the value of the test statistic.

$$z = \frac{\overline{x} - \mu_0}{\sigma / \sqrt{n}}$$

- Use α to develop the rule for rejecting H_0.
  - Reject H_0 if $z \leq -z_\alpha$ (if lower-tail test)
  - Reject H_0 if $z \geq z_\alpha$ (if upper-tail test)
  - Reject H_0 if p-value $\leq \alpha$
- Compare the test statistic to the critical value(s) in the rejection rule, or compute the p -value based on the test statistic and compare it to α, to determine whether or not to reject H_0.

Two-Tailed Tests About a Population Mean: σ Known

p-Values for Two-Tailed Tests
- In a two-tailed test, the p-value is found by doubling the area in the tail.
- The doubling of the area in the tail is done so that the p-value can be compared directly to α and the same rejection rule can be maintained, that is reject H_0 if p-value $\le \alpha$.
- Without the doubling of the area in the tail, a p-value rule based on the tail area of $\alpha/2$ would be needed.

Steps of Hypothesis Testing: Two-Tailed Case
- The steps are the same as in the one-tailed case with the following exceptions:
  - Hypotheses
$$H_0 : \mu = \mu_0 \text{ and } H_a : \mu \neq \mu_0$$
  - Rejection Rule
    Reject H_0 if $z \le -z_{\alpha/2}$ or if $z \ge z_{\alpha/2}$ or if p-value $\le \alpha$

Confidence Interval Approach to a Two-Tailed Hypothesis Test
- The steps are the same as above with one exception, the rejection rule.
- Reject H_0 if the confidence interval does <u>not</u> contain the hypothesized value μ_0.

Sample Size Considerations for the σ Known Case
- A sample size of $n \ge 30$ is always adequate when using the hypothesis testing procedures described for the σ known case.
- If the population is normally distributed, the procedures described are appropriate for any sample size.
- If the population is not normally distributed but is roughly symmetric, sample sizes as small as 15 can be used.

One-Tailed Tests About a Population Mean: σ Unknown

Steps of Hypothesis Testing
- The steps are the same as in the σ known case with the following exceptions.
- Test statistic:
  - The test statistic has a t distribution with $n - 1$ degrees of freedom.
$$t = \frac{\bar{x} - \mu_0}{s/\sqrt{n}}$$

- Rejection rule:
  - Reject H_0 if $t \le -t_\alpha$ (if lower-tail test)
  - Reject H_0 if $t \ge t_\alpha$ (if upper-tail test)
  - Reject H_0 if p-value $\le \alpha$

Two-Tailed Tests About a Population Mean: σ Unknown

Steps of Hypothesis Testing
- The steps are the same as the two-tail case with the following exceptions.
- Hypotheses: $H_0 : \mu = \mu_0 \text{ and } H_a : \mu \neq \mu_0$
- Rejection rule: Reject H_0 if $t \le -t_{\alpha/2}$ or $t \ge t_{\alpha/2}$ or p-value $\le \alpha$

Sample Size Considerations for the σ Unknown Case
- If the population is normally distributed, the procedures described for the σ unknown case are appropriate for any sample size.
- If the population is <u>approximately</u> normally distributed, an $n < 15$ is acceptable.
- If the population cannot be approximated by a normal distribution, sample sizes of $n \geq 15$ will provide acceptable results as long as the population is not highly skewed.

Tests About a Population Proportion

Summary of Forms for Hypotheses about a Population Proportion
- The equality part of the hypotheses always appears in the null hypothesis.
- A hypothesis test about the value of a population proportion p must take one of the following three forms (where p_0 is the hypothesized value of the population proportion):

$$H_0 : p \geq p_0 \qquad H_0 : p \leq p_0 \qquad H_0 : p = p_0$$
$$H_a : p < p_0 \qquad H_a : p > p_0 \qquad H_a : p \neq p_0$$

One- and Two-Tailed Tests About a Population Proportion

Steps of Hypothesis Testing
- The steps are the same as in the one- and two-tailed, σ known test of a population mean with the following exception.
- Test statistic:

$$z = \frac{\bar{p} - p_0}{\sigma_{\bar{p}}}$$

$$\text{where:} \quad \sigma_p = \sqrt{\frac{p_0(1 - p_0)}{n}}$$

KEY CONCEPTS

CONCEPT	EXAMPLES	EXERCISES
Tests About a Population Mean		
Developing Null and Alternative Hypotheses	1,2,4,5	1,2,3,4
One-Tailed Test: σ Known	①	1
Two-Tailed Test: σ Known	②	2
One-Tailed Test: σ Unknown	④	4
Two-Tailed Test: σ Unknown	⑤	5
Confidence Interval Approach	③	3
Tests About a Population Proportion		
Developing Null and Alternative Hypotheses	6	6
Two-Tailed Test	⑥	6

◯ Excel Used

EXAMPLES

EXAMPLE 1

One-Tailed Test about a Population Mean: σ Known

A major west coast city provides one of the most comprehensive emergency medical services in the world. Operating in a multiple hospital system with approximately 20 mobile medical units, the service goal is to respond to medical emergencies with a mean time of 12 minutes or less.

The director of medical services wants to conduct a hypothesis test, using a sample of emergency response times, to determine whether or not the service goal of 12 minutes or less is being achieved. A random sample of 40 emergencies was taken. The average response time was 13.25 minutes. The director of medical services knows, based on past studies, that the population of response times is normally distributed with a standard deviation of 3.2 minutes.

Complete the hypothesis test with $\alpha = .05$ and draw your conclusion using both the critical value and *p*-value approaches.

SOLUTION 1

Using a Calculator

We illustrate below each step of this one-tailed (upper-tailed) hypothesis test.

Step 1: Determine the null and alternative hypotheses

H_0: $\mu \le 12$ The emergency service is meeting the response goal.
No follow-up action is necessary.

H_a: $\mu > 12$ The emergency service is not meeting the response goal.
Appropriate follow-up action is necessary.

where: μ = mean response time for the population of medical emergency requests.

Step 2: Select the test statistic to be used to decide whether to reject H_0

With $n \ge 30$ and σ known, the appropriate test statistic is:

$$z = \frac{\bar{x} - \mu_0}{s / \sqrt{n}}$$

Step 3: Specify the level of significance α

$\alpha = .05$

Step 4: Develop the rejection rule based on the level of significance

Reject H_0 if $z \ge 1.645$ (critical value approach), or
Reject H_0 if *p*-value $\le .05$ (*p*-value approach)

Step 5: Collect the data and compute the value of the test statistic

With $n = 40$, $\bar{x} = 13.25$ minutes, and $\sigma = 3.2$ minutes, the value of z is:

$$z = \frac{\bar{x} - \mu_0}{\sigma / \sqrt{n}} = \frac{13.25 - 12}{3.2 / \sqrt{40}} = 2.47$$

Step 6: a) Compare the value of the test statistic to the critical value(s)

$z = 2.47 > 1.645$, or

b) Compute the p-value and compare it to α

With $z = 2.47$, upper tail area $= 1.0 - .9932 = .0068$. p-value $= .0068 < .05$

Step 7: State your conclusion regarding H_0

Reject H_0. We are 95% confident that Metro EMS is not meeting the response goal of 12 minutes or less. Appropriate action should be taken to improve service.

Using Excel's *NORMSDIST* Function

Enter Data: The response times for the sample of 40 emergencies are entered.

Enter Functions and Formulas: The COUNT function is used to determine the sample size. The AVERAGE function is used to compute the sample mean. Then, the value of the population standard deviation and hypothesized value of the population mean are entered.

Next, we obtain an estimate of the standard error of the mean by dividing the population standard deviation by the square root of the sample size. The value of the test statistic z is computed by dividing the difference between the sample mean and the hypothesized population mean by the standard error.

The p-value for the lower tail is computed using the NORMSDIST function. The p-value for the upper tail equals 1 minus the p-value for the lower tail. The p-value if this was a two-tailed test would be 2 times the lesser of the lower tail and upper tail p-values.

Formula Worksheet:

	A	B	C
1	**Response Time**	**Sample Size**	=COUNT(A2:A41)
2	19.5	**Sample Mean**	=AVERAGE(A2:A41)
3	15.2		
4	11.0	**Popul. Std. Dev.**	3.2
5	12.8	**Hypothesized Value**	12
6	12.4		
7	20.3	**Standard Error**	=C4/SQRT(C1)
8	9.6	**Test Statistic z**	=(C2-C5)/C7
9	10.9		
10	16.2	**p-Value (Lower Tail)**	=NORMSDIST(C8)
11	13.4	**p-Value (Upper Tail)**	=1-C10
12	19.7	**p-Value (Two Tail)**	=2*MIN((C10,C11))

Note: Rows 13-41 are not shown.

We see in the resulting worksheet below that the values of the test statistic and *p*-value agree with the results from our earlier, manual calculations.

Value Worksheet:

	A	B	C
1	Response Time	Sample Size	40
2	19.5	Sample Mean	13.25
3	15.2		
4	11.0	Popul. Std. Dev.	3.2
5	12.8	Hypothesized Value	12
6	12.4		
7	20.3	Standard Error	0.506
8	9.6	Test Statistic z	2.47
9	10.9		
10	16.2	*p*-Value (Lower Tail)	0.9933
11	13.4	*p*-Value (Upper Tail)	0.0067
12	19.7	*p*-Value (Two Tail)	0.0134

Note: Rows 13-41 are not shown.

EXAMPLE 2

Two-Tailed Test about a Population Mean: σ Known

The production line for Glow toothpaste is designed to fill tubes of toothpaste with a mean weight of 6 ounces.

Periodically, a sample of 30 tubes will be selected in order to check the filling process. Quality assurance procedures call for the continuation of the filling process if the sample results are consistent with the assumption that the mean fill weight for the population of toothpaste tubes is 6 ounces; otherwise the filling process will be stopped and adjusted. The process fill weights are known to be normally distributed with a standard deviation of .2 ounces.

The mean for the most recent sample was 6.1 ounces. Using both the critical value and *p*-value approaches, conduct a hypothesis test with $\alpha = .02$ to determine if the process requires adjustment.

SOLUTION 2

Using a Calculator

A two-tailed hypothesis test about the population mean (with σ known) can be used to help determine whether the filling process should be allowed to continue or be stopped and adjusted.

Step 1: Determine the null and alternative hypotheses

H_0: $\mu = 6$ The population mean equals the desired mean of 6 ounces. No process adjustment is necessary.

H_a: $\mu \neq 6$ The population mean does not equal the desired mean of 6 oz. Appropriate corrective action is necessary.

Step 2: Select the test statistic to be used to decide whether to reject H_0

With $n \geq 30$ and σ known, the appropriate test statistic is:

$$z = \frac{\bar{x} - \mu_0}{s/\sqrt{n}}$$

Step 3: Specify the level of significance α

$\alpha = .02$

Step 4: Develop the rejection rule(s) based on the level of significance

Reject H_0 if $z \leq -2.33$ or if $z \geq 2.33$ (critical value approach), or

Reject H_0 if p-value $\leq .02$ (p-value approach)

Step 5: Collect the data and compute the value of the test statistic

With $n = 30$, $\bar{x} = 6.1$ ounces, and $\sigma = .2$ ounces, the value of z is:

$$z = \frac{\bar{x} - \mu_0}{\sigma/\sqrt{n}} = \frac{6.1 - 6.0}{.2/\sqrt{30}} = 2.74$$

Step 6: a) Compare the value of the test statistic to the critical value(s)

$z = 2.74 > 2.33$, or

b) Compute the p-value and compare it to α

With $z = 2.74$, the upper tail area = $1.0 - .9969 = .0031$

$p = 2(.0031) = .0062 < .02$ (Note: p-value is doubled; this is a two-tailed test.)

Step 7: State your conclusion regarding H_0

Reject H_0. We are 98% confident that the mean filling weight of the toothpaste tubes is not 6 ounces.

Using Excel's *NORMSDIST* Function

Now we will use Excel to conduct a two-tailed hypothesis test about a population mean (with σ known). The steps involved are identical to those outlined in the solution to Example 1 for a one-tailed test.

Enter Data: The fill weights for the sample of 30 toothpaste tubes are entered.

Enter Functions and Formulas: The COUNT function is used to determine the sample size. The AVERAGE function is used to compute the sample mean. Then, the value of the population standard deviation and hypothesized value of the population mean are entered.

Next, we obtain an estimate of the standard error of the mean by dividing the sample standard deviation by the square root of the sample size. The value of the test statistic z is computed by dividing the difference between the sample mean and the hypothesized population mean by the standard error.

The p-value for the lower tail is computed using the NORMSDIST function. The p-value for the upper tail equals 1 minus the p-value for the lower tail. The p-value for this two-tailed test is 2 times the lesser of the lower tail and upper tail p-values.

Formula Worksheet:

	A	B	C
1	Fill Weight	Sample Size	=COUNT(A2:A31)
2	6.04	Sample Mean	=AVERAGE(A2:A31)
3	5.99		
4	5.92	Popul. Std. Dev.	0.2
5	6.03	Hypothesized Value	6
6	6.01		
7	5.95	Standard Error	=C4/SQRT(C1)
8	6.09	Test Statistic z	=(C2-C5)/C7
9	6.07		
10	6.07	p-Value (Lower Tail)	=NORMSDIST(C8)
11	5.97	p-Value (Upper Tail)	=1-C10
12	5.96	p-Value (Two Tail)	=2*MIN((C10,C11))

Note: Rows 13-31 are not shown.

Value Worksheet:

	A	B	C
1	Fill Weight	Sample Size	30
2	6.04	Sample Mean	6.1
3	5.99		
4	5.92	Popul. Std. Dev.	0.2
5	6.03	Hypothesized Value	6
6	6.01		
7	5.95	Standard Error	0.0365
8	6.09	Test Statistic z	2.74
9	6.07		
10	6.07	p-Value (Lower Tail)	0.9969
11	5.97	p-Value (Upper Tail)	0.0031
12	5.96	p-Value (Two Tail)	0.0062

Note: Rows 13-31 are not shown.

EXAMPLE 3

Confidence Interval Approach to Hypothesis Testing

Refer to the Glow toothpaste study in Example 2. Conduct the same hypothesis test, but this time use a confidence interval approach rather than the critical value or *p*-value approach.

SOLUTION 3

Using a Calculator

The interval estimate is computed as:

Point Estimate of μ +/- Margin of Error

We use the sample mean, $\bar{x}$, as the point estimate of μ. The margin of error is the product of $z_{\alpha/2}$ times the standard error of the mean. The value of $z_{\alpha/2}$ is 2.33. The standard error of the mean equals the sample standard deviation divided by the square root of the sample size. Hence, we can compute a 98% confidence interval for μ as follows:

$$\bar{x} \pm z_{\alpha/2}\frac{s}{\sqrt{n}} = 6.1 \pm 2.33(.2/\sqrt{30}) = 6.1 \pm .08508$$

Hence, we are 98% confident that the value of μ is in the interval 6.01492 to 6.18508. Since the hypothesized value for the population mean, $\mu_0 = 6$, is not in this interval, the conclusion is that the null hypothesis, H_0: $\mu = 6$, should be rejected.

Using Excel's NORMSINV Function

Enter Data: The fill weights for the 30 tubes of toothpaste are entered into column A..

Enter Functions and Formulas: The sample size *n* is determined using the COUNT function. The AVERAGE function is used to compute the sample mean, $\bar{x}$.

The values for the population standard deviation and the confidence coefficient are entered into the worksheet. The level of significance is 1 minus the confidence coefficient.

The margin of error is found by using the CONFIDENCE function, which has three parameters: 1) level of significance, 2) population standard deviation, and 3) sample size.

The point estimate of the population mean is simply the sample mean. The lower limit of the confidence interval is the point estimate minus the margin of error. To find the upper limit of the confidence interval the margin of error is added to the point estimate.

Formula Worksheet:

	A	B	C
1	Fill Weight	Sample Size	=COUNT(A2:A31)
2	6.04	Sample Mean	=AVERAGE(A2:A31)
3	5.99		
4	5.92	Popul. Std. Deviation	0.2
5	6.03	Confidence Coefficient	0.98
6	6.01	Level of Significance	=1-C5
7	5.95		
8	6.09	Margin of Error	=CONFIDENCE(C6,C4,C1)
9	6.07		
10	6.07	Point Estimate	=C2
11	5.97	Lower Limit	=C10-C8
12	5.96	Upper Limit	=C10+C8

Note: Rows 13-31 are not shown.

We see in the resulting worksheet below that the interval estimate and the test conclusion agree with the results from our earlier, manual calculations. The confidence interval (6.015 to 6.185) does not include the hypothesized value of the population mean (6.0).

Value Worksheet:

	A	B	C
1	Fill Weight	Sample Size	30
2	6.04	Sample Mean	6.1
3	5.99		
4	5.92	Popul. Std. Deviation	0.2
5	6.03	Confidence Coefficient	0.98
6	6.01	Level of Significance	0.02
7	5.95		
8	6.09	Margin of Error	0.085
9	6.07		
10	6.07	Point Estimate	6.1
11	5.97	Lower Limit	6.015
12	5.96	Upper Limit	6.185

Note: Rows 13-31 are not shown.

EXAMPLE 4

One-Tailed Test about a Population Mean: σ Unknown

A State Highway Patrol periodically samples vehicle speeds at various locations on a particular roadway. The sample of vehicle speeds is used to test the hypothesis H_0: $\mu \le 65$ mph. The locations where H_0 is rejected are deemed the best locations for radar traps.

At Location F, a sample of 16 vehicles shows a mean speed of 68.2 mph with a standard deviation of 3.8 mph. Use the critical value and p-value approaches to test the hypothesis with $\alpha = .05$. (The population of vehicle speeds at Location F is believed to be approximately normally distributed.)

SOLUTION 4

Using a Calculator

Step 1: Determine the null and alternative hypotheses

H_0: $\mu \le 65$ The population of vehicles have a mean speed of 65 or less. Location F is not a good location for a radar trap.

H_a: $\mu > 65$ The population mean speed is greater than 65. Location F is a good location for a radar trap.

Step 2: Select the test statistic to be used to decide whether to reject H_0

With σ unknown, the appropriate test statistic is:

$$t = \frac{\bar{x} - \mu_0}{s/\sqrt{n}}$$

Step 3: Specify the level of significance α

$\alpha = .05$

Step 4: Develop the rejection rule(s) based on the level of significance

Reject H_0 if $t \ge 1.753$ (based on $\alpha = .05$ and d.f. = 16 - 1 = 15), or

Reject H_0 if p-value $\le .05$

Step 5: Collect the data and compute the value of the test statistic

With $n = 16$, $\bar{x} = 68.2$ mph, and $s = 3.8$ mph, the value of t is:

$$t = \frac{\bar{x} - \mu_0}{s/\sqrt{n}} = \frac{68.2 - 65.0}{3.8/\sqrt{16}} = 3.37$$

Step 6: a) Compare the value of the test statistic to the critical value(s)

$t = 3.37 > 1.753$, or

b) Compute the p-value and compare it to α

Generally, it is not possible to be very precise with the p-value approach when doing the problem manually (without the aid of Excel).

Step 7: State your conclusion regarding H_0

Reject H_0. We are 95% confident that that the mean speed of all vehicles in Location F is greater than 65 mph. Location F is a good location for a radar trap.

Using Excel's *TDIST* Function

The steps involved are nearly identical to those outlined in the solution to Example 1. The primary difference is that here, because this is σ unknown case, we must use t, rather than z, as the test statistic.

Enter Data: The vehicle speeds for the sample of 16 vehicles are entered into column A.

Enter Functions and Formulas: The COUNT function is used to determine the sample size. The AVERAGE function is used to compute the sample mean. The STDEV function is used to compute the value of the sample standard deviation. Then, the hypothesized value of the population mean is entered.

Next, we obtain an estimate of the standard error of the mean by dividing the sample standard deviation by the square root of the sample size. The value of the test statistic t is computed by dividing the difference between the sample mean and the hypothesized population mean by the standard error. Then, the degrees of freedom are found by subtracting 1 from the sample size.

The p-value for the lower tail is computed using the TDIST function. TDIST's first argument is the test statistic value. The function's second argument is the degrees of freedom value. The third argument is the number of tails in the test, which in this case is 1.

The p-value for the upper tail equals 1 minus the p-value for the lower tail. The p-value if this was a two-tailed test would be 2 times the lesser of the lower tail and upper tail p-values.

Formula Worksheet:

	A	B	C
1	**Vehicle Speed**	Sample Size	=COUNT(A2:A17)
2	69.6	Sample Mean	=AVERAGE(A2:A17)
3	73.5	Sample Std. Dev.	=STDEV(A2:A17)
4	74.1		
5	64.4	Hypothesized Value	65
6	66.3		
7	68.7	Standard Error	=C3/SQRT(C1)
8	69.0	Test Statistic t	=(C2-C8)/C9
9	65.2	Degrees of Freedom	=C1-1
10	71.1		
11	70.8	*p*-Value (Lower Tail)	=IF(C8<0,TDIST(-C8,C9,1),1-TDIST(C8,C9,1))
12	64.6	*p*-Value (Lower Tail)	=1-C11
13	67.4	*p*-Value (Two Tail)	=2*MIN(C11,C12)

Note: Rows 14-17 are not shown.

Value Worksheet:

	A	B	C
	Vehicle Speed		
1		**Sample Size**	16
2	69.6	**Sample Mean**	68.2
3	73.5	**Sample Std. Dev.**	3.8
4	74.1		
5	64.4	**Hypothesized Value**	65
6	66.3		
7	68.7	**Standard Error**	0.949
8	69.0	**Test Statistic t**	3.372
9	65.2	**Degrees of Freedom**	15
10	71.1		
11	70.8	***p*-Value (Lower Tail)**	0.9979
12	64.6	***p*-Value (Upper Tail)**	0.0021
13	67.4	***p*-Value (Two Tail)**	0.0042

Note: Rows 14-17 are not shown.

We see in the worksheet above that the upper-tail *p*-value (.0021) is less than α = .05, so we reject the null hypothesis. This is consistent with our conclusion using the critical value approach.

EXAMPLE 5

Two-Tailed Test about a Population Mean: σ Unknown

Refer to the Glow toothpaste study in Example 2. Recall that the sample mean was 6.1 ounces and the population standard deviation was known to be .2 ounces. Conduct the same two-tailed hypothesis test, but this time assume that the population standard deviation is unknown and the sample standard deviation equals .2 ounces. Should we again reject the null hypothesis?

SOLUTION 5

A two-tailed hypothesis test about the population mean (with σ unknown) can be used to help determine whether the filling process should be allowed to continue or be stopped and adjusted.

Step 1: Determine the null and alternative hypotheses

H_0: $\mu = 6$ The population mean equals the desired mean of 6 ounces.
No process adjustment is necessary.

H_a: $\mu \neq 6$ The population mean does not equal the desired mean of 6 oz.
Appropriate corrective action is necessary.

Step 2: Select the test statistic to be used to decide whether to reject H_0

With σ unknown, the appropriate test statistic is:

$$t = \frac{\bar{x} - \mu_0}{s / \sqrt{n}}$$

Step 3: Specify the level of significance α

$\alpha = .02$

Step 4: Develop the rejection rule(s) based on the level of significance

Reject H_0 if $t \leq -2.462$ or if $t \geq 2.462$ (based on $\alpha = .02$ and d.f. = 30 - 1 = 29), or

Reject H_0 if p-value $\leq .02$

Step 5: Collect the data and compute the value of the test statistic

With $n = 30$, $\bar{x} = 6.1$ ounces, and $s = .2$ ounces, the value of t is:

$$t = \frac{\bar{x} - \mu_0}{s / \sqrt{n}} = \frac{6.1 - 6.0}{.2 / \sqrt{30}} = 2.739$$

Step 6: a) Compare the value of the test statistic to the critical value(s)

$t = 2.739 > 2.462$

or b) Compute the p-value and compare it to α

Generally, it is not possible to be very precise with the p-value approach when doing the problem manually (without the aid of Excel).

Step 7: State your conclusion regarding H_0

Reject H_0. We are 98% confident that that the mean filling weight of the toothpaste tubes is not 6 ounces.

EXAMPLE 6

Test about a Population Proportion

For a Christmas and New Year's week, the National Safety Council estimated that 500 people would be killed and 25,000 injured on the nation's roads. The NSC claimed that drunk driving would cause 50% of the accidents.

A sample of 120 accidents showed that 67 were caused by drunk driving. Use these data to test the NSC's claim with $\alpha = 0.05$. Use the critical value and p-value approaches to conduct this hypothesis testing.

SOLUTION 6

Using a Calculator

A two-tailed hypothesis test about the population proportion can be used to help determine whether 50% of all the accidents during the holiday week were caused by drunk driving.

Step 1: Determine the null and alternative hypotheses

H_0: $p = .5$ The population proportion equals .5

H_a: $p \neq .5$ The population proportion does not equal .5

Step 2: Select the test statistic to be used to decide whether to reject H_0

$$z = \frac{\bar{p} - p_0}{\sqrt{\dfrac{p_0(1 - p_0)}{n}}}$$

Step 3: Specify the level of significance α

$\alpha = .05$

Step 4: Develop the rejection rule(s) based on the level of significance

Reject H_0 if $z \leq -1.96$ or if $z \geq 1.96$ (critical value approach), or

Reject H_0 if p-value $\leq .05$ (p-value approach)

Step 5: Collect the data and compute the value of the test statistic

With $n = 120$, $\bar{p} = 67/120 = .5583$, the value of z is:

$$z = \frac{\bar{p} - p_0}{\sqrt{\dfrac{p_0(1 - p_0)}{n}}} = \frac{.5583 - .5}{\sqrt{\dfrac{.5(1 - .5)}{120}}} = 1.278$$

Step 6: a) Compare the value of the test statistic to the critical value(s)

$z = 1.278 < 1.96$, or

b) Compute the p-value and compare it to α

With $z = 1.28$, the upper tail area $= 1.0 - .8997 = .1003$

p-value $= 2(.1003) = .2006 > .05$ (Note: p-value is doubled; this is a two-tailed test.)

Step 7: State your conclusion regarding H_0

Do not reject H_0. We are <u>not</u> 95% confident that the proportion of all accidents during the holiday week caused by drunk driving was .5.

Using Excel's *NORMSDIST* Function

Enter Data: The Yes and No responses for the sample of 120 accidents are entered into column A.

Enter Functions and Formulas: The COUNTA function is used to determine the sample size. The COUNTIF function is used to count the number of "Yes" responses in the sample. The value of the sample proportion is computed by dividing the number of "Yes" responses by the sample size.

Then, the hypothesized proportion of "Yes" responses in the population is entered. Next, we compute the standard error of the proportion using the SQRT function. The value of the test statistic *t* is computed by dividing the difference between the sample proportion and the hypothesized population proportion by the standard error.

The *p*-value for the lower tail is computed using the NORMSDIST function. The *p*-value for the upper tail equals 1 minus the *p*-value for the lower tail. The *p*-value for this two-tailed test is 2 times the lesser of the lower tail and upper tail *p*-values.

Formula Worksheet:

	A	B	C
1	Drunk Driving	Sample Size	120
2	No	Response of Interest	Yes
3	Yes	Count for Response	=COUNTA(A2:A121,C2)
4	No	Sample Proportion	=C3/C1
5	Yes		
6	No	Hypothesized Value	0.5
7	Yes		
8	Yes	Standard Error	=SQRT(C6*(1-C6)/C1)
9	No	Test Statistic	=(C4-C6)/C8
10	No		
11	Yes	*p*-Value (Lower Tail)	=NORMSDIST(C9)
12	Yes	*p*-Value (Upper Tail)	=1-C11
13	Yes	*p*-Value (Two Tail)	=2*MIN(C11,C12)

Note: Rows 14-121 are not shown.

Value Worksheet:

	A	B	C
1	Drunk Driving	Sample Size	120
2	No	Response of Interest	Yes
3	Yes	Count for Response	67
4	No	Sample Proportion	0.5583
5	Yes		
6	No	Hypothesized Value	0.5
7	Yes		
8	Yes	Standard Error	0.0456
9	No	Test Statistic	1.278
10	No		
11	Yes	*p*-Value (Lower Tail)	0.8995
12	Yes	*p*-Value (Upper Tail)	0.1005
13	Yes	*p*-Value (Two Tail)	0.2010

EXERCISES

EXERCISE 1

One-Tailed Test about a Population Mean: σ Known

A radio talk show host in Brockdale has complained that the average monthly rent for an efficiency apartment in that city is $500 or more. The Brockdale Landlords Association (BLA) believes that this claim is an exaggeration. BLA takes a random sample of 70 efficiency apartments in the city, inquiring about the monthly rent charged for each. The data, in dollars, collected from the 70-apartment sample is presented below.

```
440 575 580 435 600 435 435 600 615 425
440 515 525 445 525 445 445 550 570 450
450 485 490 450 490 460 460 500 500 465
480 480 480 475 475 475 472 470 470 465
510 500 500 490 480 465 460 450 450 450
510 440 440 525 445 535 549 445 450 615
575 440 435 590 435 600 600 430 430 570
```

Conduct a hypothesis test with $\alpha = .05$ and draw your conclusion using both the critical value and *p*-value approaches. (Assume the standard deviation for all efficiency apartment rents in this city is known to be about $55.)

EXERCISE 2

Two-Tailed Test about a Population Mean: σ Known

Fast 'n Clean operates 12 laundromats on the east side of the city. All of Fast 'n Clean's clothes dryers have a label stating "20 minutes for $1.00." You question the accuracy of the dryers' clocks and decide to conduct an observational study. You randomly select 36 dryers in several different Fast 'n Clean locations, put $1.00 in each and time the drying cycle. The sample mean drying time is 20 minutes and 25 seconds. The manufacturer of the dryer states that the standard deviation for 20-minute drying cycles is 1 minute.

Using the sample data and $\alpha = .05$, test the validity of the label on the dryers. Apply the *p*-value and critical value approaches to conducting the hypothesis test.

EXERCISE 3

Two-Tailed Test about a Population Mean: σ Known

Refer to the Fast 'n Clean problem in Exercise 2. Conduct the same two-tailed hypothesis test, but this time use the confidence interval approach to hypothesis testing.

EXERCISE 4

One-Tailed Test about a Population Mean: σ Unknown

Laura Naples, Manager of Heritage Inn, periodically collects and tabulates information about a sample of the hotel's overnight guests. This information aids her in pricing and scheduling decisions she must make. The table below lists data on ten randomly selected hotel registrants, collected as the registrants checked out. The data listed are:

- Number of people in the group
- Hotel's shuttle service used: yes or no
- Total telephone charges incurred
- Reason for stay: business or personal

Name of Registrant	Number in Group	Shuttle Used	Telephone Charges ($)	Reason for Stay
Adam Sandler	1	yes	0.00	personal
Michelle Pepper	2	no	8.46	business
Claudia Shepler	1	no	3.20	business
Annette Rodriquez	2	no	2.90	business
Tony DiMarco	1	yes	3.12	personal
Amy Franklin	3	yes	4.65	business
Tammy Roberts	2	no	6.35	personal
Edward Blackstone	4	yes	2.10	personal
Mary Silverman	1	no	1.85	business
Todd Atherton	1	no	5.80	business

Before cell telephones became so common, the average telephone charge per registered group was at least $5.00. Laura suspects that the average has dropped. Test H_0: $\mu \geq 5$ and H_a: $\mu < 5$ using a .05 level of significance. Use both the critical value and p-value approaches to hypothesis testing.

EXERCISE 5

Two-Tailed Test about a Population Mean: σ Unknown

Refer to the Heritage Inn data in Exercise 4. In the past, Laura has made some important managerial decisions based on the assumption that the average number of people in a registered group is 2.5. Now she wonders if the assumption is still valid. Test the assumption with $\alpha = .05$ and use both the critical value and p-value approaches.

EXERCISE 6

Test about a Population Proportion

The board of directors of a corporation has agreed to allow the human resources manager to move to the next step in planning day care service for employees' children if the manager can prove that at least 25% of the employees have interest in using the service.

The HR manager polls 300 employees and 90 say they would seriously consider utilizing the service. At the $\alpha = .10$ level of significance, is there enough interest in the service to move to the next planning step?

SELF-TEST

TRUE/FALSE

___ 1. The p-value approach and critical value approach will always provide the same hypothesis testing conclusion.

___ 2. Hypothesis testing is proof by contradiction.

___ 3. A Type I error is not rejecting H_0 when H_a is true.

___ 4. The larger the p-value, the less likely it is that the sample results came from a population where the null hypothesis is true.

___ 5. Generally, the research hypothesis is the null hypothesis.

FILL-IN-THE-BLANK

1. By never directly accepting H_0, the statistician avoids the risk of making a

    _____.

2. A manufacturer's claim is usually given the benefit of the doubt and stated as the _____ hypothesis.

3. If the cost of making a Type I error is high, a small value should be chosen for the

    _____.

4. When the rejection region is in the lower tail of the sampling distribution, the _____ is the area under the curve less than or equal to the test statistic.

5. The z-value that establishes the boundary of the rejection region is called the

    _____.

MULTIPLE CHOICE

___ 1. Reducing the risk of a Type I error in a hypothesis test would result from doing any one of the following except
   a) increasing the sample size
   b) increasing the value of α
   c) decreasing the confidence coefficient
   d) decreasing the level of significance

___ 2. In tests about a population proportion, p_0 represents the
   a) hypothesized population proportion
   b) observed sample proportion
   c) observed p-value
   d) probability of $p - \bar{p} = 0$

_____ 3. For large-sample hypothesis tests involving population proportions, we can assume the sampling distribution of $\bar{p}$ approximately follows
   a) a normal probability distribution
   b) a uniform probability distribution
   c) an exponential probability distribution
   d) a Poisson probability distribution

_____ 4. Which one of the following is an improper form of the null and alternative hypotheses?
   a) $H_0 : \mu \leq \mu_0$ and $H_a : \mu > \mu_0$
   b) $H_0 : \mu = \mu_0$ and $H_a : \mu \neq \mu_0$
   c) $H_0 : \mu < \mu_0$ and $H_a : \mu \geq \mu_0$
   d) $H_0 : \mu \geq \mu_0$ and $H_a : \mu < \mu_0$

_____ 5. For a two-tailed hypothesis test about μ, we can use any of the following approaches except
   a) compare the confidence interval estimate of μ to the hypothesized value of μ
   b) compare the *p*-value to the value of α
   c) compare the value of the test statistic to the critical value
   d) compare the level of significance to the confidence coefficient

ANSWERS

EXERCISES

1) $z = -1.40 > -1.645$ and *p*-value = .0808 > .05; Do not reject H_0: $\mu \geq 500$

2) $z = 2.50 > 1.96$ and *p*-value = .0124 < .05; Reject H_0: $\mu = 20$

3) Confidence interval is 20.09 to 20.74, which does not include 20.00; Reject H_0: $\mu = 20$

4) *p*-value = .0877 > .05, $t = -1.471 > -1.833$; Do not reject H_0: $\mu \geq 5$

5) *p*-value = .0607 > .05, $t = -2.1433 > -2.2622$; Do not reject H_0: $\mu = 2.5$

6) *p*-value = .0228 < .10, $z = 2.00 > 1.28$; Reject H_0: $p \leq .25$; move to next planning step

TRUE/FALSE	FILL-IN-THE-BLANK	MULTIPLE CHOICE
1) True	1) Type II error	1) d
2) True	2) null	2) a
3) False	3) level of significance	3) a
4) False	4) *p*-value	4) c
5) False	5) critical value	5) d

CHAPTER 10

Comparisons Involving Means

Inferences About the Difference Between
Two Population Means: σ_1 and σ_2 Known

Inferences About the Difference Between
Two Population Means: σ_1 and σ_2 Unknown

Inferences About the Difference Between
Two Population Means: Matched Samples

Introduction to Analysis of Variance

Analysis of Variance:
Testing for the Equality of k Population Means

LEARNING OBJECTIVES

1. Be able to develop interval estimates and conduct hypothesis tests about the difference between two population means.

2. Know the properties of the sampling distribution of the difference between two means $(\bar{x}_1 - \bar{x}_2)$.

3. Be able to use the *t* distribution to conduct statistical inferences about the difference between the means of two normal populations with unequal variances.

4. Learn how to analyze the difference between two population means when the samples are independent and when the samples are matched.

5. Understand how the analysis of variance procedure can be used to determine if the means of more than two populations are equal.

6. Know the assumptions necessary to use the analysis of variance procedure.

7. Understand the use of the *F* distribution in performing the analysis of variance procedure.

8. Know how to set up an ANOVA table and interpret the entries in the table.

9. Be able to use output from computer software packages to solve analysis of variance problems.

REVIEW

Inferences About the Difference Between Two Population Means
- Let μ_1 = the mean of population 1 and μ_2 = the mean of population 2.
- The difference between the two population means is $\mu_1 - \mu_2$.
- To estimate $\mu_1 - \mu_2$, we select a simple random sample of n_1 items from population 1 and n_2 items from population 2.
- Let $\bar{x}_1$ = the sample mean for the n_1 items and $\bar{x}_2$ = the sample mean for the n_2 items.
- The point estimator of the difference between the means of two populations is:

$$\bar{x}_1 - \bar{x}_2$$

Sampling Distribution of $\bar{x}_1 - \bar{x}_2$ (with σ_1 and σ_2 known):
- The expected value is:

$$E(\bar{x}_1 - \bar{x}_2) = \mu_1 - \mu_2$$

- The standard error of $\bar{x}_1 - \bar{x}_2$ deviation is:

$$\sigma_{\bar{x}_1 - \bar{x}_2} = \sqrt{\frac{\sigma_1^2}{n_1} + \frac{\sigma_2^2}{n_2}}$$

where: σ_1 = standard deviation of population 1
σ_2 = standard deviation of population 2

- The distribution form is approximately normally distributed if both populations have a normal distribution or if the sample sizes are large enough that the central limit theorem applies.

Interval Estimate of $\mu_1 - \mu_2$ (with σ_1 and σ_2 known):
- With σ_1 and σ_2 known, the interval estimate is:

$$\overline{X}_1 - \overline{X}_2 \pm z_{\alpha/2}\sqrt{\frac{\sigma_1^2}{n_1} + \frac{\sigma_2^2}{n_2}}$$

where $1 - \alpha$ is the confidence coefficient

Hypothesis Tests about $\mu_1 - \mu_2$ (with σ_1 and σ_2 known):
- Hypotheses:
  - H_0: $\mu_1 - \mu_2 \geq D_0$ and H_a: $\mu_1 - \mu_2 < D_0$ (lower-tailed)
  - H_0: $\mu_1 - \mu_2 \leq D_0$ and H_a: $\mu_1 - \mu_2 > D_0$ (upper-tailed)
  - H_0 : $\mu_1 - \mu_2 = D_0$ and H_a : $\mu_1 - \mu_2 \neq D_0$ (two-tailed)

- Test statistic:

$$z = \frac{(\overline{X}_1 - \overline{X}_2) - D_0}{\sqrt{\dfrac{\sigma_1^2}{n_1} + \dfrac{\sigma_2^2}{n_2}}}$$

- Rejection rule:
  - Reject H_0 if $z \leq -z_\alpha$ (lower-tailed)
  - Reject H_0 if $z \geq z_\alpha$ (upper-tailed)
  - Reject H_0 if $z \leq -z_{\alpha/2}$ or $z \geq z_{\alpha/2}$ (two-tailed)

Inferences About the Difference Between Two Population Means: σ_1 and σ_2 Unknown

Interval Estimate of $\mu_1 - \mu_2$ (with σ_1 and σ_2 unknown):
- With σ_1 and σ_2 unknown, the interval estimate is:

$$\overline{X}_1 - \overline{X}_2 \pm t_{\alpha/2}\sqrt{\frac{s_1^2}{n_1} + \frac{s_2^2}{n_2}}$$

where:

$1 - \alpha$ is the confidence coefficient, and the

t value is based on the t distribution with df computed as

$$df = \frac{\left(\dfrac{s_1^2}{n_1} + \dfrac{s_2^2}{n_2}\right)^2}{\dfrac{1}{n_1 - 1}\left(\dfrac{s_1^2}{n_1}\right)^2 + \dfrac{1}{n_2 - 1}\left(\dfrac{s_2^2}{n_2}\right)^2}$$

Hypothesis Tests about $\mu_1 - \mu_2$ (with σ_1 and σ_2 unknown):

- Hypotheses:
  - H_0: $\mu_1 - \mu_2 \geq D_0$ and H_a: $\mu_1 - \mu_2 < D_0$ (lower-tailed)
  - H_0: $\mu_1 - \mu_2 \leq D_0$ and H_a: $\mu_1 - \mu_2 > D_0$ (upper-tailed)
  - H_0: $\mu_1 - \mu_2 = D_0$ and H_a: $\mu_1 - \mu_2 \neq D_0$ (two-tailed)

- Test statistic:

$$t = \frac{(\bar{x}_1 - \bar{x}_2) - D_0}{\sqrt{\dfrac{s_1^2}{n_1} + \dfrac{s_2^2}{n_2}}}$$

- Rejection rule:
  - Reject H_0 if $t \leq -t_\alpha$ (lower-tailed)
  - Reject H_0 if $t \geq t_\alpha$ (upper-tailed)
  - Reject H_0 if $t \leq -t_{\alpha/2}$ or $t \geq t_{\alpha/2}$ (two-tailed)

Inferences about the Difference Between Two Population Means: Matched Samples

- With a matched-sample design each sampled item provides a pair of data values.
- The matched-sample design can be referred to as blocking.
- This design often leads to a smaller sampling error than the independent-sample design because variation between sampled items is eliminated as a source of sampling error.
- The key to this analysis is to realize that we consider only the n differences.
- The sample mean is:

$$\bar{d} = \frac{\sum d_i}{n}$$

- The sample standard deviation is:

$$s_d = \sqrt{\frac{\sum (d_i - \bar{d})^2}{n-1}}$$

Hypothesis Tests about $\mu_1 - \mu_2$: Matched Samples

- Hypotheses:
  - H_0: $\mu_d \geq 0$ and H_a: $\mu_d < 0$ (lower-tailed)
  - H_0: $\mu_d \leq 0$ and H_a: $\mu_d > 0$ (lower-tailed)
  - H_0: $\mu_d = 0$ and H_a: $\mu_d \neq 0$ (two-tailed)
    where: μ_d = the mean of the difference values
- Test statistic:

$$t = \frac{\bar{d} - \mu_d}{s_d / \sqrt{n}}$$

- Rejection rule:
  - Reject H_0 if $t \leq -t_\alpha$ (lower-tailed)
  - Reject H_0 if $t \geq t_\alpha$ (upper-tailed)
  - Reject H_0 if $t \leq -t_{\alpha/2}$ or $t \geq t_{\alpha/}$ (two-tailed)

Interval Estimate of $\mu_1 - \mu_2$: Matched Samples
- The single population methodology of Chapter 8 is used.

$$\bar{d} \pm t_{\alpha/2} \frac{s_d}{\sqrt{n}}$$

where $1 - \alpha$ is the confidence coefficient

Introduction to Analysis of Variance
- Analysis of Variance (ANOVA) can be used to test for the equality of three or more population means using data obtained from observational or experimental studies.
- We want to use the sample results to test the following hypotheses.

$$H_0: \; \mu_1 = \mu_2 = \mu_3 = \cdots = \mu_k$$
$$H_a: \; \text{Not all population means are equal}$$

- If H_0 is rejected, we cannot conclude that all population means are different.
- Rejecting H_0 means that at least two population means have different values.
- Terminology:
  - The response variable is the dependent variable.
  - The factor is the independent variable.
  - The treatments are the levels of the factor.

Assumptions for Analysis of Variance
- For each population, the response variable is normally distributed. (This is not a concern if the sample sizes are equal.)
- The variance of the response variable, denoted s^2, is the same for all of the populations.
- The observations must be independent.

Analysis of Variance: Testing the Equality of k Population Means
- Notation is: x_{ij} = value of observation i for treatment j
       n_j = number of observations for treatment j
       $\bar{x}_j$ = sample mean for treatment j
       s_j^2 = sample variance for treatment j
       s_j = sample standard deviation for treatment j
- Sample mean for treatment j is:

$$\bar{x}_j = \frac{\sum_{i=1}^{n_j} x_{ij}}{n_j}$$

- Sample variance for treatment j is:

$$s_j^2 = \frac{\sum_{i=1}^{n_j} (x_{ij} - \bar{x}_j)^2}{n_j - 1}$$

- Overall sample mean is:

$$\bar{\bar{x}} = \frac{\sum_{j=1}^{k} \sum_{i=1}^{n_j} x_{ij}}{n_T}$$

Between-Treatments Estimate of Population Variance

- Sum of squares due to treatments is:

$$SSTR = \sum_{j=1}^{k} n_j(\bar{x}_j - \bar{\bar{x}})^2$$

- Mean of squares due to treatments is:

$$MSTR = \frac{SSTR}{k-1}$$

Within-Treatments Estimate of Population Variance

- Sum of squares due to error is:

$$SSE = \sum_{j=1}^{k} (n_j - 1)s_j^2$$

- Mean of squares due to error is:

$$MSE = \frac{SSE}{n_T - k}$$

Comparing the Variance Estimates: The *F* Test

- If the null hypothesis is true and the ANOVA assumptions are valid, the sampling distribution of MSTR/MSE is an *F* distribution with MSTR d.f. equal to $k - 1$ and MSE d.f. equal to $n_T - k$.
- If the means of the k populations are not equal, the value of MSTR/MSE will be inflated because MSTR overestimates s^2.
- Hence, we will reject H_0 if the resulting value of MSTR/MSE appears to be too large to have been selected at random from the appropriate *F* distribution.
- Hypotheses:

    H_0: $\mu_1 = \mu_2 = \mu_3 = \cdots = \mu_k$
    H_a: Not all population means are equal

- Test statistic:

    $F = MSTR/MSE$

- Rejection rule:

    Reject H_0 if $F > F_\alpha$
    where the value of F_α is based on an *F* distribution
    with $k - 1$ numerator degrees of freedom and
    $n_T - 1$ denominator degrees of freedom.

ANOVA Table

- An ANOVA table is used to summarize the analysis of variance computations and results.
- The general form of the table is:

Source of Variation	Sum of Squares	Degrees of Freedom	Mean Square	F
Treatments	SSTR	$k - 1$	MSTR	MSTR/MSE
Error	SSE	$n_T - k$	MSE	
Total	SST	$n_T - 1$		

KEY CONCEPTS

CONCEPT	EXAMPLES	EXERCISES
Interval Estimate of $\mu_1 - \mu_2$: Independent Samples		
σ_1 and σ_2 Known	①	1
σ_1 and σ_2 Unknown	②	2
Hypothesis Test about $\mu_1 - \mu_2$: Independent Samples		
σ_1 and σ_2 Known	③	3
σ_1 and σ_2 Unknown	④	4
Hypothesis Test about $\mu_1 - \mu_2$: Matched Samples	⑤	5
Test for the Equality of k Population Means	⑥	6

◯ Excel Used

EXAMPLES

EXAMPLE 1

Interval Estimate of $\mu_1 - \mu_2$: σ_1 and σ_2 Known

Par, Inc. is a manufacturer of golf equipment and has developed a new golf ball that has been designed to provide "extra distance." In a test of driving distance using a mechanical driving device, a sample of Par golf balls was compared with a sample of golf balls made by Rap, Ltd., a competitor. The sample data are below.

	Sample #1	Sample #2
Sample Size	n_1 = 120 balls	n_2 = 80 balls
Mean	$\bar{x}$ = 275 yards	$\bar{x}$ = 258 yards

Based on data from previous driving distance tests, the two population standard deviations are known with σ_1 = 15 yards and σ_2 = 20 yards.

a) What is the point estimate of the difference between the two population means?

b) Provide a 90% confidence interval for the difference between the two population means.

SOLUTION 1

Using a Calculator

a) The point estimate of the difference between the two population means is the difference between the two sample means.

Let: μ_1 = mean distance for the population of Par, Inc. golf balls

μ_2 = mean distance for the population of Rap, Ltd. golf balls

Point estimate of $\mu_1 - \mu_2 = \bar{x}_1 - \bar{x}_2$ = 275 - 258 = 17 yards.

b) With $z_{\alpha/2} = z_{.05}$ = 1.645, a 90% confidence interval is computed as:

$$\bar{x}_1 - \bar{x}_2 \pm z_{\alpha/2}\sqrt{\frac{\sigma_1^2}{n_1} + \frac{\sigma_2^2}{n_2}} = 17 \pm 1.645\sqrt{\frac{(15)^2}{120} + \frac{(20)^2}{80}}$$

$$= 17 \pm 4.3132 \text{ or } 12.69 \text{ yards to } 21.31 \text{ yards.}$$

We are 90% confident that the difference between the mean driving distances of Par, Inc. balls and Rap, Ltd. balls lies in the interval of 12.69 to 21.31 yards.

Using Excel's *NORMSINV* Function

Enter Data: Column A contains the driving distances for the 120 Par golf balls sampled. Column B contains the driving distances for the 80 Rap golf balls sampled.

Enter Functions and Formulas: The computations, line by line, are as follows. The sample statistics needed to compute the interval estimate are computed. The known population standard deviations are entered into the worksheet.

Using the two population standard deviations and two sample sizes, a point estimate of the standard error of the difference in the two sample means is computed using the SQRT function.

The confidence coefficient is entered and the corresponding level of significance is computed. The NORMSINV function is used to compute the z value needed to develop the interval. The margin of error is computed by multiplying the z value times the standard error.

The difference in the sample means is used to compute the point estimate of the difference in the two population means. The lower limit of the confidence interval is computed by subtracting the margin of error from the point estimate. The upper limit is computed by adding the margin of error to the point estimate.

Formula Worksheet:

	A	B	C	D	E
1	Par	Rap		Par, Inc.	Rap, Ltd.
2	195	226	Sample Size	=COUNT(A2:A121)	=COUNT(B2:B81)
3	230	198	Sample Mean	=AVERAGE(A2:A121)	=AVERAGE(B2:B81)
4	254	203			
5	205	237	Population Std. Dev.	20	15
6	260	235	Standard Error	=SQRT(D5^2/D2+E5^2/E2)	
7	222	204			
8	241	199	Confidence Coeff.	0.90	
9	217	202	Level of Signif.	=1-D9	
10	228	240	z Value	=NORMSINV(1-D9/2)	
11	255	221	Margin of Error	=D6*D10	
12	209	206			
13	251	201	Pt. Est. of Difference	=D3-E3	
14	229	233	Lower Limit	=D13-D11	
15	220	194	Upper Limit	=D13+D11	

Note: Rows 16-121 are not shown.

We see in the resulting worksheet below that the 90% confidence interval estimate developed using Excel agrees with our earlier, manual calculations.

Value Worksheet:

	A	B	C	D	E
1	Par	Rap		Par, Inc.	Rap, Ltd.
2	195	226	Sample Size	120	80
3	230	198	Sample Mean	275	258
4	254	203			
5	205	237	Population Std. Dev.	20	15
6	260	235	Standard Error	2.622	
7	222	204			
8	241	199	Confidence Coeff.	0.90	
9	217	202	Level of Signif.	0.10	
10	228	240	z Value	1.645	
11	255	221	Margin of Error	4.31281	
12	209	206			
13	251	201	Pt. Est. of Difference	17	
14	229	233	Lower Limit	12.69	
15	220	194	Upper Limit	21.31	

Note: Rows 16-121 are not shown.

EXAMPLE 2

Interval Estimate of $\mu_1 - \mu_2$: σ_1 and σ_2 Unknown

Specific Motors of Detroit has developed a new vehicle known as the M-car. 24 M-cars and 28 J-cars (from Japan) were road tested to compare miles-per-gallon (mpg) performance. The sample statistics are shown below.

	Sample #1 M-Cars	Sample #2 J-Cars
Sample Size	$n_1 = 24$ cars	$n_2 = 28$ cars
Sample Mean	$\bar{x} = 29.8$ mpg	$\bar{x} = 27.3$ mpg
Sample Std. Dev.	$s_1 = 2.56$ mpg	$s_2 = 1.81$ mpg

Provide a 90% confidence interval for the difference between the two population means.

SOLUTION 2

Using a Calculator

The point estimate of the difference between the two population means is the difference between the two sample means.

Let: μ_1 = mean miles-per-gallon for the population of M-cars
μ_2 = mean miles-per-gallon for the population of J-cars

Point estimate of $\mu_1 - \mu_2 = \bar{x}_1 - \bar{x}_2$ = 29.8 - 27.3 = 2.5 mpg.

In order to use the *t* distribution, we must determine the appropriate degrees of freedom.

$$df = \frac{\left(\dfrac{s_1^2}{n_1} + \dfrac{s_2^2}{n_2}\right)^2}{\dfrac{1}{n_1 - 1}\left(\dfrac{s_1^2}{n_1}\right)^2 + \dfrac{1}{n_2 - 1}\left(\dfrac{s_2^2}{n_2}\right)^2} = \frac{\left(\dfrac{2.56^2}{24} + \dfrac{1.81^2}{28}\right)^2}{\dfrac{1}{24 - 1}\left(\dfrac{2.56^2}{24}\right)^2 + \dfrac{1}{28 - 1}\left(\dfrac{1.81^2}{28}\right)^2} = 24.07 \approx 24$$

For *df* = 24 and α = .10, the appropriate *t* value is $t_{.05}$ = 1.711.

$$\bar{x}_1 - \bar{x}_2 \pm t_{\alpha/2}\sqrt{\frac{s_1^2}{n_1} + \frac{s_2^2}{n_2}} = 29.8 - 27.3 \pm 1.711\sqrt{\frac{2.56^2}{24} + \frac{1.81^2}{28}}$$

$$= 2.5 + 1.711(.625)$$

$$= 2.5 \pm 1.07 \text{ or } 1.43 \text{ to } 3.57 \text{ miles per gallon.}$$

We are 90% confident that the difference between the mean mpg ratings of the two car types is from 1.43 to 3.57 mpg (with the M-car having the higher mpg).

Using Excel's *TINV* Function

Enter Data: Column A contains the mpg performance for the 24 M-cars sampled. Column B contains the mpg performance for the 28 J-cars sampled.

Enter Functions and Formulas: The computations, line by line, are as follows. The sample statistics (size, mean, and standard deviation) needed to compute the interval estimate are computed.

Using the two sample sizes and sample standard deviations, an estimate of the variance is computed. The standard error is computed using the SQRT function.

The confidence coefficient is entered and the corresponding level of significance is computed. The degrees of freedom needed for the *t* distribution is computed. The TINV function is used to compute the *t* value needed to develop the interval. The margin of error is computed by multiplying the *t* value times the standard error.

The difference in the sample means is used to compute the point estimate of the difference in the two population means. The lower limit of the confidence interval is computed by subtracting the margin of error from the point estimate. The upper limit is computed by adding the margin of error to the point estimate.

Formula Worksheet:

	A	B	C	D	E
1	M Car	J Car		**M-Car**	**J-Car**
2	26.1	25.6	**Sample Size**	=COUNT(A2:A25)	=COUNT(B2:B29)
3	32.5	28.1	**Sample Mean**	=AVERAGE(A2:A25)	=AVERAGE(B2:B29)
4	31.8	27.9	**Sample Std. Dev.**	=STDEV(A2:A25)	=STDEV(B2:B29)
5	27.6	25.3			
6	28.5	30.1	**Est. of Variance**	=D4^2/D2+E4^2/E2	
7	33.6	27.5	**Standard Error**	=SQRT(D6)	
8	31.7	26.0			
9	25.2	28.8	**Confidence Coeff.**	0.90	
10	26.0	30.6	**Level of Signif.**	=1-D6	
11	32.0	24.4	**Degr. of Freedom**	=D6^2/((1/(D2-1))*(D4^2/D2)^2+(1/(E2-1))*(E4^2/E2	
12	31.7	27.3	*t* **Value**	=TINV(D10,D11)	
13	30.4	27.5	**Margin of Error**	=D12*D7	
14	27.6	26.3			
15	32.3	25.5	**Pt. Est. of Diff.**	=D3-E3	
16	30.6	26.3	**Lower Limit**	=D15-D13	
17	29.5	24.3	**Upper Limit**	=D15+D13	

Note: Rows 18-29 are not shown.

We see in the resulting worksheet below that the 90% confidence interval estimate developed using Excel agrees with our earlier, manual calculations.

Value Worksheet:

	A	B	C	D	E
1	M Car	J Car		M-Car	J-Car
2	26.1	25.6	Sample Size	24	28
3	32.5	28.1	Sample Mean	29.8	27.3
4	31.8	27.9	Sample Std. Dev.	2.56	1.81
5	27.6	25.3			
6	28.5	30.1	Est. of Variance	0.390	
7	33.6	27.5	Standard Error	0.625	
8	31.7	26.0			
9	25.2	28.8	Confidence Coeff.	0.90	
10	26.0	30.6	Level of Signif.	0.10	
11	32.0	24.4	Degr. of Freedom	24.07	
12	31.7	27.3	t Value	1.711	
13	30.4	27.5	Margin of Error	1.07	
14	27.6	26.3			
15	32.3	25.5	Pt. Est. of Diff.	2.5	
16	30.6	26.3	Lower Limit	1.43	
17	29.5	24.3	Upper Limit	3.57	

Note: Rows 18-29 are not shown.

EXAMPLE 3

Hypothesis Test about $\mu_1 - \mu_2$: σ_1 and σ_2 Known

Refer to the golf equipment problem in Example 1. Can we conclude, using a .01 level of significance, that the mean driving distance of Par, Inc. golf balls is greater than the mean driving distance of Rap, Ltd. golf balls?

SOLUTION 3

Using a Calculator

This problem calls for a one-tailed hypothesis test to determine if the mean of one population (Par golf balls) is greater than the mean of the other population (Rap golf balls).

Step 1: Determine the null and alternative hypotheses

H_0: $\mu_1 - \mu_2 \leq 0$ The mean driving distance of Par golf balls is less than or equal to the mean driving distance of Rap golf balls.

H_a: $\mu_1 - \mu_2 > 0$ The mean driving distance of Par golf balls is greater than the mean driving distance of Rap golf balls.

where: μ_1 = mean distance for the population of Par, Inc. golf balls
μ_2 = mean distance for the population of Rap, Ltd. golf balls

Step 2: Select the test statistic to be used to decide whether to reject H_0

$$z = \frac{(\bar{x}_1 - \bar{x}_2) - D_0}{\sqrt{\dfrac{\sigma_1^2}{n_1} + \dfrac{\sigma_2^2}{n_2}}}$$

Step 3: Specify the level of significance α

$\alpha = .01$

Step 4: Develop the rejection rule based on the level of significance

Reject H_0 if $z \geq 2.33$

Step 5: Collect the data and compute the value of the test statistic

$$z = \frac{(\bar{x}_1 - \bar{x}_2) - D_0}{\sqrt{\dfrac{\sigma_1^2}{n_1} + \dfrac{\sigma_2^2}{n_2}}} = \frac{(275 - 258) - 0}{\sqrt{\dfrac{(15)^2}{120} + \dfrac{(20)^2}{80}}} = \frac{17}{2.62} = 6.49$$

Step 6: a) Compare the value of the test statistic to the critical value(s)

$z = 6.49 > 2.33$, or

b) Compute the *p*-value and compare it to α

With $z = 6.49$, the upper tail area $= 1.0 - .9999 = .0001$ (approximately)

$p = .0001 < .01$

Step 7: State your conclusion regarding H_0

Reject H_0. We are 99% confident that Par golf balls have a mean driving distance greater than the mean driving distance of Rap golf balls.

Excel's *z*-TEST: TWO SAMPLE FOR MEANS Tool

We will continue with the worksheet we developed in Example 1.

Enter Data: The data are already entered in columns A and B (see Solution 1).

Enter Functions and Formulas: There are no functions or formulas to enter.

Apply Tools: We use Excel "z-Test: Two Sample for Means" Tool to conduct the hypothesis test about the difference between the population means in the golf ball study.

Step 1 Select the **Tools** pull-down menu
Step 2 Choose the **Data Analysis** option
Step 3 Choose **z-Test: Two Sample for Means** from the list of Analysis Tools

Excel Dialog Box

```
z-Test: Two Sample for Means                                    [?] [X]
┌─Input─────────────────────────────────────┐    ┌──────────┐
│ Variable 1 Range:        $A$1:$A$121   [▤] │    │    OK    │
│                                            │    └──────────┘
│ Variable 2 Range:        $B$1:$B$81    [▤] │    ┌──────────┐
│                                            │    │  Cancel  │
│ Hypothesized Mean Difference:   [0     ]   │    └──────────┘
│                                            │    ┌──────────┐
│ Variable 1 Variance (known):    [225   ]   │    │   Help   │
│                                            │    └──────────┘
│ Variable 2 Variance (known):    [400   ]   │
│                                            │
│ ☑ Labels                                   │
│                                            │
│ Alpha:  [0.01 ]                            │
├─Output options─────────────────────────────┤
│ ◉ Output Range:          [$D$1        ][▤] │
│ ○ New Worksheet Ply:     [            ]     │
│ ○ New Workbook                             │
└────────────────────────────────────────────┘
```

Value Worksheet:

	A	B	C	D	E	F
1	Par	Rap		z-Test: Two Sample for Means		
2	195	226				
3	230	198			Par, Inc.	Rap, Ltd.
4	254	203		Mean	235	218
5	205	237		Known Variance	225	400
6	260	235		Observations	120	80
7	222	204		Hypothesized Mean Difference	0	
8	241	199		z	6.483545607	
9	217	202		P(Z<=z) one-tail	4.50145E-11	
10	228	240		z Critical one-tail	2.326341928	
11	255	221		P(Z<=z) two-tail	9.00291E-11	
12	209	206		z Critical two-tail	2.575834515	

Note: Rows 13-121 are not shown.

The value of the test statistic, 6.48, is shown in cell E8 of the worksheet above. The critical value 2.33, labeled z Critical one-tail, is shown in cell E10. Because $z = 6.48$ is in the rejection region, we can conclude that the mean driving distance of Par golf balls is greater than the mean driving distance of Rap golf balls.

Alternatively, we can use the *p*-value to make the hypothesis-testing decision. The *p*-value, labeled P(Z < z) one-tail, is shown in cell E10. Because the *p*-value is less than the level of significance, $\alpha = .01$, we have sufficient statistical evidence to reject the null hypothesis.

EXAMPLE 4

Hypothesis Test about $\mu_1 - \mu_2$: σ_1 and σ_2 Unknown

Refer to the Specific Motors problem in Example 2. Can we conclude, using a .01 level of significance, that the miles-per-gallon (mpg) performance of M-cars is greater than the miles-per-gallon performance of J-cars?

SOLUTION 4

Using a Calculator

This problem calls for a one-tailed hypothesis test to determine if the mean of one population (M-cars) is greater than the mean of the other population (J-cars). Our approach will be similar to that of Example 3, but here we do not know the population standard deviations.

Step 1: Determine the null and alternative hypotheses

H_0: $\mu_1 - \mu_2 \leq 0$ The mean miles-per-gallon of M-cars is less than or equal to the mean miles-per-gallon of J-cars.

H_a: $\mu_1 - \mu_2 > 0$ The mean miles-per-gallon of M-cars is greater than the mean miles-per-gallon of J-cars..

where: μ_1 = mean miles-per-gallon for the population of M-cars
μ_2 = mean miles-per-gallon for the population of J-cars

Step 2: Select the test statistic to be used to decide whether to reject H_0

$$t = \frac{(\bar{X}_1 - \bar{X}_2) - D_0}{\sqrt{\dfrac{s_1^2}{n_1} + \dfrac{s_2^2}{n_2}}}$$

Step 3: Specify the level of significance α

$\alpha = .01$

Step 4: Develop the rejection rule based on the level of significance

df = 40 was computed in Solution 2

Reject H_0 if $t \geq 2.423$ ($\alpha = .01$, d.f. = 40)

Step 5: <u>Collect the data and compute the value of the test statistic</u>

$$t = \frac{(29.8 - 27.3) - 0}{\sqrt{\dfrac{2.56^2}{24} + \dfrac{1.81^2}{28}}} = \frac{2.5}{.6246} = 4.003$$

Step 6: a) <u>Compare the value of the test statistic to the critical value(s)</u>

$t = 4.003 > 2.423$, or

b) <u>Compute the p-value and compare it to α</u>

(It is difficult to determine a precise p-value from the t Distribution table.)

Step 7: <u>State your conclusion regarding H_0</u>

Reject H_0. We are 95% confident that M-cars have a mean mpg greater than the mean mpg of J-cars.

Excel's t-TEST: TWO SAMPLE ASSUMING UNEQUAL VARIANCES Tool

Enter Data: The data is already entered in columns A and B (see Solution 2).

Enter Functions and Formulas: There are no functions or formulas to enter.

Apply Tools: The following steps describe how to use Excel "t-Test: Assuming Unequal Variances" tool.

Step 1 Select the **Tools** pull-down menu
Step 2 Choose the **Data Analysis** option
Step 3 Choose **t-Test: Two Sample Assuming Unequal Variances** from the list of Analysis Tools

Excel Dialog Box

Value Worksheet:

	A	B	C	D	E	F
1	**M Car**	**J Car**		t-Test: Two-Sample Assuming Unequal Variances		
2	26.1	25.6				
3	32.5	28.1			*M Car*	*J Car*
4	31.8	27.9		Mean	29.795833	27.303571
5	27.6	25.3		Variance	6.5551993	3.272209
6	28.5	30.1		Observations	24	28
7	33.6	27.5		Hypothesized Mean Diff.	0	
8	31.7	26.0		df	41	
9	25.2	28.8		t Stat	3.9908237	
10	26.0	30.6		P(T<=t) one-tail	0.0001329	
11	32.0	24.4		t Critical one-tail	2.420802	
12	31.7	27.3		P(T<=t) two-tail	0.0002658	
13	30.4	27.5		t Critical two-tail	2.7011811	

Note: Rows 14-29 are not shown.

Excel computed the value of the test statistic to 3.991 (in cell E9), compared to our manually calculated value of 4.003. The critical value 2.421, labeled t Critical one-tail, is shown in cell E11. Because $t = 3.991$ is in the rejection region, we can conclude that the mean mpg of M-cars is greater than the mean mpg of J-cars.

Alternatively, we can use the *p*-value to make the hypothesis-testing decision. The *p*-value, labeled P(T < t) one-tail, is shown in cell E10. Because the *p*-value (.0001) is less than the level of significance, $\alpha = .01$, we have sufficient statistical evidence to reject the null hypothesis.

EXAMPLE 5

Hypothesis Test about $\mu_1 - \mu_2$: Matched Samples

A Chicago-based firm has documents that must be quickly distributed to district offices throughout the U.S. The firm must decide between two delivery services, UPX (United Parcel Express) and INTEX (International Express), to transport its documents. In testing the delivery times of the two services, the firm sent two reports to a random sample of ten district offices with one report carried by UPX and the other report carried by INTEX.

Do the data that follow indicate a difference in mean delivery times for the two services at the .05 level of significance?

	Delivery Time (Hours)		
District Office	UPX	INTEX	Difference
Seattle	32	25	7
Los Angeles	30	24	6
Boston	19	15	4
Cleveland	16	15	1
New York	15	13	2
Houston	18	15	3
Atlanta	14	15	-1
St. Louis	10	8	2
Milwaukee	7	9	-2
Denver	16	11	5

SOLUTION 5

Using a Calculator

In this problem we are conducting a two-tailed hypothesis test about the difference between two population means based on matched samples. We are conducting a test to determine if the mean delivery time for UPX is equal to the mean delivery time for Intex.

Step 1: Determine the null and alternative hypotheses

Let μ_d = the mean of the difference values for the two
delivery services for the population of district offices.
H_0: $\mu_d = 0$
H_a: $\mu_d \neq 0$

Step 2: Select the test statistic to be used to decide whether to reject H_0

$$t = \frac{\bar{d} - \mu_d}{s_d / \sqrt{n}}$$

where:

$$s_d = \sqrt{\frac{\Sigma(d_i - \bar{d})^2}{n - 1}}$$

Step 3: Specify the level of significance α

$\alpha = .05$

Step 4: Develop the rejection rule based on the level of significance

Assuming the population of difference values is approximately normally distributed, the t distribution with $n - 1$ degrees of freedom applies.
With $\alpha = .05$, $t_{.025} = 2.262$ (9 degrees of freedom).

Reject H_0 if $t \leq -2.262$ or if $t \geq 2.262$

Step 5: Collect the data and compute the value of the test statistic

$$\bar{d} = \frac{\sum d_i}{n} = \frac{(7+6+\ldots+5)}{10} = 2.7$$

$$s_d = \sqrt{\frac{\sum (d_i - \bar{d})^2}{n-1}} = \sqrt{\frac{76.1}{9}} = 2.9$$

$$t = \frac{\bar{d} - \mu_d}{s_d / \sqrt{n}} = \frac{2.7 - 0}{2.9 / \sqrt{10}} = 2.94$$

Step 6: a) Compare the value of the test statistic to the critical value(s)

$t = 2.94 > 2.262,$ or

b) Compute the *p*-value and compare it to α

(It is difficult to determine a precise *p*-value from the *t* Distribution table.)

Step 7: State your conclusion regarding H_0

Reject H_0. We are 95% confident that there is a difference between the mean delivery times for the two services.

Excel's *t*-TEST: PAIRED TWO SAMPLE FOR MEANS Tool

Excel's "*t*-Test: Paired Two Sample for Means" Tool

Step 1 Select the **Tools** pull-down menu
Step 2 Choose the **Data Analysis** option
Step 3 Choose *t*-**Test: Paired Two Sample for Means** from the list of Analysis Tools

Excel Dialog Box

Value Worksheet:

	A	B	C	D	E	F	G
1	**Office**	**UPX**	**INTEX**				
2	Seattle	32	25		t-Test: Paired Two Sample for Means		
3	Los Angeles	30	24				
4	Boston	19	15			*UPX*	*INTEX*
5	Cleveland	16	15		Mean	17.7	15
6	New York	15	13		Variance	62.011	31.778
7	Houston	18	15		Observations	10	10
8	Atlanta	14	15		Pearson Correlation	0.9612	
9	St. Louis	10	8		Hypothesized Mean Difference	0	
10	Milwaukee	7	9		df	9	
11	Denver	16	11		t Stat	2.9362	
12					P(T<=t) one-tail	0.0083	
13					t Critical one-tail	1.8331	
14					P(T<=t) two-tail	0.0166	
15					t Critical two-tail	2.2622	

The value of the test statistic, 2.936, is shown in cell F11 of the worksheet above. The critical value 2.262, labeled t Critical two-tail, is shown in cell F15. Because $t = 2.936$ is in the rejection region, we can conclude that the mean delivery times for the two services are not equal. Alternatively, we can use the *p*-value approach. The *p*-value, labeled P(T < t) two-tail, is shown in cell F14. Because the *p*-value = .017 is less than $\alpha = .05$, we have sufficient statistical evidence to reject the null hypothesis.

EXAMPLE 6

Test for the Equality of *k* Population Means

J. R. Reed would like to know if the mean number of hours worked per week is the same for the department managers at her three manufacturing plants (Buffalo, Pittsburgh, and Detroit).

A simple random sample of 5 managers from each of the three plants was taken and the number of hours worked by each manager for the previous week is shown below.

Observation	Plant 1 Buffalo	Plant 2 Pittsburgh	Plant 3 Detroit
1	48	73	51
2	54	63	63
3	57	66	61
4	54	64	54
5	62	74	56
Sample Mean	55	68	57
Sample Variance	26.0	26.5	24.5

Using $\alpha = .05$, test for any significant difference in hours worked at the three plants.

SOLUTION 6

Using a Calculator

In this problem we are using analysis of variance to test for the equality of the mean number of hours worked at three plants.

Step 1: Determine the null and alternative hypotheses

H_0: $\mu_1 = \mu_2 = \mu_3$
H_a: Not all the means are equal

Let: μ_1 = mean number of hours worked per week by the managers at Plant 1
μ_2 = mean number of hours worked per week by the managers at Plant 2
μ_3 = mean number of hours worked per week by the managers at Plant 3

Step 2: Select the test statistic to be used to decide whether to reject H_0

F = MSTR/MSE

Step 3: Specify the level of significance α

α = .05

Step 4: Develop the rejection rule based on the level of significance

Assuming α = .05, $F_{.05}$ = 3.89 (2 d.f. numerator, 12 d.f. denominator).
Reject H_0 if $F \geq 3.89$ (found in the F Distribution table in the textbook)
Reject H_0 if p-value $\leq$ .05

Step 5: Collect the data and compute the value of the test statistic

Mean Square Treatment (MSTR) is found by:
x = (55 + 68 + 57)/3 = 60
SSTR = $5(55 - 60)^2 + 5(68 - 60)^2 + 5(57 - 60)^2$ = 490
MSTR = 490/(3 - 1) = 245

Mean Square Error (MSE) is found by:
SSE = 4(26.0) + 4(26.5) + 4(24.5) = 308
MSE = 308/(15 - 3) = 25.667

F = MSTR/MSE = 245/25.667 = 9.55

Step 6: a) Compare the value of the test statistic to the critical value(s)

F = 9.55 > 3.89

or b) Compute the p-value and compare it to α

(It is difficult to determine a precise p-value of the F Distribution table.)

Step 7: State your conclusion regarding H_0

F = 9.55 > $F_{.05}$ = 3.89, so we reject H_0. The mean number of hours worked per week by department managers is not the same at all of the plant.

Using Excel's ANOVA: SINGLE FACTOR Tool

Enter Data: Column A is used to identify the observations at each of the plants. Columns B, C, and D contain the hours worked data for the managers at the three plants.

Apply Tools: The following steps describe how to use Excel's Anova: Single Factor tool.

Step 1   Select the **Tools** menu
Step 2   Choose **Data Analysis** option
Step 3   Choose **Anova: Single Factor** from the list of Analysis Tools
Step 4   When the Anova: Single Factor dialog box appears:
       Enter B1:D6 in the **Input Range** box
       Select Grouped By **Columns**
       Select **Labels in First Row**
       Enter .05 in the **Alpha** box
       Select **Output Range**
       Enter A8 (your choice) in the **Output Range** box
       Click **OK**

Value Worksheet:

	A	B	C	D	E	F	G
1	Observation	Buffalo	Pittsb.	Detroit			
2	1	48	73	51			
3	2	54	63	63			
4	3	57	66	61			
5	4	54	64	54			
6	5	62	74	56			
7							
8	Anova: Single Factor						
9							
10	SUMMARY						
11	*Groups*	*Count*	*Sum*	*Average*	*Variance*		
12	Buffalo	5	275	55	26		
13	Pittsburgh	5	340	68	26.5		
14	Detroit	5	285	57	24.5		
15							
16							
17	ANOVA						
18	*Source of Variation*	*SS*	*df*	*MS*	*F*	*P-value*	*F crit*
19	Between Groups	490	2	245	9.54545	0.00331	3.88529
20	Within Groups	308	12	25.6667			
21							
22	Total	798	14				

The value of the test statistic, 9.55, is shown in cell E19 of the worksheet above. The critical value of F, 3.89, is shown in cell G19. Because $F = 9.55$ is in the rejection region (9.55 > 3.89), we can conclude that the mean number of hours worked at the three plants are not all equal. Alternatively, we can use the p-value to make the test decision. The p-value, .0033, is shown in cell F19. Because the p-value is less than the level of significance, $\alpha = .05$, we have sufficient statistical evidence to reject the null hypothesis.

EXERCISES

EXERCISE 1

Interval Estimate of $\mu_1 - \mu_2$: σ_1 and σ_2 Known

Starting annual salaries for business school graduates majoring in finance and management information systems (MIS) were collected in two independent random samples. Use the following data to develop a 95% confidence interval estimate of the difference between the starting salaries for the two majors. Based on previous studies, the population standard deviations for Finance and MIS salaries are estimated to be $2,100 and $2,600, respectively.

Finance	MIS
$n_1 = 60$	$n_2 = 50$
$\bar{x}_1 = \$43,200$	$\bar{x}_2 = \$46,500$

EXERCISE 2

Interval Estimate of $\mu_1 - \mu_2$: σ_1 and σ_2 Unknown

A manager is thinking of providing, on a regular basis, in-house training for employees preparing for an inventory management certification exam. In the past, some employees received the in-house training before taking the exam, while others did not. Independent random samples taken from the company's records provided the following exam scores for 10 workers who did not receive in-house training and 8 workers who did receive training. (The manager is confident that the distributions of both populations' exam scores are approximately normal.)

No Training	Training
76	80
80	66
60	71
91	79
73	94
77	74
82	83
68	78
75	
86	

Develop a 95% confidence interval estimate for the difference between the average test scores for the two populations of employees.

EXERCISE 3

Hypothesis Test about $\mu_1 - \mu_2$: σ_1 and σ_2 Known

Refer to the starting salary statistics in Exercise 1. Using $\alpha = .10$, test to determine if the average starting salary for an MIS graduate is $4,000 more than the starting salary for a finance graduate. Use both the critical value and p-value approaches to hypothesis testing. (Hint: the null hypothesis is H_0: $\mu_1 - \mu_2 = \$4,000$, where μ_1 is the average starting salary of MIS graduates.)

EXERCISE 4

Hypothesis Test about $\mu_1 - \mu_2$: σ_1 and σ_2 Unknown

Refer to the certification exam score data in Exercise 2. Using $\alpha = .05$, test for any difference between the average test scores for the two populations of employees.

EXERCISE 5

Hypothesis Test about $\mu_1 - \mu_2$: Matched Samples

A survey was recently conducted to determine if consumers spend more on computer-related purchases via the Internet or store visits. Assume a sample of 8 respondents provided the following data on their computer-related purchases during a 30-day period. Using a .05 level of significance, can we conclude that consumers spend more on computer-related purchases by way of the Internet than by visiting stores?

Respondent	Expenditures (dollars) In-Store	Internet
1	132	225
2	90	24
3	119	95
4	16	55
5	85	13
6	248	105
7	64	57
8	49	0

EXERCISE 6

Test for the Equality of *k* Population Means

Regional Manager Sue Collins would like to know if the mean number of telephone calls made per 8-hour shift is the same for the telemarketers at her three call centers (Austin, Las Vegas, and Albuquerque).

A simple random sample of 6 telemarketers from each of the three call centers was taken and the number of telephone calls made in eight hours by each observed employee is shown below.

Observation	Center 1 Austin	Center 2 Las Vegas	Center 3 Albuquerque
1	82	72	71
2	68	63	81
3	77	74	73
4	80	60	68
5	69	70	76
6	78	73	80
Sample Mean	75.667	68.667	74.833
Sample Variance	33.867	33.467	26.167

Using $\alpha = .10$, test for any significant difference in the mean number of telephone calls made at the three call centers.

SELF-TEST

TRUE/FALSE

____ 1. The independent-sample design generally leads to a smaller sampling error than the matched-sample design.

____ 2. In a two-tailed hypothesis test, the p-value is found by doubling the area in the tail corresponding to the value of the test statistic.

____ 3. When making comparisons of population means using an independent sample design, the sizes of the samples do not have to be equal.

____ 4. If the appropriate confidence interval estimate contains the hypothesized difference in two population means, we can reject the null hypothesis.

____ 5. If we reject the hypothesis H_0: $\mu_1 = \mu_2 = \mu_3$, we can conclude that all three population means are different.

FILL-IN-THE-BLANK

1. The process of combining the results of two independent random samples to provide one estimate of σ^2 is referred to as _____.

2. _____ is the sum of SSTR and SSE.

3. The d in the notation s_d and $\bar{d}$ is a reminder that the matched sample provides _____ data.

4. The null hypothesis H_0: $\mu_d = 0$ is appropriate for a test of the difference between two population means using a _____ design.

5. The _____ distribution of a point estimator provides the basis for developing interval estimates and in testing hypotheses about parameters of interest.

MULTIPLE CHOICE

____ 1. Which one of the following is an improper form of the null hypothesis in a test about the difference between the means of two populations?
a) $H_0 : \mu_1 - \mu_2 = 0$
b) $H_0 : \mu_1 - \mu_2 \leq 0$
c) $H_0 : \mu_1 - \mu_2 > 0$
d) $H_0 : \mu_1 - \mu_2 \geq D_0$

____ 2. The test statistic F is the ratio
a) MSE/MST
b) MSTR/MSE
c) SSTR/SSE
d) SSTR/SSE

___ 3. In testing for the equality of k population means, the number of treatments is
   a) k
   b) $k - 1$
   c) n_T
   d) $n_T - k$

___ 4. The within-treatments estimate of σ^2 is called the
   a) sum of squares due to error
   b) mean square due to error
   c) sum of squares due to treatments
   d) mean square due to treatments

___ 5. If we are testing for the equality of 3 population means, we should use the
   a) test statistic F
   b) test statistic t
   c) test statistic z
   d) none of the above

ANSWERS

EXERCISES

1) MIS is higher by $2,404.62 to $4,195.38

2) -10.02 to 7.37 (thus, $\mu_1 - \mu_2$ could be 0)

3) $z = -1.53 > -1.645$; do not reject H_0

4) $t = -0.325 > -2.131$, p-value $= .75 > .05$; do not reject H_0: $\mu_1 - \mu_2 = 0$

5) t $= 1.12 < 1.89$, p-value $= .15 > .05$; do not reject H_0: $\mu_d \leq 0$

6) $F = 2.815 > 2.695$, p-value $= .092 < .10$; Reject H_0 ; not all means are equal

TRUE/FALSE

1) False
2) True
3) True
4) False
5) False

FILL-IN-THE-BLANK

1) pooling
2) SST
3) difference
4) matched sample
5) sampling

MULTIPLE CHOICE

1) c
2) b
3) a
4) b
5) a

CHAPTER 11

Comparisons Involving Proportions and a Test of Independence

Inferences about the Difference Between
Two Population Proportions

Hypothesis Test for Proportions
of a Multinomial Population

Test of Independence

LEARNING OBJECTIVES

1. Be able to develop interval estimates and conduct hypothesis tests about the difference between the proportions of two populations.

2. Know the properties of the sampling distribution of the difference between two proportions $(\bar{p}_1 - \bar{p}_2)$.

3. Know how to use sample data to test for independence of two variables.

4. Understand the role of the chi-square distribution in conducting tests of goodness of fit and independence.

5. Be able to conduct a goodness of fit test for cases where the population is hypothesized to have a multinomial probability distribution.

6. For a test of independence, be able to set up a contingency table, determine the observed and expected frequencies, and determine if the two variables are independent.

REVIEW

Inference about the Difference Between Two Population Proportions
- Let p_1 = the proportion of population 1 and p_2 = the proportion of population 2.
- The difference between the two population proportions is given by $p_1 - p_2$.
- To estimate $p_1 - p_2$, we select a simple random sample of n_1 items from population 1 and n_2 items from population 2.
- Let $\bar{p}_1$ = the sample proportion for the n_1 items and $\bar{p}_2$ = the sample proportion for the n_2 items.
- The point estimator of $p_1 - p_2$ is the difference between the two sample proportions.

Sampling Distribution of $\bar{p}_1 - \bar{p}_2$

- The sampling distribution of a point estimator provides the basis for developing interval estimates and in testing hypotheses about parameters of interest.
- The expected value is:

$$E(\bar{p}_1 - \bar{p}_2) = p_1 - p_2$$

- The standard deviation is:

$$\sigma_{\bar{p}_1 - \bar{p}_2} = \sqrt{\frac{p_1(1-p_1)}{n_1} \frac{p_2(1-p_2)}{n_2}}$$

- If the sample sizes are large (n_1p_1, $n_1(1 - p_1)$, n_2p_2, and $n_2(1 - p_2)$ are all greater than or equal to 5), the sampling distribution of $\bar{p}_1 - \bar{p}_2$ can be approximated by a normal probability distribution.

Interval Estimation of p_1 - p_2

- Computing $\sigma_{\bar{p}_1 - \bar{p}_2}$ requires knowing the values of p_1 and p_2, which will not be known in practice. So, $\bar{p}_1$ and $\bar{p}_2$ are used to estimate p_1 and p_2.
- Interval Estimate of the Difference Between the Proportions of Two Populations:

$$\bar{p}_1 - \bar{p}_2 \pm z_{\alpha/2} \sqrt{\frac{\bar{p}_1(1-\bar{p}_1)}{n_1} + \frac{\bar{p}_2(1-\bar{p}_2)}{n_2}}$$

Hypothesis Tests about $p_1 - p_2$

- The possible hypotheses are:
    - $H_0 : p_1 - p_2 \geq 0$, $H_a : p_1 - p_2 < 0$ (lower-tailed test)
    - $H_0 : p_1 - p_2 \leq 0$, $H_a : p_1 - p_2 > 0$ (upper-tailed test)
    - $H_0 : p_1 - p_2 = 0$, $H_a : p_1 - p_2 \neq 0$ (two-tailed test)
- The two sample proportions are "pooled" to provide one estimate of p given by $\bar{p}$.

$$\bar{p} = \frac{n_1\bar{p}_1 + n_2\bar{p}_2}{n_1 + n_2}$$

- The test statistic is computed as:

$$z = \frac{(\bar{p}_1 - \bar{p}_2)}{\sqrt{\bar{p}(1-\bar{p})(\frac{1}{n_1} + \frac{1}{n_2})}}$$

- The rejection rule for the two-tailed test is:
  Reject H_0 if $z \leq -z_{\alpha/2}$ or $z \geq z_{\alpha/2}$

Hypothesis Test for Proportions of a Multinomial Population

- Here we are concerned with the proportion of elements in a population belonging to each of several classes or categories.
- The multinomial probability distribution can be viewed as an extension of the binomial distribution to the case of three or more categories of outcomes.
- Here, conducting a hypothesis test involves performing a goodness of fit test.
- The goodness of fit test is based on a comparison of the sample of observed results with the expected results under the assumption that the null hypothesis is true.
- The test for goodness of fit is always a one-tailed test with the rejection region located in the upper tail of the chi-square distribution.

Multinomial Distribution Goodness of Fit Test: A Summary

- Set up the null and alternative hypotheses:
    - H_0: The population follows a multinomial probability distribution with specified probabilities for each of k categories.
    - H_a: The population does not follow a multinomial probability distribution with specified probabilities for each of k categories.
- Select a random sample and record the observed frequencies f_i for each category.
- Assuming the null hypothesis is true, determine the expected frequency e_i in each category by multiplying the category probability by the sample size.

- Compute the value of the test statistic:

$$\chi^2 = \sum_{i=1}^{k} \frac{(f_i - e_i)^2}{e_i}$$

- Rejection rule:

  Using p-value: Reject H_0 if p-value $\leq \alpha$

  Using test statistic: Reject H_0 if $\chi^2 \geq \chi_\alpha^2$

  where: α is the level of significance for the test
  and there are $k - 1$ degrees of freedom.

Test of Independence

- A test of independence addresses the question of whether one variable is independent of another variable.
- The test of independence uses the contingency table format (cross-tabulation) and for that reason is sometimes referred to as the contingency table test.

Test of Independence: A Summary

- Set up the null and alternative hypotheses:

  H_0: The column variable is independent of the row variable
  H_a: The column variable is not independent of the row

- Select a random sample and record the observed frequencies for each cell of the contingency table.
- Compute the expected frequency e_{ij} for each cell:

$$e_{ij} = \frac{(\text{Row } i \text{ Total})(\text{Column } j \text{ Total})}{\text{Sample Size}}$$

- Compute the value of the χ^2 test statistic:

$$\chi^2 = \sum_i \sum_j \frac{(f_{ij} - e_{ij})^2}{e_{ij}}$$

  where: f_{ij} = observed frequency for contingency table category
  in row i and column j

  e_{ij} = expected frequency for contingency table category in
  row i and column j based on the assumption of independence

- Rejection rule:

  Using the p-value: Reject H_0 if p-value $\leq \alpha$

  Using the test statistic: Reject H_0 if $\chi^2 \geq \chi_\alpha^2$

  where α is the level of significance; n rows and m columns
  providing $(n - 1)(m - 1)$ degrees of freedom.

KEY CONCEPTS

CONCEPT	EXAMPLES	EXERCISES
Interval Estimation of $p_1 - p_2$	①	1
Hypothesis Test of $p_1 - p_2$	②	2
Multinomial Distribution Goodness of Fit Test	③	3
Test of Independence	④	4

◯ Excel Used

EXAMPLES

EXAMPLE 1

Interval Estimation of $p_1 - p_2$

MRA (Market Research Associates) is conducting research to evaluate the effectiveness of a client's new advertising campaign. Before the new campaign began, a telephone survey of 150 households in the test market area was conducted. Each household was asked if they were aware of the client's product and the Yes or No response was recorded. The new campaign was initiated with TV and newspaper advertisements for three weeks and then a second survey, involving 250 households, was conducted. Again, each household was asked if they were aware of the client's product and the Yes or No response was recorded.

MRA tallied the survey data and found there were 60 Yes responses in the first study and 120 Yes responses in the second study. Do these results support the position that the advertising campaign has provided an increased awareness of the client's product? Develop an interval estimate of the difference between the proportions of the two populations, using a .05 level of significance, as the basis for your decision.

SOLUTION 1

Using a Calculator

Let us solve this problem manually, to demonstrate the mathematical operations, and then we will use Excel. The first step is to determine a point estimate of the difference in the proportions of the two populations, $p_1 - p_2$.

$$p_1 - p_2 = \bar{p}_1 - \bar{p}_2 = \frac{120}{250} - \frac{60}{150} = .48 - .40 = .08$$

where: p_1 = proportion of the population of households
"aware" of the product <u>after</u> the new campaign
p_2 = proportion of the population of households
"aware" of the product <u>before</u> the new campaign
$\bar{p}_1$ = sample proportion of households "aware" of
the product <u>after</u> the new campaign
$\bar{p}_2$ = sample proportion of households "aware" of
the product <u>before</u> the new campaign

The point estimate, .08, <u>suggests</u> that the percentage of households aware of the product after the campaign is 8 percentage points greater than the percentage before the campaign. However, we should not base our decision on a suggestion that ignores the possible impact of sampling error.

The interval estimate of the difference between the proportions of "aware" households before and after the advertising campaign is computed as:

$$\bar{p}_1 - \bar{p}_2 \pm z_{\alpha/2} \sqrt{\frac{\bar{p}_1(1-\bar{p}_1)}{n_1} + \frac{\bar{p}_2(1-\bar{p}_2)}{n_2}} \qquad .48 - .40 \pm 1.96 \sqrt{\frac{.48(.52)}{250} + \frac{.40(.60)}{150}}$$

$$.08 \pm 1.96(.0510)$$
$$.08 \pm .10$$
$$\text{or} \quad -.02 \text{ to } +.18$$

At a 95% confidence level, the interval estimate of the difference between the proportion of households aware of the client's product before and after the new advertising campaign is -.02 to +.18. Notice that the interval ranges from a <u>slight decrease</u> in awareness to a <u>significant increase</u> in awareness. On the basis of the interval estimate, the data does not support the position that the advertising campaign has provided an increased awareness of the client's product.

Using Excel's COUNTIF and NORMSINV Functions

Enter Data: The 250 responses from the later survey are entered into column A. The 150 responses from the earlier survey are entered into column B.

Enter Functions and Formulas: The COUNTA function is used to determine the sample sizes. The COUNTIF function is used to count the number of Yes responses from in each sample. Then, the sample proportions are computed.

The confidence coefficient is entered and the corresponding level of significance is computed. The NORMSINV function to compute the z value needed.

The standard error of the difference in the two sample proportions is computed. The margin of error is computed by multiplying the z value by the standard error.

The point estimate of the difference in the two population proportions is the difference in the two sample proportions. The lower (and upper) limit of the confidence interval is computed by subtracting (adding) the margin of error from (to) the point estimate.

Formula Worksheet:

	A	B	C	D	E
1	Late Surv.	Early Surv.		Later Survey (from Population 1)	Earlier Survey (from Population 2)
2	No	Yes	Sample Size	=COUNTA(A2:A251)	=COUNTA(B2:B151)
3	Yes	No	Response of Int.	Yes	Yes
4	Yes	Yes	Count of Resp.	=COUNTIF(A2:A251,D3)	=COUNTIF(B2:B151,E3)
5	No	Yes	Samp. Propor.	=D4/D2	=E4/E2
6	Yes	No			
7	No	No	Confid. Coeff.	0.95	
8	No	Yes	Lev. Of Signif.	=1-D7	
9	Yes	No	z Value	=NORMSINV(1-D8/2)	
10	No	No			
11	Yes	Yes	Std. Error	=SQRT(D5*(1-D5)/D2+E5*(1-E5)/E2)	
12	Yes	No	Marg. of Error	=D9*D11	
13	Yes	Yes			
14	No	Yes	Pt. Est. of Diff.	=D5-E5	
15	Yes	Yes	Lower Limit	=D14-D12	
16	Yes	No	Upper Limit	=D14+D12	

Note: Rows 17-251 are not shown.

Value Worksheet:

	A	B	C	D	E
1	Late Surv.	Early Surv.		Later Survey (from Population 1)	Earlier Survey (from Population 2)
2	No	Yes	Sample Size	250	150
3	Yes	No	Response of Int.	Yes	Yes
4	Yes	Yes	Count of Resp.	120	60
5	No	Yes	Samp. Propor.	0.48	0.4
6	Yes	No			
7	No	No	Confid. Coeff.	0.95	
8	No	Yes	Lev. Of Signif.	0.05	
9	Yes	No	z Value	1.96	
10	No	No			
11	Yes	Yes	Std. Error	0.051	
12	Yes	No	Marg. of Error	0.0999	
13	Yes	Yes			
14	No	Yes	Pt. Est. of Diff.	0.08	
15	Yes	Yes	Lower Limit	-0.02	
16	Yes	No	Upper Limit	0.18	

Note: Rows 17-251 are not shown.

We see in the value worksheet that the 95% confidence interval estimate of the difference in the two population proportions is -.02 to .18. These numbers agree with the results of our manual calculations earlier.

EXAMPLE 2

Hypothesis Test about $p_1 - p_2$

Refer to the Market Research Associates problem in Example 1. Can we conclude, using a .05 level of significance, that the proportion of households aware of the client's product increased after the new advertising campaign?

SOLUTION 2

Using a Calculator

Let us solve this problem manually, to demonstrate the mathematical operations, and then we will use Excel. The first step is to define our notation. Let:

p_1 = proportion of the population of households
"aware" of the product <u>after</u> the new campaign
p_2 = proportion of the population of households
"aware" of the product <u>before</u> the new campaign

Hypotheses:

H_0: $p_1 - p_2 \le 0$
H_a: $p_1 - p_2 > 0$

Rejection Rule: Reject H_0 if $z \ge 1.645$

Test Statistic:

$$\bar{p} = \frac{250(.48) + 150(.40)}{250 + 150} = \frac{180}{400} = .45$$

$$z = \frac{(\bar{p}_1 - \bar{p}_2)}{\sqrt{\bar{p}(1-\bar{p})\left(\frac{1}{n_1} + \frac{1}{n_2}\right)}} = \frac{(.48 - .40)}{.0514} = \frac{.08}{.0514} = 1.56$$

Conclusion: Do not reject H_0. The test statistic value, 1.56, is less than the critical value, 1.645. Our confidence in rejecting the null hypothesis is less than 95%.

Using Excel's NORMSDIST Function

Enter Data: The 250 responses from the later survey are entered into column A. The 150 responses from the earlier survey are entered into column B.

Enter Functions and Formula: The COUNTA function is used to determine the sample sizes. The COUNTIF function is used to count the number of Yes responses in each sample. Then, the sample proportions are computed.

Next, the hypothesized value of the difference in the population proportions is entered. The difference in the sample proportions is used to compute a point estimate of the difference in the two population proportions.

Then, using the two sample proportions and sample sizes, a pooled estimate of p is computed. Using the pooled estimate of p, the standard error of the difference in the two sample proportions is computed. Then, the test statistic is computed.

We use the NORMSINV function to compute the p-value for the lower tail. The upper tail p-value equals 1 minus the lower tail p-value. The two-tail p-value equals two times the minimum of the lower and upper tail p-values.

Formula Worksheet:

	A	B	C	D	E
1	Late Surv.	Early Surv.		Later Survey (from Population 1)	Earlier Survey (from Population 2)
2	No	Yes	Sample Size	=COUNTA(A2:A251)	=COUNTA(B2:B151)
3	Yes	No	Response of Int.	Yes	Yes
4	Yes	Yes	No. of "Yes"	=COUNTIF(A2:A251,D3)	=COUNTIF(B2:B151,E3)
5	No	Yes	Samp. Propor.	=D4/D2	=E4/E2
6	Yes	No			
7	No	No	Hypoth. Value	0	
8	No	Yes	Pt. Est. of Diff.	=D5-E5	
9	Yes	No			
10	No	No	Pool. Est. of p	=(D2*D5+E2*E5)/(D2+E2)	
11	Yes	Yes	Standard Error	=SQRT(D10*(1-D10)*(1/D2+1/E2))	
12	Yes	No	Test Statistic	=(D8-D7)/D11	
13	Yes	Yes			
14	No	Yes	p-Value (Lower Tail)	=NORMSDIST(1-D12)	
15	Yes	Yes	p-Value (Upper Tail)	=1-NORMSDIST(D12)	
16	Yes	No	p-Value (Two Tail)	=2*MIN(D14,D15)	

Note: Rows 17-251 are not shown.

We see below that the p-value (.06) is greater than the level of significance (.05) and the test statistic (1.557) is less than the critical value (1.645). We should <u>not</u> reject H_0.

Value Worksheet:

	A	B	C	D	E
1	Late Surv.	Early Surv.		Later Survey (from Population 1)	Earlier Survey (from Population 2)
2	No	Yes	Sample Size	250	150
3	Yes	No	Response of Int.	Yes	Yes
4	Yes	Yes	No. of "Yes"	120	60
5	No	Yes	Samp. Propor.	0.48	0.40
6	Yes	No			
7	No	No	Hypoth. Value	0	
8	No	Yes	Pt. Est. of Diff.	0.08	
9	Yes	No			
10	No	No	Pool. Est. of p	0.450	
11	Yes	Yes	Standard Error	0.0514	
12	Yes	No	Test Statistic	1.557	
13	Yes	Yes			
14	No	Yes	p-Value (Lower Tail)	0.94	
15	Yes	Yes	p-Value (Upper Tail)	0.06	
16	Yes	No	p-Value (Two Tail)	0.12	

EXAMPLE 3

Goodness of Fit Test: A Multinomial Population

Finger Lakes Homes manufactures four styles of prefabricated homes, a two-story colonial, a ranch, a split-level, and an A-frame. To help in production planning, management would like to determine if previous customer purchases indicate that there is a preference in the style selected.

The number of homes sold of each style for 100 sales over the past two years is shown below.

Style:	Colonial	Ranch	Split-Level	A-Frame
# Sold:	30	20	35	15

Use $\alpha = .05$ to determine if there is a preference in the home style selected by customers. In other words, determine if there are any differences in the proportion of home styles among all the styles sold.

SOLUTION 3

Using a Calculator

This problem calls for a multinomial distribution goodness of fit test. The first step is to define our notation.

Let: p_C = population proportion that purchase a colonial style
p_R = population proportion that purchase a ranch style
p_S = population proportion that purchase a split-level style
p_A = population proportion that purchase an A-frame style

Hypotheses:

H_0: $p_C = p_R = p_S = p_A = .25$
H_a: The population proportions are not
$p_C = .25$, $p_R = .25$, $p_S = .25$, and $p_A = .25$

Expected Frequencies:

$e_1 = .25(100) = 25$ $e_2 = .25(100) = 25$
$e_3 = .25(100) = 25$ $e_4 = .25(100) = 25$

Test Statistic:

$$\chi^2 = \frac{(30-25)^2}{25} + \frac{(20-25)^2}{25} + \frac{(35-25)^2}{25} + \frac{(15-25)^2}{25}$$

$$= 1 + 1 + 4 + 4$$
$$= 10$$

Rejection Rule:

Reject H_0 if $\chi^2 \geq 7.815$

(based on $\alpha = .05$ and $k - 1 = 4 - 1 = 3$ degrees of freedom)

or Reject H_0 if p-value $\leq .05$

Conclusion:

Reject the null hypothesis

The test statistic value (10) is greater than the critical value (7.815), so we reject the null hypothesis. Alternatively, we reject H_0 because the p-value (which is between .01 and .025, using the Chi-Square Distribution table) is less than $\alpha = .05$. Therefore, we reject the assumption there is no home style preference, at the .05 level of significance. The sample strongly suggests that there is a preference in home style selected by customers.

Using Excel's CHIDIST Function

Enter Data: The home styles (C for Colonial, R for Ranch, S for Split-Level, and A for A-Fame) of the 100 homes in the sample are entered into column A. The four home style categories are entered into column B. The hypothesized proportions (.25, .25, .25, and .25) are entered into column C. The number of categories is entered into cell D9.

Enter Functions and Formulas: The COUNTIF function is used in column D to compute the number of customers that preferred each of the home styles.

To compute the expected frequency of the each home style, the respective hypothesized proportion is multiplied by the total frequency. Then, for each home style, the difference between the observed frequency and the expected frequency is computed. Next, the squared differences between the observed and expected frequencies are computed. Then, for each home style, the squared difference is divided by the expected frequency. The values that result are summed to get the value of the test statistic.

The degrees of freedom for the chi-square distribution are 1 minus the number of categories. And last, the p-value is found using the CHIDIST function. The function has two arguments, the value of the test statistic and the degrees of freedom.

Formula Worksheet:

	A	B	C	D	E	F	G	H
1	Style		Hyp.	Observed	Exp.		Sqrd.	Sq.Dif./
2	C	Categ.	Prop.	Frequency	Freq.	Diff.	Diff.	Exp.Freq.
3	R	Col (C)	0.25	=COUNTIF(A2:A101,"C")	=D3*E7	=D3-E3	=F3^2	=G3/E3
4	R	Ran (R)	0.25	=COUNTIF(A2:A101,"R")	=D4*E7	=D4-E4	=F4^2	=G4/E4
5	A	Split (S)	0.25	=COUNTIF(A2:A101,"S")	=D5*E7	=D5-E5	=F5^2	=G5/E5
6	C	A-Fr (A)	0.25	=COUNTIF(A2:A101,"A")	=D6*E7	=D6-E6	=F6^2	=G6/E6
7	S		Total	=SUM(D3:D6)				=SUM(H3:H6)
8	A							
9	C	No. of Categ.		4				
10	A							
11	R	Test Statistic		=H7				
12	S	Degr. of Freed.		=D9-1				
13	S							
14	C	p-Value		=CHIDIST(D11,D12)				

Note: Rows 15-101 are not shown.

Looking at the results in the value worksheet below, we see the p-value (.0186) is less than the level of significance (.05). Our conclusion is to reject the null hypothesis. This result is consistent, as it should be, with the result of our manual calculations.

Value Worksheet:

	A	B	C	D	E	F	G	H
1	Style		Hyp.	Observed	Exp.		Sqrd.	Sq.Dif./
2	C	Categ.	Prop.	Frequency	Freq.	Diff.	Diff.	Exp.Freq.
3	R	Col (C)	0.25	30	25	5	25	1.0
4	R	Ran (R)	0.25	20	25	-5	25	1.0
5	A	Split (S)	0.25	35	25	10	100	4.0
6	C	A-Fr (A)	0.25	15	25	-10	100	4.0
7	S		Total	100				10.0
8	A							
9	C	No. of Categ.		4				
10	A							
11	R	Test Statistic		10.0				
12	S	Degr. of Freed.		3				
13	S							
14	C	p-Value		0.0186				

Note: Rows 15-101 are not shown.

EXAMPLE 4

Test of Independence

Finger Lakes Homes manufactures prefabricated homes. Each home sold can be classified according to price and to style. The Finger Lakes Homes manager would like to determine if the price of the home and the style of the home are independent variables.

The number of homes sold for each style and price for the past two years is shown below. For convenience, the price of the home is listed as either *$99,000 or less* or *more than $99,000*.

Price	Colonial	Ranch	Split-Level	A-Frame
$\leq$ $99,000	18	6	19	12
> $99,000	12	14	16	3

Conduct a test of independence using $\alpha = .05$ to address the question of whether the home price preference is independent of the home style preference.

SOLUTION 4

Using a Calculator

Hypotheses:
H_0: Price of the home is independent of the style of the home that is purchased
H_a: Price of the home is not independent of the style of the home that is purchased

Expected Frequencies:

Price	Colonial	Ranch	Split-Level	A-Frame	Total
$\leq$ $99,000	18	6	19	12	55
> $99,000	12	14	16	3	45
Total	30	20	35	15	100

Test Statistic:

$$\chi^2 = \frac{(18-16.5)^2}{16.5} + \frac{(6-11)^2}{11} + \ldots + \frac{(3-6.75)^2}{6.75}$$

$$= .1364 + 2.2727 + \ldots + 2.0833$$
$$= 9.1486$$

Rejection Rule:

Reject H_0 if $\chi^2 \geq 7.8147$

(based on $\alpha = .05$ and $(2-1)(4-1) = 3$ degrees of freedom)

or Reject H_0 if p-value $\leq .05$

Conclusion:

The test statistic (9.1486) is greater than the critical value (7.8147). Alternatively, the p-value (between .025 and .05, using the Chi-Square Distribution table) is less than $\alpha = .05$. Reject H_0. We reject the assumption that the price of the home is independent of the style of the home that is purchased.

Using Excel's PIVOT TABLE REPORT Tool
and CHITEST Function

Enter Data: Column A is used to identify each of the 100 sold homes in the study. Column B shows the price and column C shows the style of each home sold.

Data Worksheet:

	A	B	C	D	E	F	G
1	Home	Price ($)	Style				
2	1	>99,000	Colonial				
3	2	<=99,000	Ranch				
4	3	>99,000	Ranch				
5	4	<=99,000	A-Frame				
6	5	<=99,000	Colonial				

Note: Rows 7-101 are not shown.

Apply Tools: Next, we use Excel's PivotTable Report tool to develop a crosstabulation. The steps involved are as follows:

Using the PivotTable Report

    Step 1 Select the **Data** menu
    Step 2 Choose **PivotTable and PivotChart Report**
    Step 3 When the **PivotTable and PivotChart Wizard Step 1 of 3** dialog box appears:
        Choose **Microsoft Office Excel list or database**
        Choose **PivotTable**
        Click **Next >**
    Step 4 When the **PivotTable and PivotChart Wizard Step 2 of 3** dialog box appears:
        Enter A1:C101 in the **Range** box
        Click **Next >**
    Step 5 When the **PivotTable and PivotChart Wizard Step 3 of 3** dialog box appears:
        Select **New Worksheet**
        Click **Layout**
        When the **PivotTable and PivotChart Wizard – Layout** diagram appears:
            Drag the **Price ($)** field button to the **ROW** section of the diagram
            Drag the **Style** field button to the **COLUMN** section of the diagram
            Drag the **Home** field button to the **DATA** section of the diagram
            Double click the **Sum of Home** field button in the DATA section
            When the **PivotTable Field** dialog box appears:
                Choose **Count** under **Summarized by**:
                Click **OK**
            Click **OK**
        When the **PivotTable and PivotChart Wizard Step 3 of 3** dialog box reappears:
            Click **Finish >**

Value Worksheet:

D	E	F	G	H	I	J
1	Count of Home	Style				
2	Price ($)	Colonial	Ranch	Split-Lev.	A-Frame	Grand Tot.
3	<=99,000	18	6	19	12	55
4	>99,000	12	14	16	3	45
5	Grand Total	30	20	35	15	100

Note: Columns A-C and rows 6-101 are not shown.

Enter Functions and Formulas: Now we ready to compute the expected frequencies for the Finger Lakes Homes contingency table under the assumption of independence. To compute the expected number of homes sold that are a Colonial style and priced at $\leq 99,000$, we enter the formula =F5*J3/J5 into cell F9. To compute the expected number of homes sold that are a Colonial style and priced at $> 99,000$, we enter the formula =F5*J4/J5 into cell F10. Similar formulas are entered into cells G9:I10 to compute the expected frequencies for the remaining style-price combinations.

At this point we have the observed frequencies and expected frequencies in cells F3:E4 and F9:F10, respectively. Now, to compute the p-value associated with this test of independence, we enter the following formula into cell G12:

$$=CHITEST(F3:I4,F9:I10)$$

Formula Worksheet:

D	E	F	G	H	I	J
1	Count of Home	Style				
2	Price ($)	Colonial	Ranch	Split-Lev.	A-Frame	Grand Tot.
3	<=99,000	18	6	19	12	55
4	>99,000	12	14	16	3	45
5	Grand Total	30	20	35	15	100
6						
7	Expected Frequencies					
8		Colonial	Ranch	Split-Lev.	A-Frame	
9	<=99,000	=F5*J3/J5	=G5*J3/J5	=H5*J3/J5	=I5*J3/J5	
10	>99,000	=F5*J4/J5	=G5*J4/J5	=H5*J4/J5	=I5*J4/J5	
11						
12			*p*-Value =CHITEST(F3:I4,F9:I10)			

Note: Columns A-C and Rows 13-101 are not shown.

We see below that the p-value (.0274) is less than the level of significance (.05). Therefore, our conclusion is to reject the null hypothesis. We are 95% confident that the two variables, home price and home style, are not independent.

Value Worksheet:

D	E	F	G	H	I	J
1	Count of Home	Style				
2	Price ($)	Colonial	Ranch	Split-Lev.	A-Frame	Grand Tot.
3	<=99,000	18	6	19	12	55
4	>99,000	12	14	16	3	45
5	Grand Total	30	20	35	15	100
6						
7	Expected Frequencies					
8		Colonial	Ranch	Split-Lev.	A-Frame	
9	<=99,000	16.50	11.00	19.25	8.25	
10	>99,000	13.50	9.00	15.75	6.75	
11						
12		*p*-Value	0.0274			

Note: Columns A-C and Rows 13-101 are not shown.

EXERCISES

EXERCISE 1

Interval Estimation of $p_1 - p_2$

A movie based on a best-selling novel was recently released. Six hundred viewers of the movie, 235 of whom had previously read the novel, were asked to rate the quality of the movie. The survey showed that 141 of the novel readers gave the movie a rating of excellent, while 248 of the non-readers gave the movie an excellent rating.

Develop an interval estimate of the difference between the proportions of the two populations, using a .05 level of significance, as the basis for your decision.

EXERCISE 2

Hypothesis Test about $p_1 - p_2$

Refer to Exercise 1. Can we conclude, on the basis of a hypothesis test about $p_1 - p_2$, that the proportion of the non-readers of the novel who thought the movie was excellent is greater than the proportion of readers of the novel who thought the movie was excellent? Use a .05 level of significance. (Hint: this is a one-tailed test.)

EXERCISE 3

Goodness of Fit Test: A Multinomial Population

Employee panel preferences for three proposed company logo designs follow.

Design A	Design B	Design C
78	59	66

Use $\alpha = .05$ and test to determine any difference in preference among the three logo designs.

EXERCISE 4

Test of Independence

City planners are evaluating three proposed alternatives for relieving the growing traffic congestion on a north-south highway in a booming city. The proposed alternatives are: (1) designate high-occupancy vehicle (HOV) lanes on the existing highway, (2) construct a new, parallel highway, and (3) construct a light (passenger) rail system.

In an analysis of the three proposals, a citizen group has raised the question of whether preferences for the three alternatives differ among residents near the highway and non-residents. A test of independence will address this question, with the hypotheses being:

H_0: Proposal preference is independent of the residency status of the individual
H_a: Proposal preference is not independent of the residency status of the individual

A simple random sample of 500 individuals has been selected. The crosstabulation of the residency statuses and proposal preferences of the individuals sampled is shown below.

	Proposal		
	HOV	New	Light
Residency Status	Lanes	Highway	Rail
Nearby resident	110	45	70
Distant resident	140	75	60

Conduct a test of independence using $\alpha = .05$ to address the question of whether residency status is independent of the proposal preference.

SELF-TEST

TRUE/FALSE

___ 1. The test of independence is always a one-tailed test.

___ 2. If we reject the null hypothesis H_0 in a test of independence, we are concluding that the variables are independent.

___ 3. The purpose of the hypothesis test for proportions of a multinomial population is to determine whether the proportions are equal (follow a discrete uniform distribution).

___ 4. In the test of independence, the computation of the expected frequencies is based on the assumption that the variables are independent.

___ 5. If we conclude by means of the test of independence that the variables are not independent, we can then determine from the test results exactly how the dependence comes about.

FILL-IN-THE-BLANK

1. The _____ used in the test of independence is an example of crosstabulation.

2. The formula for the point estimate of the difference between the proportions of two populations is _____.

3. Both the hypothesis test for proportions of a multinomial population and the test of independence focus on the differences between the observed frequencies and the

   _____.

4. The _____ probability distribution can be thought of as an extension of the binomial distribution to the case of three or more categories of outcomes.

5. Both the hypothesis test for proportions of a multinomial population and the test of independence employ a _____ test.

MULTIPLE CHOICE

___ 1. The test statistic for the chi-square tests in this chapter requires, for each category, an expected frequency of at least
   a) 2
   b) 5
   c) 10
   d) 30

___ 2. In conducting a hypothesis test about $p_1 - p_2$, any of the following approaches can be used <u>except</u>
    a) comparing the observed frequencies to the expected frequencies
    b) comparing the p-value to α
    c) comparing the hypothesized difference to the confidence interval
    d) comparing the test statistic to the critical value

___ 3. In the case of the test of independence, the number of degrees of freedom for the appropriate chi-square distribution is computed as
    a) $k - 1$
    b) $k - 2$
    c) $(r - 1)(c - 1)$
    d) $rc - 2$

___ 4. The properties of a multinomial experiment include all of the following <u>except</u>
    a) the experiment consists of a sequence of n identical trials
    b) three or more outcomes are possible on each trial
    c) the probability of each outcome can change from trial to trial
    d) the trials are independent

___ 5. The test of independence presented in the chapter requires that there be
    a) two variables, each having two outcomes
    b) two variables, each having two or more outcomes
    c) two or more variables, each having two outcomes
    d) two or more variables, each having two or more outcomes

ANSWERS

EXERCISES

1) .0118 to .1690 (note that 0 is not in the interval)

2) $H_0: p_{NR} - p_R \le 0$, $z = 2.274 > 1.645$, p-value $= .0115 < .05$; reject H_0

3) p-value $= .2667 > .05$; do not reject H_0 (no apparent preferences)

4) p-value $= .0277 < .05$; reject H_0 (they are not independent)

TRUE/FALSE	FILL-IN-THE-BLANK	MULTIPLE CHOICE
1) True	1) contingency table	1) b
2) False	2) $\bar{p}_1 - \bar{p}_2$	2) a
3) False	3) expected frequencies	3) c
4) True	4) multinomial	4) c
5) False	5) chi-square goodness of fit	5) b

CHAPTER 12

Simple Linear Regression

Simple Linear Regression Model

Least Squares Method

Coefficient of Determination

Model Assumptions

Testing for Significance

Excel's Regression Tool

Using the Estimated Regression Equation
for Estimation and Prediction

Residual Analysis:
Validating Model Assumptions

Outliers and Influential Observations

LEARNING OBJECTIVES

1. Understand how regression analysis can be used to develop an equation that estimates mathematically how two variables are related.

2. Understand the differences between the regression model, the regression equation, and the estimated regression equation.

3. Know how to fit an estimated regression equation to a set of sample data based upon the least-squares method.

4. Be able to determine how good a fit is provided by the estimated regression equation and compute the sample correlation coefficient from the regression analysis output.

5. Understand the assumptions necessary for statistical inference and be able to test for a significant relationship.

6. Learn how to use a residual plot to make a judgment as to the validity of the regression assumptions, recognize outliers, and identify influential observations.

7. Know how to develop confidence interval estimates of y given a specific value of x in both the case of a mean value of y and an individual value of y.

8. Be able to compute the sample correlation coefficient from the regression analysis output.

9. Know the definition of the following terms:

independent and dependent variable	confidence interval
simple linear regression	prediction interval
regression model	residual plot
regression equation	standardized residual plot
estimated regression equation	outlier
scatter diagram	influential observation
coefficient of determination	leverage
standard error of the estimate	

REVIEW

Regression Analysis
*   Managerial decisions often are based on the relationship between two or more variables.
*   A statistical procedure called regression analysis can be used to develop an equation showing how the variables are related.
*   The variable being predicted is called the dependent variable.
*   The variable(s) being used to predict the value of the dependent variable are called the independent variables.

Simple Linear Regression
*   Regression analysis involving one independent variable and one dependent variable, in which a straight line approximates the relationship between the variables, is called simple linear regression.

Simple Linear Regression Model
- The equation that describes how y is related to x and an error term is called the regression model.
- The regression model used in simple linear regression is:
$$y = \beta_0 + \beta_1 x + \varepsilon$$
- β_0 and β_1 are referred to as the parameters of the model.
- ε is a random variable referred to as the error term.
- The error term accounts for the variability in y that cannot be explained by the linear relationship between x and y.

Simple Linear Regression Equation
- One of the assumptions made here is that the mean or expected value of ε is zero.
- As a result of the above assumption, the mean or expected value of y, denoted $E(y)$, is equal to $\beta_0 + \beta_1 x$.
- The equation that describes how the mean value of y is related to x is called the simple linear regression equation.
$$E(y) = \beta_0 + \beta_1 x$$
- The graph of the simple linear regression equation is a straight line.
- β_0 is the y intercept of the regression equation; β_1 is the slope.
- $E(y)$ is the expected value of y for a given value of x.

Estimated Regression Equation
- The values of the parameters β_0 and β_1 are not known in practice and must be estimated by using sample data.
- The sample statistics b_0 and b_1 are computed as estimates of β_0 and β_1.
- The estimated simple linear regression equation is:
$$\hat{y} = b_0 + b_1 x$$
  where: $\hat{y}$ = the estimated value of y for a given value of x

  b_0 = the y intercept

  b_1 = the slope

Scatter Diagram
- A scatter diagram (introduced in Chapter 2) enables us to observe the data graphically and to draw preliminary conclusions about the possible relationship between the independent and dependent variables.
- The independent variable x is on the horizontal axis and the dependent variable y is on the vertical axis.
- We hope to observe that the relationship between the two variables appears to be approximated by a straight line.

Least Squares Method
- The least squares method is a procedure for using sample data to compute an estimated regression equation, specifically values for b_0 and b_1.
- Values are found for b_0 and b_1 that minimize the sum of the squares of the deviations between the observed values of y_i and the estimated values $\hat{y}_i$.

- The least squares criterion is:

$$\min \sum (y_i - \hat{y}_i)^2$$

where:

y_i = observed value of the dependent variable for the i th observation
$\hat{y}_i$ = estimated value of the dependent variable for the i th observation

Slope for the Estimated Regression Equation

$$b_1 = \frac{\sum x_i y_i - (\sum x_i \sum y_i)/n}{\sum x_i^2 - (\sum x_i)^2 / n}$$

y-Intercept for the Estimated Regression Equation

$$b_0 = \bar{y} - b_1 \bar{x}$$

where:

x_i = value of independent variable for i th observation
y_i = value of dependent variable for i th observation
$\bar{x}$ = mean value for independent variable
$\bar{y}$ = mean value for dependent variable
n = total number of observations

Applying the Estimated Regression Equation

- If we believe the least squares estimated regression equation adequately describes the relationship between x and y, it probably is reasonable to use the equation to predict the value of y for a given value of x.
- Plugging into the equation an x value outside the range of the x data with which the equation was developed should be done with caution because we cannot be sure the same relationship is valid.

Coefficient of Determination

- The coefficient of determination provides a measure of the goodness of fit for the estimated regression equation.
- It can also be used to measure of the goodness of fit involving relationships that are nonlinear or have two or more independent variables.

Sum of Squares Due to Error (SSE)

- The SSE is a measure of the error in using the estimated regression equation to estimate the values of the dependent variable in the sample.
- The formula for the SSE is:

$$SSE = \sum (y_i - \hat{y}_i)^2$$

Total Sum of Squares (SST)

- The SST is a measure of the error involved if we had used the average value of y, $\bar{y}$, to estimate y.
- The formula for the SSE is:

$$SST = \sum (y_i - \bar{y})^2$$

Sum of Squares Due to Regression (SSR)

- The SSR is a measure of how much the $\hat{y}$ values on the estimated regression line deviate from $\bar{y}$.
- The formula for the SSR is:

$$SSR = \sum(\hat{y}_i - \bar{y})^2$$

Relationship Among SST, SSR, and SSE

- SST = SSR + SSE
- SSR can be thought of as the explained portion of SST.
- SSE can be thought of as the unexplained portion of SST.
- If the regression equation provided a perfect fit, $y_i - \hat{y}_i$ would be zero for each observation, resulting in SSE = 0 and SSR/SST = 1.
- The ratio SSR/SST, which will be between 0 and 1, is used to evaluate the goodness of fit for the estimated regression equation.
- The coefficient of determination, r^2, is:

$$r^2 = SSR/SST$$

Correlation Coefficient

- The correlation coefficient is a measure of the strength of linear association between two variables, x and y. (Note – only linear association, and only two variables)
- Values of the correlation coefficient are always between –1 and +1.
- A value of +1 indicates that the two variables x and y are perfectly related in a positive linear sense (all data points are on a straight line that has a positive slope).
- A value of -1 indicates that the two variables x and y are perfectly related in a negative linear sense (all data points are on a straight line that has a negative slope).
- Values close to zero indicate that x and y are not linearly related.
- The sign for the sample correlation coefficient is positive if the estimated regression equation has a positive slope ($b_1 > 0$). The sign is negative if $b_1 < 0$.
- If the coefficient of determination, r^2, has been computed, the correlation coefficient is easily computed as follows:

$$r_{xy} = (\text{sign of } b_1)\sqrt{r^2}$$

Testing for Significance

- Determining the appropriateness of a model includes testing for the significance of the relationship.
- The tests for significance are based on the following assumptions about the error term ε:
  - The error ε is a random variable with mean of zero.
  - The variance of ε, denoted by σ^2, is the same for all values of the independent variable.
  - The values of ε are independent.
  - The error ε is a normally distributed random variable.
- To test for significance we must conduct a hypothesis test to determine whether the value of β_1 is zero. Two tests often used are the t test and F test.
- Both the t and F tests require an estimate of σ^2, the variance of ε in the regression model.

An Estimate of σ^2

- The mean square error (an estimate of σ^2) is denoted s^2 and computed as:

$$s^2 = \text{MSE} = \text{SSE}/(n-2)$$

- The standard error of the estimate (an estimate of σ) is denoted s and computed as:

$$s = \sqrt{\text{MSE}} = \sqrt{\frac{\text{SSE}}{n-2}}$$

t Test

- The t test can be summarized as follows:
  - Hypotheses:

$$H_0 : \beta_1 = 0$$
$$H_a : \beta_1 \neq 0$$

  - Test statistic:

$$t = \frac{b_1}{s_{b_1}}$$

  - Rejection rule:

Reject H_0 if $t \leq -t_{\alpha/2}$ or if $t \geq t_{\alpha/2}$
where $t_{\alpha/2}$ is based on a t distribution with $n-2$ degrees of freedom

Confidence Interval for β_1

- We can use a confidence interval for β_1 to test the hypotheses used above in the t test.
- H_0 is rejected if the hypothesized value of β_1 is not within the confidence interval for β_1.
- The form of the confidence interval is:

$$b_1 \pm t_{\alpha/2}s_{b_1}$$

F Test

- The F test can be summarized as follows:
  - Hypotheses:

$$H_0 : \beta_1 = 0$$
$$H_a : \beta_1 \neq 0$$

  - Test statistic:

$$F = \text{MSR/MSE}$$

  - Rejection rule:

Reject H_0 if $F \geq F_\alpha$
where F_α is based on an F distribution with
1 d.f. in the numerator and $n-2$ d.f. in the denominator

Interpretation of Significance Tests

- Rejecting the null hypothesis in the t or F test and concluding the relationship between x and y is significant does not prove a cause-and-effect relationship is present between x and y.
- Rejecting the null hypothesis in the t or F test does not enable us to conclude that the relationship between x and y is linear.

Using the Estimated Regression Equation for Estimation and Prediction

Point Estimation
- The estimated regression equation can be used to compute a point estimate of the mean value of *y* for a particular value of *x* or to predict an individual value of *y* for a given value of *x*. (Either way the question is stated, the results are the same.)

Interval Estimation
- Point estimates do not provide any information on the precision of the estimates.
- One type of interval estimate, a confidence interval estimate, is an interval estimate of the mean value of *y* for a given *x*.
- Another type of interval estimate, a prediction interval estimate, is an interval estimate of an individual value of *y* corresponding to a given value of *x*.

Confidence Interval Estimate of the Mean Value of *y*
- The estimate of the standard deviation of $\hat{y}_p$ is:

$$s_{\hat{y}_p} = s\sqrt{\frac{1}{n} + \frac{(x_p - \bar{x})^2}{\sum(x_i - \bar{x})^2}}$$

where: x_p = the given value of the independent variable *x*
s = the standard error of the estimate
- The confidence interval estimate of $E(y_p)$ is:

$$\hat{y}_p \pm t_{\alpha/2}s_{\hat{y}_p}$$

where: the confidence coefficient is $1 - \alpha$ and $t_{\alpha/2}$ is based on a *t* distribution with $n - 2$ degrees of freedom

Prediction Interval Estimate of an Individual Value of *y*
- The estimate of the standard deviation of an individual value of y_p is:

$$s_{ind} = s\sqrt{1 + \frac{1}{n} + \frac{(x_p - \bar{x})^2}{\sum(x_i - \bar{x})^2}}$$

where: x_p = the given value of the independent variable *x*
s = the standard error of the estimate
- The prediction interval estimate of y_p is:

$$\hat{y}_p \pm t_{\alpha/2}s_{ind}$$

where: the confidence coefficient is $1 - \alpha$ and $t_{\alpha/2}$ is based on a *t* distribution with $n - 2$ degrees of freedom

Residual Analysis: Validating Model Assumptions
- The residual for observation I is the difference between the observed value (y_i) and the estimated value ($\hat{y}_i$) of the dependent variable.
- Residual analysis is the primary tool for determining whether the assumed regression model is appropriate because:
  - The residuals provide the best information about ε.
  - It is important to determine whether the assumptions about ε are appropriate.

Residual Plot against *x*

- A residual plot against *x* is, as it sounds, a graph with residuals (represented by the vertical axis) corresponding to the independent variable (represented by the horizontal axis) plotted.
- The plotted points should give an overall impression of a horizontal band of points if:
  - The assumption that the variance of ε is the same for all values of *x*.
  - The assumed regression model is an adequate representation of the relationship between the two variables.

Standardized Residual Plot

- A residual is standardized by dividing it by its standard deviation.
- The standard deviation of the *i* th residual is:

$$s_{y_i - \hat{y}_i} = s\sqrt{1 - h_i}$$

where: *s* = the standard error of the estimate

$$h_i = \frac{1}{n} + \frac{(x_i - \overline{x})^2}{\sum (x_i - \overline{x})^2}$$

- The standardized residual for observation *i* is:

$$\frac{y_i - \hat{y}_i}{s_{y_i - \hat{y}_i}}$$

- If the error term ε has a normal distribution, we should expect to see roughly 95% of the standardized residuals between −2 and +2.

Normal Probability Plot

- This is another approach for determining the validity of the assumption that the error term has a normal distribution.
- Normal scores are on the horizontal axis.
- The corresponding standardized residuals are on the vertical axis.
- The plotted points should cluster closely around a 45-degree line passing through the origin if the standardized residuals are normally distributed.

Outliers and Influential Observations

Detecting Outliers

- An outlier is a data point that does not fit the trend shown by the remaining data.
- Outliers are suspect and warrant careful examination.
- They may be erroneous data ⟶ if so, they should be corrected.
- They may signal a violation of model assumptions ⟶ if so, another model should be considered
- They may simply be unusual values that have occurred by chance ⟶ if so, they should be retained.
- The standardized residuals can be used to identify outliers.
- A standardized residual less than −2 or greater than +2 might be considered an outlier.

Detecting Influential Observations

- An influential observation is one that has a strong influence on the regression results.
- It may correspond to a somewhat off-trend y value, somewhat extreme x value, or both.
- Observations with extreme values for the independent variables are called high leverage points.
- The leverage of an observation is determined by how far the value of the independent variable is from its mean value.
- Leverage of observation i is:

$$h_i = \frac{1}{n} + \frac{(x_i - \bar{x})^2}{\sum (x_i - \bar{x})^2}$$

- Minitab identifies observations as having high leverage if $h_i > 6/n$.
- Data points having high leverage are often influential.
- Excel does not have built-in capabilities for identifying outliers and high-leverage points.

KEY CONCEPTS

CONCEPT	EXAMPLES	EXERCISES
Scatter Diagram Approach		
Estimated Regression Equation	①	1,2,3,4
Coefficient of Determination	②	5
Correlation Coefficient	②	5
Testing for Significance		
t Test for β_1	3	6
Confidence Interval for β_1	3	6
F Test for β_1	3	6
Analysis of Variance Table	3	6
Excel's *Regression* Tool		
Interpretation of Output	④	7
Using the Estimated Regression Equation		
Confidence Interval Estimate of $E(y_p)$	⑤	8
Prediction Interval Estimate of y_p	⑤	8
Residual Analysis	⑥	9

◯ Excel Used

EXAMPLES

EXAMPLE 1

Estimated Regression Equation

Reed Auto periodically has a special week-long sale. As part of the advertising campaign Reed runs one or more television commercials during the weekend preceding the sale. Data from a sample of 5 previous sales are shown below.

Number of TV Ads	Number of Cars Sold
1	14
3	24
2	18
1	17
3	27

a) Develop a scatter diagram for these data.

b) Develop the estimated regression equation by computing the values of b_0 and b_1.

c) Use the estimated regression equation to predict the number of cars sold when two television ads are run.

SOLUTION 1

Using a Calculator

a) See the application of Excel below for the scatter diagram.

b) Slope for the estimated regression equation:

$$b_1 = \frac{\sum(x_i - \bar{x})(y_i - \bar{y})}{\sum(x_i - \bar{x})^2} \quad \text{or} \quad b_1 = \frac{\sum x_i y_i - (\sum x_i \sum y_i)/n}{\sum x_i^2 - (\sum x_i)^2/n}$$

$$b_1 = \frac{220 - (10)(100)/5}{24 - (10)^2/5} = \frac{20}{4} = 5$$

y-Intercept for the estimated regression equation:

$$b_0 = \bar{y} - b_1\bar{x} = 20 - 5(2) = 10$$

Estimated regression equation:

$$\hat{y} = 10 + 5x$$

c) $\hat{y} = 10 + 5x = 10 + 5(2) = 10 + 10 = 20$ cars sold

Using Excel's *Scatter Diagram* and *Trendline* Tools

Excel's Chart Wizard can be used to construct a scatter diagram. Once the scatter diagram has been developed, Excel's Chart menu provides options for computing the estimated regression equation and displaying the regression line.

Enter Data: The labels Week, TV Ads, and Cars Sold are entered into cells A1:C1 of the worksheet. To identify each of the 5 observations, we enter the number 1 through 5 into cells A2:A6. The sample data are entered into cells B2:C6.

Data Worksheet:

	A	B	C	D	E	F
1	Week	TV Ads	Cars Sold			
2	1	1	14			
3	2	3	24			
4	3	2	18			
5	4	1	17			
6	5	3	27			
7						

Enter Functions and Formulas: There are none to be entered.

Apply Tools: First we will produce the scatter diagram using Chart Wizard and then we will add the trend line. The steps are as follows:

Producing a Scatter Diagram

    Step 1 Select cells B1:C6
    Step 2 Click the **Chart Wizard** button on the standard toolbar
    Step 3 When the **Chart Type (Step 1 of 4)** dialog box appears:
            Choose **XY (Scatter)** in the **Chart type** list
            Choose **Scatter** from the **Chart sub-type** display
            Click **Next >**
    Step 4 When the **Chart Source Data (Step 2 of 4)** dialog box appears
            Click **Next >**
    Step 5 When the **Chart Options (Step 3 of 4)** dialog box appears:
            Select the **Titles** tab and then
                Delete **Cars Sold** in the Chart title box
                Enter **TV Ads** in the **Value (X)** axis box
                Enter **Cars Sold** in the **Value (Y)** axis box
            Select the **Legend** tab and then
                Remove the check in the **Show Legend** box
                Click **Next >**
    Step 6 When the **Chart Location (Step 4 of 4)** dialog box appears:
            Specify the location for the new chart
            Click **Finish**

Adding the Trendline

Step 1 Position the mouse pointer over any data point
        and right click to display the **Chart** menu
Step 2 Select the **Add Trendline** option
Step 3 When the **Add Trendline** dialog box appears:
        On the **Type** tab select **Linear**
        On the **Options** tab select the **Display equation on chart** box
        Click **OK**

Scatter Diagram with Regression Line and Regression Equation:

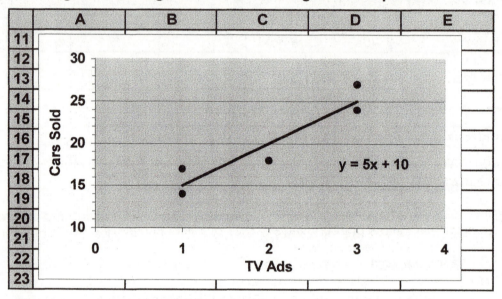

EXAMPLE 2

Coefficient of Determination and Correlation Coefficient

Refer to the Reed Auto problem in Example 1. The estimated regression equation for these data is $\hat{y} = 10 + 5x$.

a) Compute SSE, SST, and SSR.

b) Compute the coefficient of determination r^2. Comment on the goodness of fit.

c) Compute the correlation coefficient.

SOLUTION 2

Using a Calculator

a) $SST = SSR + SSE = \sum(y_i - \bar{y})^2 = \sum(\hat{y}_i - \bar{y})^2 + \sum(y_i - \hat{y}_i)^2 = 100 + 14 = 114$
$SSE = 14$, $SST = 114$, and $SSR = 100$

b) $r^2 = SSR/SST = 100/114 = .8772$
An $r^2 = .8772$ indicates that almost 88 % of the total sum of squares can be explained by using the estimated regression equation $\hat{y} = 10 + 5x$ to predict the number of cars sold.

c) $r_{xy} = (\text{sign of } b_1)\sqrt{r^2} = (+)\sqrt{.8772} = .9366$

Using Excel to Compute the Coefficient of Determination

Enter Data: We will continue with the worksheet we developed in Solution .

Enter Functions and Formulas: There are none to be entered.

Apply Tools: We produce the scatter diagram, added the trend line, and displayed the estimated regression equation in Solution 1.

Producing r^2

Step 1 Position the mouse pointer over any data point in the diagram and right click
Step 2 When the Chart menu appears:
      Select the **Add Trendline** option
Step 3 When the Add Trendline dialog box appears:
      On the **Options** tab, select the **Display R-squared value on chart** box
      Click **OK**

r^2 **Value Displayed on Scatter Diagram:**

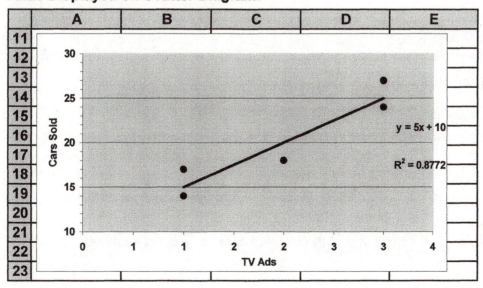

EXAMPLE 3

Testing for Significance

Refer to the Reed Auto problem in Example 1. The estimated regression equation for these data is $\hat{y} = 10 + 5x$.

a) Compute the mean square error MSE.

b) Compute the standard error of the estimate.

c) Compute the estimated standard deviation of b_1.

d) Use the t test to test the following hypotheses ($\alpha = .05$):

$$H_0 : \beta_1 = 0$$
$$H_a : \beta_1 \neq 0$$

e) Develop a 95% confidence interval estimate for β_1 to test the hypotheses in part (d).

f) Use the F test to test the hypotheses in part (d) at a .05 level of significance. Present the results in an analysis of variance table format.

SOLUTION 3

Using a Calculator

a) MSE = s^2 = SSE/(n − 2) = 14/(5 − 2) = 14/3 = 4.667
    (SSE = 14 was computed in Solution 2.)

b) $s = \sqrt{\text{MSE}} = \sqrt{4.667} = 2.1603$

c) $s_{b_1} = \dfrac{s}{\sqrt{\sum(x_i - \bar{x})^2}} = \dfrac{2.1603}{\sqrt{4}} = \dfrac{2.1603}{2} = 1.08$

d) t Test for Significance

Step 1: Determine the null and alternative hypotheses

$H_0 : \beta_1 = 0$ The mean value of y does not depend on x.
The number of TV ads run and the number of cars sold are <u>not</u> linearly related.

$H_a : \beta_1 \neq 0$ The number of TV ads run and the number of cars sold are linearly related.

where: β_1 = the slope of the simple linear regression equation.

Step 2: Select the test statistic to be used to decide whether to reject H_0

$$t = \frac{b_1}{s_{b_1}}$$

Step 3: Specify the level of significance α

$\alpha = .05$

Step 4: Develop the rejection rule based on the level of significance

Reject H_0 if p-value $\leq .05$, or
Reject H_0 if $t \leq -3.182$ or if $t \geq 3.182$ (based on 3 d.f.)

Step 5: Collect the data and compute the value of the test statistic

$$t = \frac{b_1}{s_{b_1}} = \frac{5}{1.08} = 4.63$$

Step 6: a) Compare the value of the test statistic to the critical value(s)

$t = 4.63 > 3.182$, or

b) Compute the p-value and compare it to α

p-value (between .005 and .01) $< .05$
(precise p-values are difficult to determine from the Student t table)

Step 7: State your conclusion regarding H_0

Reject H_0. We are 95% confident that the mean value of y depends on x (that the number of TV ads run and the number of cars sold are linearly related).

e) 95% Confidence Interval Estimate for β_1

We can use a 95% confidence interval for β_1 to test the hypotheses just used in the t test. H_0 is rejected if the hypothesized value of β_1 is not included in the confidence interval for β_1.

Rejection Rule

Reject H_0 if 0 is not included in the confidence interval for β_1.

95% Confidence Interval for β_1

$b_1 \pm t_{\alpha/2} s_{b_1} = 5 \pm 3.182(1.08) = 5 \pm 3.44 = 5$ +/- $3.182(1.08) = 5$ +/- $3.44 = 1.56$ to 8.44

Conclusion

Reject H_0. 0 is not in the 95% confidence interval estimate of 1.56 to 8.44.

f) *F Test*

Step 1: Determine the null and alternative hypotheses

$H_0 : \beta_1 = 0$ The mean value of y does not depend on x.
The number of TV ads run and the number of cars sold are <u>not</u> linearly related.

$H_a : \beta_1 \neq 0$ The number of TV ads run and the number of cars sold are linearly related.

where: β_1 = the slope of the simple linear regression equation.

Step 2: Select the test statistic to be used to decide whether to reject H_0
F = MSR/MSE

Step 3: Specify the level of significance α
$\alpha = .05$

Step 4: Develop the rejection rule based on the level of significance
Reject H_0 if p-value $\leq .05$, or
Reject H_0 if $F \geq 10.13$
(based on F distribution with 1 d.f. in numerator and $n - 2$ d.f. in denominator)

Step 5: Collect the data and compute the value of the test statistic
$F = 100/4.667 = 21.43$

Step 6: a) Compare the value of the test statistic to the critical value(s)
$F = 21.43 > 10.13$, or

b) Compute the p-value and compare it to α
Precise p-values are difficult to determine from the Student t Table.

Step 7: State your conclusion regarding H_0
Reject H_0. We are 95% confident that the mean value of y depends on x (that the number of TV ads run and the number of cars sold are linearly related).

ANALYSIS OF VARIANCE TABLE

Source of Variation	Sum of Squares	Degrees of Freedom	Mean Square	F
Regression	100	1	100	21.43
Residual	14	3	4.67	
Total	114	4		

EXAMPLE 4

Interpretation of Excel's Regression Output

Refer to the Reed Auto problem in Example 1. Use Excel's Regression tool to perform a complete regression analysis. Interpret the output.

SOLUTION 4

Using Excel's *Regression* Tool

Excel's Regression tool can be used to perform a complete regression analysis. All of the analysis we performed in Examples 1, 2, and 3 will automatically be performed using the Regression tool.

Enter Data: The data and labels are already entered (see Solution 1).

Enter Functions and Formulas: There are none to be entered.

Apply Tools: The following steps describe how to use Excel's Regression tool:

Step 1 Select the **Tools** pull-down menu
Step 2 Choose the **Data Analysis** option
Step 3 Choose **Regression** from the list of Analysis Tools

Regression Dialog Box:

Value Worksheet:

	A	B	C	D	E	F	G	H	I
1	Week	TV Ads	Cars Sold						
2	1	1	14						
3	2	3	24						
4	3	2	18						
5	4	1	17						
6	5	3	27						
7									
8	SUMMARY OUTPUT								
9									
10	*Regression Statistics*								
11	Multiple R	0.93658581							
12	R Square	0.87719298							
13	Adjusted R Sq.	0.83625731							
14	Standard Error	2.1602469							
15	Observations	5							
16									
17	ANOVA								
18		*df*	*SS*	*MS*	*F*	*Signific. F*			
19	Regression	1	100	100	21.4286	0.01898623			
20	Residual	3	14	4.66667					
21	Total	4	114						
22									
23		*Coeffic.*	*Std. Error*	*t Stat*	*P-value*	*Low. 95%*	*Up. 95%*	*Low. 95.0%*	*Up. 95.0%*
24	Intercept	10	2.36643191	4.22577	0.02424	2.46895044	17.5310496	2.46895044	17.5310496
25	TV Ads	5	1.08012345	4.6291	0.01899	1.56256189	8.43743811	1.56256189	8.43743811

We see above that the regression output, titled SUMMARY OUTPUT, begins with row 8. The first section of the output, titled *Regression Statistics*, contains summary statistics such as the coefficient of determination (R Square). The second section, titled ANOVA, contains the analysis of variance table. The third section, which is not titled, contains the estimated regression coefficients and related information.

The values you solved for in Examples 1, 2, and 3 can be found in the worksheet above among the output generated by Excel's Regression tool.

Items to note in the *Regression Statistics* section shown below:

- The MULTIPLE R value of .9366 in cell B11 is the sample correlation coefficient value we calculated in Example 2, part (c).
- The R Square value of .8872 in cell B12 is the coefficient of determination value we calculated in Example 2, part (b).
- The Standard Error value of 2.16 in cell B14 is the standard error of the estimate value we calculated in Example 3, part (b).

Regression Statistics Ouput:

	A	B	C	D	E	F
10	*Regression Statistics*					
11	Multiple R	0.9365858				
12	R Square	0.877193				
13	Adjusted R Sq.	0.8362573				
14	Standard Error	2.1602469				
15	Observations	5				

Items to note in the ANOVA section shown below:
- The ANOVA table generated by Excel is virtually the same as the table we constructed in Example 3, part (f).
- The label in cell A20 is Residual, whereas the textbook uses the label Error.
- The degrees of freedom (*df*) and sum of squares (*SS*) columns are in reverse order here compared with the table in the textbook.
- The values in cells C19:C21 correspond to the SSR, SSE, and SST values we computed in Example 2, part (a).
- The *F* value in cell E19 is the test statistic value we computed in Example 3, part (f).
- The *Signific. F* value in cell F19 is the *p*-value for the *F* test. When we compare the *p*-value .019 with the level of significance .05, we clearly have overwhelming reason to reject the null hypothesis.

ANOVA Output:

	A	B	C	D	E	F
17	ANOVA					
18		*df*	*SS*	*MS*	*F*	*Signific. F*
19	Regression	1	100	100	21.429	0.0189862
20	Residual	3	14	4.6667		
21	Total	4	114			

Items to note in the Estimated Regression Equation (unlabeled) section shown below:
- The *Coeffic.* Values in cells B24 and B25 are the b_0 and b_1 values we computed in Example 1, part (b).
- The *Std. Error* value of 1.08 in cell C25 is the estimated standard deviation of b_1 value we computed in Example 3, part (c).
- The *t Stat* value of 4.23 in cell D24 is the *t* value we computed in Example 3, part (d).
- The values 1.56 and 8.44 in cells F25 and G24 are the lower and upper limits of the confidence interval estimate for β_1 that we computed in Example 3, part (e).

Estimated Regression Equation Output:

	A	B	C	D	E	F	G
22							
23		*Coeffic.*	*Std. Error*	*t Stat*	*P-value*	*Low. 95%*	*Up. 95%*
24	Intercept	10	2.3664319	4.2258	0.0242	2.4689504	17.53105
25	TV Ads	5	1.0801234	4.6291	0.019	1.5625619	8.4374381
26							

EXAMPLE 5

Confidence and Prediction Interval Estimates

Refer to the Reed Auto problem in Example 1.

a) Develop a 95% confidence interval estimate of the mean number of cars sold when 3 TV ads are run.

b) Develop a 95% prediction interval estimate for the number of cars sold when 3 TV ads are run.

SOLUTION 5

Using a Calculator

a) 95% Confidence Interval Estimate:

s = standard error of the estimate = 2.1603 (refer to Solution 3)
x_p = the given value of the independent variable = 3

$$\sum(x_i - \bar{x})^2 = (1-2)^2 + (3-2)^2 + (2-2)^2 + (1-2)^2 + (3-2)^2 = 4$$

$$s_{\hat{y}_p} = s\sqrt{\frac{1}{n} + \frac{(x_p - \bar{x})^2}{\sum(x_i - \bar{x})^2}} = 2.1603\sqrt{\frac{1}{5} + \frac{(3-2)^2}{4}} = 1.4492$$

t = 3.182 (based $\alpha/2$ = .025 and df = $n - 2 = 3$)
$\hat{y}_p = b_0 + b_1x = 10 + 5(3) = 25$

$$\hat{y}_p \pm t_{\alpha/2}s_{\hat{y}_p}$$

$$25 \pm 3.182(1.4492)$$

$$25 \pm 4.61$$

20.39 to 29.61

b) 95% Prediction Interval Estimate:

$$s_{ind} = s\sqrt{1 + \frac{1}{n} + \frac{(x_p - \bar{x})^2}{\sum(x_i - \bar{x})^2}} = 2.1603\sqrt{1 + \frac{1}{5} + \frac{(3-2)^2}{4}} = 2.6013$$

$$\hat{y}_p \pm t_{\alpha/2}s_{ind}$$

$$25 \pm 3.182(2.6013)$$

$$25 \pm 8.28$$

16.72 to 33.28

Using Excel's *DEVSQ* Function

The general expression for a confidence or prediction interval is:

Point Estimate +/- Margin of Error

Excel's Regression tool does not have an option for computing confidence and prediction intervals. However, formulas can be designed to compute these intervals along with the output provided by the Regression tool.

Confidence Interval Estimate

Enter Data: The data (cells B2:C6) and regression output (A8:I25) that were developed in Example 4 are used as a starting point here.

Enter Functions and Formulas: We enter the value 3 for x_p into cell F2. The AVERAGE function is used to compute $\bar{x}$ in cell F3. The formula =F2-F3 is entered into cell F4 to compute the value of $x_p - \bar{x}$. The formula =F4^2 is entered into cell F5 to compute the value of $(x_p - \bar{x})^2$. The DEVSQ function is used to compute $\Sigma(x_i - \bar{x})^2$ by entering the formula =DEVSQ(B2:B6) into cell F6.

We can now compute $s_{\hat{y}_p}^2$ by entering the formula =D20*(1/B15+F5/F6) into cell F7. We then enter the formula =SQRT(F7) into cell F8 to compute $s_{\hat{y}_p}$. To compute the t value required, we enter the formula =TINV(0.05,3) into cell F9. Finally, the margin of error is computed by entering the formula =F9*F8 into cell F10.

To compute the point estimate, we enter the formula =B24+B25*F2 into cell F11. The lower and upper limits of the 95% confidence interval are then computed by entering the formulas =F11-F10 and =F11+F10 into cells F12 and F13, respectively.

Formula Worksheet:

	D	E	F
1		CONFIDENCE INTERVAL	
2		Given value of x	3
3		xbar	=AVERAGE(B2:B6)
4		x-xbar	=F2-F3
5		(x-xbar)sq	=F4^2
6		Sum of (x-xbar)sq	=DEVSQ(B2:B6)
7		Var of yhat	=D20*(1/B15+F5/F6)
8		Stdev of yhat	=SQRT(F7)
9		t Value	=TINV(0.05,3)
10		Margin of Error	=F9*F8
11		Point Estimate	=B24+B25*F2
12		Lower Limit	=F11-F10
13		Upper Limit	=F11+F10

We see in the resulting worksheet below that the 95% confidence interval estimate of the mean number of cars sold when 3 TV ads are run is 20.39 to 29.61 cars.

Value Worksheet:

	D	E	F
1		CONFIDENCE INTERVAL	
2		Given value of x	3
3		xbar	2.0
4		x-xbar	1.0
5		(x-xbar)sq	1.0
6		Sum of (x-xbar)sq	4.0
7		Variance of yhat	2.1000
8		Stdev of yhat	1.4491
9		t Value	3.1824
10		Margin of Error	4.6118
11		Point Estimate	25.0
12		Lower Limit	20.39
13		Upper Limit	29.61

Prediction Interval Estimate

Enter Functions and Formulas: To compute $s_{ind}^2 = s^2 + s_{\hat{y}_p}^2$ we enter the formula =D20+F7 into cell I2. In cell I3 we enter the formula =SQRT(I2) to compute s_{ind}. To compute the margin of error the formula =F9*I3 is entered into cell I4. The formulas =F11-I4 and =F11+I4 are entered into cells I5 and I6 respectively to compute the lower and upper limits..

Formula Worksheet:

	H	I
1	PREDICTION INTERVAL	
2	Var of yind	=D20+F7
3	Stdev of yind	=SQRT(I2)
4	Margin of Error	=F9*I3
5	Lower Limit	=F11-I4
6	Upper Limit	=F11+I4

We see in the resulting worksheet below that the 95% prediction interval estimate for the number of cars sold when 3 TV ads run is 16.72 to 33.28 cars.

Value Worksheet:

	H	I
1	PREDICTION INTERVAL	
2	Var of yind	6.76667
3	Stdev of yind	2.60128
4	Margin of Error	8.27844
5	Lower Limit	16.72
6	Upper Limit	33.28

EXAMPLE 6

Residual Analysis

Refer to the Reed Auto problem in Example 1. Develop a plot of the residuals against the independent variable, number of TV ads run. Do the assumptions about the error terms seem to be satisfied?

SOLUTION 6

Using Excel's *Regression* Tool for Residual Plot

The steps outlined earlier in Example 4 to obtain the regression output are performed with one change. When the Regression dialog box appears, we must also select the **Residual Plot** option. The output will include two new items:
- a plot of the residuals against the independent variable, and
- a list of predicted values of *y* and the corresponding residual values.

Residual Plot:

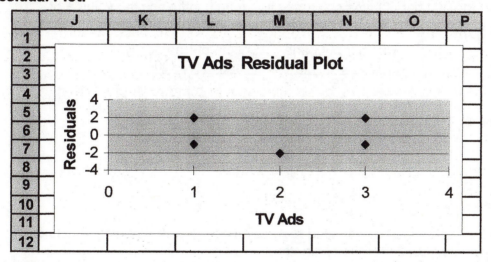

Residual Ouput:

	A	B	C
28			
29	RESIDUAL OUTPUT		
30			
31	*Observation*	*Predicted Cars Sold*	*Residuals*
32	1	15	-1
33	2	25	-1
34	3	20	-2
35	4	15	2
36	5	25	2

If the assumption that the variance of the error term is the same for all values of x, the residual plot should give an overall impression of a horizontal band of points, which is what we see in the Residual Plot above.

On the other hand, if the absolute value of the residuals is greater for larger values of x, the assumption of a constant variance of ε is violated. Fortunately, this is not true here. We see that when x is smallest (15) the error is 2 and when x is the largest (25) the error is 2 again. We conclude that the assumed regression model is an adequate representation of the relationship between the number of TV ads run and the number of cars sold.

EXERCISES

EXERCISE 1

Estimated Regression Equation

Connie Harris, in charge of office supplies at First Capital Mortgage Corp., would like to predict the quantity of paper used in the office photocopying machines per month. She believes that the number of loans originated in a month influence the volume of photocopying performed. She has compiled the following recent monthly data:

Number of Loans Originated in Month	Sheets of Photocopy Paper Used (000's)
45	22
25	13
50	24
60	25
40	21
25	16
35	18
40	25

a) Develop the least-squares estimated regression equation that relates sheets of photocopy paper used to loans originated.

b) Use the regression equation developed in part (a) to forecast the amount of paper used in a month when 42 loan originations are expected.

EXERCISE 2

Estimated Regression Equation

Four months ago, the Bank Drug Company introduced Jeffrey William brand designer bandages. Advertised using the slogan, "What the best dressed cuts are wearing", weekly sales for this period (in 1000's) have been as follows:

Week	Sales	Week	Sales	Week	Sales
1	12.8	7	20.6	12	23.8
2	14.6	8	18.5	13	25.1
3	15.2	9	19.9	14	24.7
4	16.1	10	23.6	15	26.5
5	15.8	11	24.2	16	28.9
6	17.2				

a) Plot a graph of sales vs. weeks. Does linear trend appear reasonable?

b) Assuming linear trend, forecast sales for weeks 17, 18, 19, and 20.

EXERCISE 3

Estimated Regression Equation

At a local car dealership the following is a record of sales for the past 12 months:

Month	Sales	Month	Sales
Jan	36	Jul	25
Feb	34	Aug	22
Mar	28	Sep	26
Apr	30	Oct	22
May	27	Nov	21
Jun	24	Dec	19

a) Using the method of least squares, determine a trend line for forecasting future sales.

b) Using your model in part (a), determine how long it will be before zero sales are forecasted.

c) Consider your answer to part (b). What will be the forecasted sales for the month after that? Does this make sense? Comment on the validity of the model. What assumption about the model appears to be in error?

EXERCISE 4

Estimated Regression Equation

Scott Bell Builders would like to predict the total number of labor hours spent framing a house based on the square footage of the house. The following data has been compiled on ten houses recently built.

Square Footage (100's)	Framing Labor Hours	Square Footage (100's)	Framing Labor Hours
20	195	27	225
21	170	29	240
23	220	31	225
23	200	32	275
26	230	35	260

a) Develop the least-squares estimated regression equation that relates framing labor hours to house square footage.

b) Use the regression equation developed in part (a) to predict framing labor hours when the house size is 3350 square feet.

EXERCISE 5

Coefficient of Determination and Correlation Coefficient

Refer to the First Capital Mortgage Corp. problem in Exercise 1.

a) Compute SSE, SST, and SSR.

b) Compute the coefficient of determination r^2. Comment on the goodness of fit.

c) Compute the correlation coefficient.

EXERCISE 6

Testing for Significance

Refer to the First Capital Mortgage Corp. problem in Exercise 1.

a) Compute the mean square error MSE.

b) Compute the standard error of the estimate.

c) Compute the estimated standard deviation of b_1.

d) Use the t test to test the following hypotheses ($\alpha = .05$):

e) Develop a 95% confidence interval estimate for β_1 to test the hypotheses in part (d).

f) Use the F test to test the hypotheses in part (d) at a .05 level of significance. Present the results in an analysis of variance table format.

EXERCISE 7

Interpretation of Excel's Regression Output

Refer to the Scott Bell Builders problem in Exercise 4. Use Excel's Regression tool to perform a complete regression analysis. Interpret the output.

EXERCISE 8

Confidence and Prediction Interval Estimates

Refer to the First Capital Mortgage Corp. problem in Exercise 1.

a) Develop a 95% confidence interval estimate of the mean number of sheets of paper used when 38 mortgages are originated.

b) Develop a 95% prediction interval estimate for the number of sheets of paper used when 38 mortgages are originated.

EXERCISE 9

Residual Analysis

Refer to the First Capital Mortgage Corp. problem in Exercise 1. Develop a plot of the residuals against the independent variable, number of mortgages originated. Do the assumptions about the error terms seem to be satisfied?

SELF-TEST

TRUE/FALSE

____ 1. Rejecting the null hypothesis H_0: $\beta_1 = 0$ as the result of a t test enables us to conclude that a cause-and-effect relationship is present between x and y.

____ 2. In the context of simple linear regression, the t test and the F test provide the same conclusion regarding β_1.

____ 3. Residuals represent the difference between the actual y values and the mean of the y values.

____ 4. A correlation coefficient (r) value of -1 indicates a perfect linear relationship between x and y.

____ 5. If the sign of the sample correlation coefficient is negative, we know the estimated regression equation has a negative slope.

FILL-IN-THE-BLANK

1. The _____ is a measure of the strength of the linear relationship between two variables.

2. The interval estimate of the mean value of *y* for a given value of *x* is the _____ interval estimate..

3. A scatter diagram is constructed with the values of the _____ variable on the horizontal axis.

4. In every ANOVA table the total sum of squares is the sum of the regression sum of squares and the _____.

5. The _____ variable is the variable doing the predicting or explaining.

MULTIPLE CHOICE

____ 1. The proportion of the variation in the dependent variable y that is explained by the estimated regression equation is measured by the
   a) correlation coefficient
   b) standard error of the estimate
   c) coefficient of determination
   d) confidence interval estimate

____ 2. The least squares criterion is
   a) min $\sum (x_i - y_i)^2$
   b) min $\sum (y_i - \bar{y})^2$
   c) min $(\sum y_i - \hat{y}_i)^2$
   d) min $\sum (y_i - \hat{y}_i)$

____ 3. In a residual plot that does not suggest we should challenge the assumptions of our regression model, we would expect to see
   a) a horizontal band of points centered near zero
   b) a widening band of points
   c) a band of points having a slope consistent with that of the regression equation
   d) a parabolic band of points

____ 4. The difference between the observed value of the dependent variable and the value predicted by using the estimated regression equation is the
   a) standard error
   b) residual
   c) prediction interval
   d) variance

____ 5. As the goodness of fit for the estimated regression equation increases,
   a) the absolute value of the regression equation's slope increases
   b) the value of the regression equation's y intercept decreases
   c) the value of the coefficient of determination increases
   d) the value of the correlation coefficient increases

ANSWERS

EXERCISES

1) a) $\hat{y} = 7.5 + .325x$
   b) $\hat{y} = 21,150$ sheets.

2) a) Yes
   b) Week 17: 29.0; Week 18: 30.0;
      Week 19: 31.0; Week 20: 32.0

3) a) $F_t = 34.80 - 1.329t$
   b) 26 months
   c) After 27 months sales will be approximately -1 cars; this is clearly impossible; the assumption of a continued linear decline is inappropriate.

4) a) $\hat{y} = 80.8757 + 5.3605(x)$
   b) $\hat{y} = 260.45245$ hours

5) a) 32.38, 138.00, 105.63
   b) $r^2 = .7654$; very good fit
   c) $r = .8749$

6) a) 5.3958
   b) 2.3229
   c) 0.0735
   d) p-value = .0045; Reject H_0
   e) .145 to .505; Reject H_0
   f) $F = 19.575$

7) $r^2 = .7608$; very good fit
   p-value = .001; Reject H_0
   Confid. Interval = 2.91 to 7.81; Reject H_0

8) a) 17.83 to 21.87
   b) 13.82 to 25.88

9) Residual range: -2.6 to 4.5;
   Approx. horizontal band of pts; yes

TRUE/FALSE

1) False
2) True
3) False
4) True
5) True

FILL-IN-THE-BLANK

1) correlation coefficient
2) confidence
3) independent
4) error sum of squares
5) independent

MULTIPLE CHOICE

1) c
2) c
3) a
4) b
5) c

CHAPTER 13

Multiple Regression

Multiple Regression Model

Least Squares Method

Multiple Coefficient of Determination

Model Assumptions

Testing for Significance

Using the Estimated Regression Equation
for Estimation and Prediction

Qualitative Independent Variables

LEARNING OBJECTIVES

1. Understand how multiple regression analysis can be used to develop relationships involving one dependent variable and several independent variables.

2. Be able to interpret the coefficients in a multiple regression analysis.

3. Know the assumptions necessary to conduct statistical tests involving the hypothesized regression model.

4. Understand the role of Excel in performing multiple regression analysis.

5. Be able to interpret and use Excel's Regression tool output to develop the estimated regression equation.

6. Be able to determine how good a fit is provided by the estimated regression equation.

7. Be able to test for the significance of the regression equation.

8. Understand how multicollinearity affects multiple regression analysis.

REVIEW

Regression Analysis
- Managerial decisions often are based on the relationship between two or more variables.
- A statistical procedure called regression analysis can be used to develop an equation showing how the variables are related.
- The variable being predicted is called the dependent variable.
- The variable(s) being used to predict the value of the dependent variable are called the independent variables.

Multiple Regression
- Multiple regression analysis is the study of how one dependent variable is related to two or more independent variables.
- Multiple regression analysis enables us to consider more factors and thus obtain better estimates than are possible with simple linear regression.

Multiple Regression Model
- The equation that describes how y is related to the independent variables $x_1, x_2, \ldots x_p$ and an error term is called the regression model.
- The multiple regression model is:
$$y = \beta_0 + \beta_1 x_1 + \beta_2 x_2 + \ldots + \beta_p x_p + \varepsilon$$
where: p = number of independent variables
- $\beta_0, \beta_1, \ldots \beta_p$ are re referred to as the parameters of the model.
- The error term ε accounts for the variability in y that cannot be explained by the linear effect of the p independent variables.

Multiple Regression Equation

- One of the assumptions made here is that the mean or expected value of ε is zero.
- As a result of the above assumption, the mean or expected value of y, denoted $E(y)$, is equal to $\beta_0 + \beta_1 x_1 + \beta_2 x_2 + \ldots + \beta_p x_p$.
- The multiple regression equation is:

$$E(y) = \beta_0 + \beta_1 x_1 + \beta_2 x_2 + \ldots + \beta_p x_p$$

- The values of β_0, β_1, β_2, ... β_p are not known, so we take a simple random sample and compute sample statistics b_0, b_1, b_2, ... b_p that are used as point estimators.

Estimated Multiple Regression Equation

- The estimated multiple regression equation is:

$$\hat{y} = b_0 + b_1 x_1 + b_2 x_2 + \ldots + b_p x_p$$

where: $\hat{y}$ = estimated value of the dependent variable

b_0, b_1, b_2, ... b_p are the estimates of β_0, β_1, β_2, ... β_p

Least Squares Method

- The least squares method is a procedure for using sample data to compute an estimated regression equation, specifically values for b_0, b_1, b_2, ... b_p.
- Values are found for b_0, b_1, b_2, ... b_p that minimize the sum of the squares of the deviations between the observed values of y_i and the estimated values $\hat{y}_i$.
- The least squares criterion is:

$$\min \sum (y_i - \hat{y}_i)^2$$

where: y_i = observed value of the dependent variable for the i th observation
$\hat{y}_i$ = estimated value of the dependent variable for the i th observation

- The formulas for the regression coefficients b_0, b_1, b_2, ... b_p involve the use of matrix algebra. We will rely on Excel to perform the calculations.

Excel's Regression Tool

- Excel's Regression Tool in its Data Analysis package performs a complete regression analysis, including statistical tests of significance.
- The resulting Summary Output has three sections:
  - Regression Statistics
  - ANOVA (Analysis of Variance)
  - Estimated Regression Equation Output
- The Regression Statistics section contains summary statistics, including the coefficient of determination, sample correlation coefficient, standard deviation of the error term ε, and number of observations.
- The ANOVA section is a relatively standard ANOVA table showing, most importantly, the test statistic F and the critical value of F.
- The Estimated Regression Equation Output section (it's not labeled) provides information about the y intercept and slope of the estimated regression line. This information can be used to conduct hypothesis tests for significance and develop confidence interval estimates.

Note on Interpretation of Coefficients
- In multiple regression, we must be careful when interpreting the regression coefficients.
- We interpret each coefficient as follows: b_i represents an estimate of the change in y corresponding to a one-unit increase in x_i when all other independent variables are held constant.

Multiple Coefficient of Determination
- The multiple coefficient of determination provides a measure of the goodness of fit for the estimated regression equation.
- R^2 is the proportion of the variability in the dependent variable that can be explained by the estimated regression equation.
- The multiple coefficient of determination, R^2, is computed using the same formula as is used in simple regression:

$$R^2 = SSR/SST$$

where:

$$SST = \sum(y_i - \bar{y})^2 = \text{total sum of squares}$$

$$SSR = \sum(\hat{y}_i - \bar{y})^2 = \text{sum of squares due to regression}$$

$$SSE = \sum(y_i - \hat{y}_i)^2 = \text{sum of squares due to error}$$

Relationship Among SST, SSR, and SSE
- SST = SSR + SSE
- SSR can be thought of as the explained portion of SST.
- SSE can be thought of as the unexplained portion of SST.
- If the regression equation provided a perfect fit, $y_i - \hat{y}_i$ would be zero for each observation, resulting in SSE = 0 and SSR/SST = 1.
- The ratio SSR/SST, which will be between 0 and 1, is used to evaluate the goodness of fit for the estimated regression equation.

Adjusted Multiple Coefficient of Determination
- If a variable is added to the model, $R2$ becomes larger even if the variable added is not statistically significant.
- The adjusted multiple coefficient of determination compensates for the number of independent variables in the model.
- The adjusted multiple coefficient of determination is computed as follows:

$$R_a^2 = 1 - (1 - R^2)\frac{n-1}{n-p-1}$$

where: n = number of observations
p = number of independent variables

Assumptions About the Error Term ε
- The error ε is a random variable with mean or expected value of zero. $E(\varepsilon) = 0$.
- The variance of ε is denoted by σ^2 and is the same for all values of the independent variables.
- The values of ε are independent.
- The error ε is a normally distributed random variable reflecting the deviation between the y value and the expected value of y given by $\beta_0 + \beta_1 x_1 + \beta_2 x_2 + \ldots + \beta_p x_p$.

Testing for Significance

- In multiple regression, the t and the F test have different purposes.
- The F test determines whether there is a significant relationship between the dependent variable and the set of all independent variables. (a test for overall significance)
- A separate t test is conducted for each of the independent variables. (a test for individual significance)

  - ### F Test
    - Hypotheses:
      $H_0: \beta_1 = \beta_2 = \ldots = \beta_p = 0$
      H_a: One or more of the parameters is not equal to zero
    - Test Statistic:
      $F = MSR/MSE$
    - Rejection Rule:
      Using test statistic: Reject H_0 if $F \geq F_\alpha$
      where F_α is based on an F distribution with p d.f. in the numerator and $(n - p - 1)$ d.f. in the denominator.
      Using p-value: Reject H_0 if p-value $\leq \alpha$

  - ### t Test
    - Hypotheses:
      $H_0 : \beta_i = 0$
      $H_a : \beta_i \neq 0$
    - Test Statistic:

      $$t = \frac{b_i}{s_{b_i}}$$

    - Rejection Rule:
      Using test statistic: Reject H_0 if $t \leq -t_{\alpha/2}$ or $t \geq t_{\alpha/2}$
      where $t_{\alpha/2}$ is based on a t distribution
      with $(n - p - 1)$ degrees of freedom
      Using p-value: Reject H_0 if p-value $\leq \alpha$

Multicollinearity

- Most independent variables in a multiple regression problem are correlated to some degree with one another.
- Multicollinearity refers to the correlation among the independent variables.
- When the independent variables are highly correlated, it is not possible to determine the separate effect of any particular independent variable on the dependent variable.
- Every attempt should be made to avoid including independent variables that are highly correlated.
- Multicollinearity is a potential problem if the absolute value of the sample correlation coefficient exceeds .7 for any two independent variables.

Point Estimation

- Estimating the mean value of y and an individual value of y in multiple regression is similar to that in simple regression. The given values of each of the independent variables are substituted into the estimated regression equation and the corresponding value of $\hat{y}$ is the point estimate.

Interval Estimation
- The estimated multiple regression equation can be used to make two interval estimates:
  - a confidence interval estimate of the mean value of *y*
  - a prediction interval estimate of an individual value of *y*
- The formulas required for these estimates are beyond the scope of the textbook.
- Excel's Regression tool does not have this capability, but the PredInt.xls macro included on the data disk will produce these estimates.

Qualitative Independent Variables
- A qualitative variable can be represented as one or more quantitative variables.
- In this case, the quantitative variable is called a dummy or indicator variable.
- If a qualitative variable has *k* levels, *k* − 1 dummy variables are required.
- Each dummy variable is coded as 0 or 1.
- A qualitative variable with 3 levels - high, medium, and low – can be represented by 2 dummy variables, x_1 and x_2.
  - High could be coded $x_1 = 0$ and $x_2 = 0$.
  - Medium could be coded $x_1 = 1$ and $x_2 = 0$.
  - Low could be coded $x_1 = 0$ and $x_2 = 1$.
- Care must be taken in defining and interpreting the dummy variables.

KEY CONCEPTS

CONCEPT	EXAMPLES	EXERCISES
Estimated Multiple Regression Equation	①	1
Interpretation of Coefficients	2	2
Coefficient of Determination	③	3
F Test for Overall Significance	④	4
t Test for Individual Significance	④	4
Qualitative Variables	⑤	5

◯ Excel Used

EXAMPLES

EXAMPLE 1

Estimated Multiple Regression Equation

Cortland Software, Inc. collected data for a sample of 20 computer programmers. A suggestion was made that regression analysis could be used to determine if salary was related to the years of experience and the score on the firm's programmer aptitude test.

The years of experience, score on the aptitude test, and corresponding annual salary ($1000s) for a sample of 20 programmers are shown below.

Experience	Test Score	Salary	Experience	Test Score	Salary
4	78	24.0	9	88	38.0
7	100	43.0	2	73	26.6
1	86	23.7	10	75	36.2
5	82	34.3	5	81	31.6
8	86	35.8	6	74	29.0
10	84	38.0	8	87	34.0
0	75	22.2	4	79	30.1
1	80	23.1	6	94	33.9
6	83	30.0	3	70	28.2
6	91	33.0	3	89	30.0

Suppose we believe that salary (y) is related to the years of experience (x_1) and the score on the programmer aptitude test (x_2) by the following regression model:

$$y = b_0 + b_1x_1 + b_2x_2 + e$$

where: y = annual salary ($000) for a programmer
x_1 = years of programming experience
x_2 = score on programmer aptitude test

Use years of experience and test score as two independent variables and salary as the dependent variable.

a) What is the estimated multiple regression equation?

b) Estimate the salary for a programmer with 4.5 years of experience and a score of 82 on the aptitude test.

SOLUTION 1

Using Excel's *Regression* Tool for Multiple Regression

To develop the estimated multiple regression equation, we will use Excel's Regression tool. (The calculations involve matrix algebra and are beyond the scope of the textbook.)

Enter Data: The appropriate labels are entered into cells A1:D1 of the worksheet. To identify each of the 20 observations, we enter the number 1 through 20 into cells A2:A21. The sample data are entered into cells B2:D21.

Data Worksheet:

	A	B	C	D	E	F
1	Program-mer	Exper-ience	Test Score	Salary ($1000)		
2	1	4	78	24.0		
3	2	7	100	43.0		
4	3	1	86	23.7		
5	4	5	82	34.3		
6	5	8	86	35.8		
7	6	10	84	38.0		
8	7	0	75	22.2		
9	8	1	80	23.1		

Note: Rows 10-21 are not shown.

Enter Functions and Formulas: There are none to enter.

Apply Tools: The following steps describe how to use the Regression tool for multiple regression analysis:

Performing the Multiple Regression Analysis

    Step 1 Select the **Tools** menu
    Step 2 Choose **Data Analysis** option
    Step 3 Choose **Regression** from the list of Analysis Tools

Regression Dialog Box:

Regression [?][X]

Input
- Input Y Range: $D$1:$D$21
- Input X Range: $B$1:$C$21
- ☑ Labels ☐ Constant is Zero
- ☑ Confidence Level 95 %

OK
Cancel
Help

Output options
- ⦿ Output Range: A24
- ○ New Worksheet Ply:
- ○ New Workbook

Residuals
- ☐ Residuals ☐ Residual Plots
- ☐ Standardized Residuals ☐ Line Fit Plots

Normal Probability
- ☐ Normal Probability Plots

Regression Equation Output:

	A	B	C	D	E	F	G
38							
39		Coefficients	Std. Error	t Stat	P-value	Lower 95%	Upper 95%
40	Intercept	3.173936	6.156067	0.5155786	0.612789	-9.814248	16.1621201
41	Experience	1.403902	0.198567	7.0701733	1.88E-06	0.984962	1.822843
42	Test Score	0.250885	0.077354	3.2433363	0.00478	0.087682	0.414089
43							

Note: Rows 1-37 are not shown.

a) The values for b_0, b_1, and b_2 in the estimated multiple regression equation are found in cells B40:B42 of the Excel output shown above.

$$\hat{y} = 3.174 + 1.404x_1 + 0.2509x_2$$

In other words, Estimated Salary = 3.174 + 1.404(Exper) + 0.2509(Score). Note that estimated salary will be in thousands of dollars.

b) The estimated salary $\hat{y}$ for a programmer with 4.5 years of experience and a test score of 82 is:

$$\hat{y} = 3.174 + 1.404(4.5) + 0.2509(82) = 30.0658 \text{ or } \$30,065.80$$

EXAMPLE 2

Interpretation of Coefficients

In Example 1, the following estimated multiple regression equation was presented.

$$\hat{y} = 3.174 + 1.404x_1 + 0.2509x_2$$

where: $\hat{y}$ = estimated annual salary ($000) for a programmer
x_1 = years of programming experience
x_2 = score on programmer aptitude test

Interpret the coefficients b_1 and b_2 in this estimated multiple regression equation.

SOLUTION 2

Interpretation of coefficients:

b_1: With each additional year of experience, salary is expected to increase by $1,404.00, when the aptitude test score is held constant.

b_2: With each additional point scored on the aptitude test, salary is expected to increase by $250.90, when the years of experience is held constant.

EXAMPLE 3

Multiple Coefficient of Determination

In Example 1, the following estimated multiple regression equation was presented.

$$\hat{y} = 3.174 + 1.404x_1 + 0.2509x_2$$

where: $\hat{y}$ = estimated annual salary ($000) for a programmer
x_1 = years of programming experience
x_2 = score on programmer aptitude test

a) Compute the multiple coefficient of determination R^2 using the SSR and SST values provided by Excel's Regression tool. Compare your answer with the R^2 value provided by Excel.

b) Compute the adjusted coefficient of determination R_a^2. Compare your answer with the R_a^2 value provided by Excel.

c) Comment on the goodness of fit. Does the model appear to explain a large amount of variability in the data?

SOLUTION 3

The Summary Output and ANOVA Table portions of the Excel Regression output are relevant here.

Summary Output:

	A	B	C	D	E	F	G
23							
24	SUMMARY OUTPUT						
25							
26	*Regression Statistics*						
27	Multiple R	0.91333					
28	R Square	0.83418					
29	Adj. R Sq.	0.81467					
30	Std. Error	2.41876					

Note: Rows 1-22 are not shown.

ANOVA Table:

	A	B	C	D	E	F	G
32							
33	ANOVA						
34		*df*	*SS*	*MS*	*F*	*Signif. F*	
35	Regression	2	500.329	250.16	42.7601	2.3E-07	
36	Residual	17	99.457	5.8504			
37	Total	19	599.786				
38							

Note: Rows 1-31 are not shown.

a) The SSR and SST values appear in cells C35 and C37 of the ANOVA Table above.

$$R^2 = SSR/SST = 500.329/599.786 = .83418$$

This result agrees with the R^2 value appearing in cell B28 of the Summary Output above.

b) $R_a^2 = 1 - (1 - R^2)\dfrac{n-1}{n-p-1}$

where n = number of observations, and p = number of independent variables.

$$R_a^2 = 1 - (1 - .83418)\dfrac{20-1}{20-2-1} = .81467$$

This result agrees with the R_a^2 value appearing in cell B29 of the Summary Output above.

c) Goodness of Fit: Based on the R^2 value, 83.42% of the variability in programmer salaries is explained by the estimated multiple regression equation with experience and test score as the independent variables. Even after adjusting the coefficient of determination for the number of independent variables in the model, the % of variability explained by the model is high (81.47%). On this basis (without performing residual analysis) we can say that the estimated multiple regression equation fits well.

EXAMPLE 4

Testing for Significance

In Example 1, the following estimated multiple regression equation was presented.

$$\hat{y} = 3.174 + 1.404x_1 + 0.2509x_2$$

where: $\hat{y}$ = estimated annual salary ($000) for a programmer
x_1 = years of programming experience
x_2 = score on programmer aptitude test

a) Compute the mean square due to regression (MSR) and mean square error (MSE) using the SSR and SSE values provided by Excel.

b) Compute F and perform the appropriate F test. Use $\alpha = .05$.

c) Perform a t test for the significance of β_1. Use $\alpha = .05$.

d) Perform a t test for the significance of β_2. Use $\alpha = .05$.

SOLUTION 4

The Summary Output and ANOVA Table portions of the Excel output are relevant here.

a) MSR = SSR/p = 500.329/2 = 250.1645
MSE = SSE/($n - p - 1$) = 99.457/(20 – 2 – 1) = 5.8504
where: n = number of observations, and p = number of independent variables

b) F = MSR/MSE = 250.1645/5.8504 = 42.7602

   F Test for Overall Significance:

   $H_0 : \beta_1 = \beta_2 = 0$
   $H_a : \beta_1$ and/or β_2 is/are not equal to zero
   Reject H_0 if p-value $\leq \alpha$ or $F \geq F_\alpha$ (where F_α is based on p degrees of freedom in the numerator and $n - p - 1$ degrees of freedom in the denominator)

   F_α = 3.59 is found in the Appendix of the textbook.
   p-value = 2.3E-07 is found in cell F35 of the ANOVA Table output

   We reject H_0. F = 42.7602 > 3.59 and p-value = 2.3E-07 < .05.
   β_1 and/or β_2 is/are not equal to zero.

c) t Test for Significance of β_1

$H_0 : \beta_1 = 0$
$H_a : \beta_1 \neq 0$

Reject H_0 if $t \leq -t_{\alpha/2}$ or $t \geq t_{\alpha/2}$ or p-value $\leq \alpha$
where $t_{\alpha/2}$ is based on a t distribution with $n - p - 1$ degrees of freedom

$$t = \frac{b_1}{s_{b_1}} = 1.4039/.1986 = 7.0702$$

where $s_{b_1} = .1986$ is found in cell C41 of the Regression Equation output

$t_{.025} = 2.11$ is found in Appendix B of the textbook (using 17 deg. of freedom)
p-value $= 1.9E{-}06$ is found in cell E41 of the Regression Equation output

Using the t or p-value approach, we reject H_0.
$(7.0702 > 2.11$ and $1.9E{-}06 < .05)$
β_1 is not equal to zero.

d) t Test for Significance of β_2

$H_0 : \beta_2 = 0$
$H_a : \beta_2 \neq 0$

Reject H_0 if $t \leq -t_{\alpha/2}$ or $t \geq t_{\alpha/2}$ or p-value $\leq \alpha$
where $t_{\alpha/2}$ is based on a t distribution with $n - p - 1$ degrees of freedom

$$t = \frac{b_2}{s_{b_2}} = 0.25089/.07735 = 3.2436$$

where $s_{b_2} = .07735$ is found in cell C42 of the Regression Equation output

$t_{.025} = 2.11$ is found in Appendix B of the textbook (using 17 deg. of freedom)
p-value $= .00478$ is found in cell E42 of the Regression Equation output

$t = 3.2436 > 2.11$ and p-value $= .00478 < .05$.
We reject H_0. β_2 is not equal to zero.

EXAMPLE 5

Qualitative Variables

Refer again to the Cortland Software problem in Example 1. As an extension of the problem, suppose that management also believes that the annual salary is related to whether the individual has a graduate degree in computer science or information systems.

The years of experience, the score on the programmer aptitude test, whether or not the individual has a relevant graduate degree, and the annual salary ($1000) for each of the sampled 20 programmers are shown below.

Exper.	Test Score	Degree	Salary	Exper.	Test Score	Degree	Salary
4	78	No	24.0	9	88	Yes	38.0
7	100	Yes	43.0	2	73	No	26.6
1	86	No	23.7	10	75	Yes	36.2
5	82	Yes	34.3	5	81	No	31.6
8	86	Yes	35.8	6	74	No	29.0
10	84	Yes	38.0	8	87	Yes	34.0
0	75	No	22.2	4	79	No	30.1
1	80	No	23.1	6	94	Yes	33.9
6	83	No	30.0	3	70	No	28.2
6	91	Y	33.0	3	89	No	30.0

a) Develop the estimated multiple regression equation to predict the programmer's salary given the number of years of experience, score on the aptitude test, and presence or absence of a relevant graduate degree.

b) Interpret the coefficients of the regression equation.

c) Estimate the salary for a programmer with 5 years of experience, a score of 88 on the aptitude test, and a relevant graduate degree.

SOLUTION 5

Using Excel's *Regression* Tool for Multiple Regression

a) $\hat{y} = b_0 + b_1x_1 + b_2x_2 + b_3x_3$

where: $\hat{y}$ = estimated annual salary ($000)
x_1 = years of programming experience
x_2 = score on programmer aptitude test
x_3 = 0 if individual <u>does not</u> have a graduate degree
    1 if individual <u>does</u> have a graduate degree

To develop the estimated multiple regression equation, we will use Excel's Regression tool. (The calculations involve matrix algebra and are beyond the scope of the textbook.)

Enter Data: We can modify the worksheet we developed for Example 1. A new column for the Graduate Degree data is inserted between the columns containing the Test Score and Salary data.

Enter Functions and Formulas: There are none to enter.

Data Worksheet:

	A	B	C	D	E	F
1	Program-mer	Exper-ience	Test Score	Grad. Degree	Salary ($1000)	
2	1	4	78	0	24.0	
3	2	7	100	1	43.0	
4	3	1	86	0	23.7	
5	4	5	82	1	34.3	
6	5	8	86	1	35.8	
7	6	10	84	1	38.0	
8	7	0	75	0	22.2	
9	8	1	80	0	23.1	

Note: Rows 10-21 are not shown.

Apply Tools: The following steps describe how to use the Regression tool for multiple regression analysis:

Step 1 Select the **Tools** menu
Step 2 Choose **Data Analysis** option
Step 3 Choose **Regression** from the list of Analysis Tools
Step 4 When the Regression dialog box appears:
Enter E1:E21 in the **Input Y Range** box
Enter B1:D21 in the **Input X Range** box
Select **Labels**
Select **Confidence Level**
Enter 95 (for now) in the **Confidence Level** box
Select **Output Range** and enter A24 in the **Output Range** box
Click **OK**

Regression Equation Output:

	A	B	C	D	E	F	G	H	I
38									
39		Coeffic.	Std. Err.	t Stat	P-value	Lo. 95%	Up. 95%	Lo. 95.0%	Up. 95.0%
40	Intercept	7.9448	7.3808	1.0764	0.2977	-7.7017	23.5914	-7.7017	23.5914
41	Experience	1.1476	0.2976	3.8561	0.0014	0.5167	1.7785	0.5167	1.7785
42	Test Score	0.1969	0.0899	2.1905	0.0436	0.0063	0.3875	0.0063	0.3875
43	Grad. Degr.	2.2804	1.9866	1.1479	0.2679	-1.9310	6.4918	-1.9310	6.4918
44									

The values for b_0, b_1, b_2, and b_3 in the estimated multiple regression equation are found in cells B40:B43 of the Excel output shown above.

$$\hat{y} = 7.945 + 1.148x_1 + 0.197x_2 + 2.280x_3$$

That is, Estimated Salary = 7.945 + 1.148(Exper) + 0.197(Score) + 2.280(Degree). Note that estimated salary will be in thousands of dollars.

b) Interpretation of coefficients:

   b_1: With each additional year of experience, salary is expected to increase by
         $1,148.00, when the aptitude test score is held constant.
   b_2: With each additional point scored on the aptitude test, salary is expected to
         increase by $197.00, when the years of experience is held constant.
   B_3: The salary of a programmer with a relevant graduate degree is, on average,
         $2,280.00 higher than the salary of a programmer without the advanced degree.

c) The estimated salary $\hat{y}$ for a programmer with 5 years of experience, a test score of 88,
   and a relevant graduate degree is:
$$\hat{y} = 7.945 + 1.148(5) + 0.197(88) + 2.280(1) = 33.30100 \text{ or } \$33,301.00$$

EXERCISES

EXERCISE 1

Estimated Multiple Regression Equation

Tony Zamora, a real estate investor, has just moved to Clarksville and wants to learn about the city's residential real estate market. Tony has randomly selected 25 house-for-sale listings from the Sunday newspaper and collected the data listed below.

a) Use square footage, number of bedrooms, and number of bathrooms as three
   independent variables and selling price as the dependent variable. What is the
   estimated multiple regression equation?

b) A house in Clarksville is advertised as having 2,600 square feet, four bedrooms, and
   three bathrooms. Use the results in part (a) to predict the selling price for the house.

Segment of City	Selling Price ($000)	House Size (00 sq. ft.)	Number of Bedrooms	Number of Bathrooms	Garage Size (cars)
Northwest	290	21	4	2	2
South	95	11	2	1	0
Northeast	170	19	3	2	2
Northwest	375	38	5	4	3
West	350	24	4	3	2
South	125	10	2	2	0
West	310	31	4	4	2
West	275	25	3	2	2
Northwest	340	27	5	3	3
Northeast	215	22	4	3	2
Northwest	295	20	4	3	2
South	190	24	4	3	2
Northwest	385	36	5	4	3
West	430	32	5	4	2
South	185	14	3	2	1
South	175	18	4	2	2
Northeast	190	19	4	2	2
Northwest	330	29	4	4	3
West	405	33	5	4	3
Northeast	170	23	4	2	2
West	365	34	5	4	3
Northwest	280	25	4	2	2
South	135	17	3	1	1
Northeast	205	21	4	3	2
West	260	26	4	3	2

EXERCISE 2

Interpretation of Coefficients

Refer again to the Clarksville real estate problem in Exercise 1. Interpret the coefficients b_1, b_2, and b_3 in the estimated multiple regression equation.

a) How much does an additional 200 square feet add to the predicted selling price of a house? Assume this additional space will not be used for a bedroom or bathroom.

b) How much does an additional bedroom add to the predicted selling price of a home? Assume the new bedroom space will come, through remodeling, from existing space in the house.

c) How much does an additional bathroom add to the predicted selling price of a house? Assume the new bathroom space will come, through remodeling, from existing space in the house.

EXERCISE 3

Multiple Coefficient of Determination

Refer again to the Clarksville real estate problem in Exercise 1.

a) <u>Compute</u> the multiple coefficient of determination R^2 using the SSR and SST values provided by Excel's Regression tool. Compare your answer with the R^2 value provided by Excel.

b) <u>Compute</u> the adjusted coefficient of determination R_a^2. Compare your answer with the R_a^2 value provided by Excel.

c) Comment on the goodness of fit. Does the model appear to explain a large amount of variability in the data?

EXERCISE 4

Testing for Significance

Refer again to the Clarksville real estate problem in Exercise 1.

a) Compute the mean square due to regression (MSR) and mean square error (MSE) using the SSR and SSE values provided by Excel.

b) Compute F and perform the appropriate F test. Use $\alpha = .05$.

c) Perform a t test for the significance of β_1. Use $\alpha = .05$.

d) Perform a t test for the significance of β_2. Use $\alpha = .05$.

e) Perform a t test for the significance of β_3. Use $\alpha = .05$.

f) Does there appear to be a correlation among the independent variables?

EXERCISE 5

Qualitative Variables

Refer again to the Clarksville real estate problem in Exercise 1. As an extension of the problem, suppose that Tony Zamora also believes that the selling price of a house in Clarksville is related to the segment of the city in which the house is located.

a) Develop the estimated multiple regression equation to predict the selling price of a house given the square footage, number of bedrooms, number of bathrooms, and segment of the city in which it is located. (Introduce 3 dummy variables x_4, x_5, and x_6 in order to code city segments. That is, x_4, x_5, and $x_6 = 0,0,0$ for Northeast; x_4, x_5, and $x_6 = 1,0,0$ for Northwest; x_4, x_5, and $x_6 = 0,1,0$ for West; and x_4, x_5, and $x_6 = 0,0,1$ for South.)

b) Estimate the selling price of a house having 1800 square feet, 3 bedrooms, and 1.5 bathrooms and located in the South segment of Clarksville.

SELF-TEST

TRUE/FALSE

_____ 1. Rejecting the null hypothesis $H_0: \beta_1 = \beta_2 = \ldots = \beta_p = 0$ as the result of a F test enables us to conclude that the overall relationship between y and the set of independent variables is significant.

_____ 2. If a qualitative variable has k levels, $k + 1$ dummy variables are required.

_____ 3. Multiple regression analysis involves two or more dependent variables.

_____ 4. The value of the adjusted multiple coefficient of determination will always be greater than the value of the unadjusted multiple coefficient of determination.

_____ 5. Generally, if an independent variable is added to the multiple regression model, R^2 becomes larger even if the variable added is not statistically significant.

FILL-IN-THE-BLANK

1. The _____ can be interpreted as the proportion of the variability in the dependent variable that can be explained by the estimated multiple regression equation.

2. Correlation among the independent variables is known as _____.

3. The standardized residual plot is useful in identifying _____.

4. In every ANOVA table the total sum of squares is the sum of the regression sum of squares and the _____.

5. In multiple regression analysis, b_i represents an estimate of the change in y corresponding to a one-unit change in x_i when _____.

MULTIPLE CHOICE

_____ 1. The multiple coefficient of determination is computed as
     a) SSR/SSE
     b) SSE/SSR
     c) SSR/SST
     d) SSE/SST

_____ 2. The least squares criterion is
     a) $\min \sum (x_i - y_i)^2$
     b) $\min \sum (y_i - \bar{y})^2$
     c) $\min (\sum y_i - \hat{y}_i)^2$
     d) $\min \sum (y_i - \hat{y}_i)$

___ 3. In a residual plot that does <u>not</u> suggest we should challenge the assumptions of our regression model, we would expect to see
   a) a horizontal band of points centered near zero
   b) a widening band of points
   c) a band of points having a slope consistent with that of the regression equation
   d) a parabolic band of points

___ 4. The difference between the observed value of the dependent variable and the value predicted by using the estimated regression equation is the
   a) standard error
   b) residual
   c) prediction interval
   d) variance

___ 5. As the goodness of fit for the estimated multiple regression equation increases,
   a) the absolute value of the regression equation's slope increases
   b) the value of the regression equation's y intercept decreases
   c) the value of the coefficient of determination increases
   d) the value of the correlation coefficient increases

ANSWERS

EXERCISES

1)

	Coeffic.	Std. Error	t Stat	P-value
Intercept	-47.3416	44.34672	-1.06753	0.29785
Square Feet	6.020214	2.94446	2.044591	0.053633
Bedrooms	23.03526	20.8229	1.106247	0.281132
Bathrooms	27.02864	18.36005	1.472144	0.155811

a) $\hat{y} = -47.34160 + 6.020214x_1 + 23.03526x_2 + 27.02864x_3$ b) $282,410.92

2) a) b_1: With each additional 100 square feet, selling price is expected to increase by $6,020.21, when number of bedrooms and bathrooms are held constant. An additional 200 sq. ft. raises the estimated selling price by $12,040.42.
   b) b_2: With each additional bedroom, selling price is expected to increase by $23,035.26, when the square footage and number of bathrooms are held constant.
   c) b_3: With each additional bathroom, selling price is expected to increase by $27,028.64, when the square footage and number of bedrooms are held constant.

3)

Regression Statistics	
Multiple R	0.89813
R Square	0.806638
Adj. R Square	0.779015
Standard Error	44.94059
Observations	25

a) R^2 = SSR/SST = 176,931.2/219,344 = .806638

b) $R_a^2 = 1-(1-.806638)\dfrac{25-1}{25-3-1} = .779015$

c) Based on the R^2 value, 80.7% of the variability in house selling prices is explained by the estimated multiple regression equation with square footage, bedrooms, and bathrooms as the independent variables. After adjusting the coefficient of determination for the number of independent variables in the model, the % of variability explained by the model is still high (77.9%). On this basis we can say that the estimated multiple regression equation fits well.

4) a) MSR = SSR/p = 176,931.2/3 = 58,977.07
   MSE = SSE/($n-p-1$) = 42,412.79/(25 – 3 – 1) = 2,019.657

   b) F = MSR/MSE = 58,977.07/2,019.657 = 29.20153; F_α = 3.07; Reject H_0

   c) $t = \dfrac{b_1}{s_{b_1}}$ = 6.020214/2.94446 = 2.045; $t_{.025}$ = 2.080; Do **not** reject H_0

   β_1 is not statistically significant.

   d) $t = \dfrac{b_2}{s_{b_2}}$ = 23.03526/20.8229 = 1.106; $t_{.025}$ = 2.080; Do **not** reject H_0

   β_2 is not statistically significant.

   e) $t = \dfrac{b_3}{s_{b_3}}$ = 27.02864/18.36005 = 1.472; $t_{.025}$ = 2.080; Do **not** reject H_0

   β_3 is not statistically significant.

   f) Yes, because the F test indicates a relationship between the dependent variable and the set of independent variables. However, the t tests indicate no relationships between the dependent variable and the individual independent variables.

5) a) $\hat{y}$ = -2.0035 + .0042x_1 + 35.5549x_2 + 23.6697x_3 + 97.8948x_4 + 110.4917x_5 + 2.7117x_6

	Coeffic.	Std. Error	t Stat	P-value
Intercept	-2.0035	33.78591	-0.0593	0.953367
Square Feet	0.004212	1.954649	0.002155	0.998304
Bedrooms	35.55493	12.9314	2.749503	0.013186
Bathrooms	23.66965	10.83255	2.18505	0.04235
Northwest	97.89483	17.40063	5.625938	2.45E-05
West	110.4917	18.82655	5.868929	1.48E-05
South	2.7117	17.23321	0.157353	0.876718

b) $\hat{y}$ =-2.0035 + .0042(1800) + 35.5549(3) + 23.6697(1.5) + 2.7117(1) = $150,437.45

TRUE/FALSE

1) True
2) False
3) False
4) False
5) True

FILL-IN-THE-BLANK

1) multiple coefficient of determination
2) multicollinearity
3) outliers
4) error sum of squares
5) all other independent variables are held constant

MULTIPLE CHOICE

1) c
2) c
3) a
4) b
5) c

CHAPTER 14

Statistical Methods
For Quality Control

Statistical Process Control

Acceptance Sampling

LEARNING OBJECTIVES

1. Learn about the importance of quality control and how statistical methods can assist in the quality control process.

2. Learn about acceptance sampling procedures.

3. Know the difference between consumer's risk and producer's risk.

4. Be able to use the binomial probability distribution to develop acceptance sampling plans.

5. Know what is meant by multiple sampling plans.

6. Be able to construct quality control charts and understand how they are used for statistical process control.

7. Know the definitions of the following terms:

producer's risk	assignable causes
consumer's risk	common causes
acceptance sampling	control charts
acceptable criterion	upper control limit
operating characteristic curve	lower control limit

REVIEW

Quality Terminology
- Quality is "the totality of features and characteristics of a product or service that bears on its ability to satisfy given needs."
- Quality assurance refers to the entire system of policies, procedures, and guidelines established by an organization to achieve and maintain quality.
- The objective of quality engineering is to include quality in the design of products and processes and to identify potential quality problems prior to production.
- Quality control consists of making a series of inspections and measurements to determine whether quality standards are being met.

Statistical Process Control (SPC)
- The goal of SPC is to determine whether the process can be continued or whether it should be adjusted to achieve a desired quality level.
- If the variation in the quality of the production output is due to assignable causes (operator error, worn-out tooling, bad raw material, . . .) the process should be adjusted or corrected as soon as possible.
- If the variation in output is due to common causes (variation in materials, humidity, temperature, . . .) which the manager cannot control, the process does not need to be adjusted.

SPC Hypotheses
- SPC procedures are based on hypothesis-testing methodology.
- The null hypothesis H_0 is formulated in terms of the production process being in control.
- The alternative hypothesis H_a is formulated in terms of the process being out of control.
- As with other hypothesis-testing procedures, both a Type I error (adjusting an in-control process) and a Type II error (allowing an out-of-control process to continue) are possible.

Control Charts
- SPC uses graphical displays known as control charts to monitor a production process.
- Control charts provide a basis for deciding whether the variation in the output is due to common causes (in control) or assignable causes (out of control).
- Two important lines on a control chart are the upper control limit (UCL) and lower control limit (LCL).
- These lines are chosen so that when the process is <u>in</u> control, there will be a high probability that the sample finding will be between the two lines.
- Values outside of the control limits provide strong evidence that the process is out of control.
- Patterns of data within the control limits can also indicate potential quality control problems and suggest that corrective action may be warranted.
- Over time, more and more data points will be added to the control chart.
- Every time a point is plotted on the control chart, we are carrying out a hypothesis test.
- The most important use of a control chart is in improving the process.

Types of Control Charts
- An $\bar{x}$ chart is used to monitor the mean of the measurements in a sample.
- An R chart is used to monitor the range of the measurements in the sample.
- A p chart is used to monitor the proportion defective in the sample.
- An np chart is used to monitor the number of defective items in the sample.
- The major difference among the four above charts is what the vertical axis measures.

$\bar{x}$ Chart
- An $\bar{x}$ chart is used if the quality of the output is measured in terms of a variable such as length, weight, temperature, and so on.
- The decision to continue or to adjust the production process is based on the mean value, $\bar{x}$, found in a sample of the output.

Control Limits for an $\bar{x}$ Chart: Process μ and σ Known
- The general practice is to define as reasonable any value of $\bar{x}$ that is within 3 standard deviations above or below the mean value.
- The upper control limit (UCL) and lower control limit (LCL) are:
$$\text{UCL} = \mu + 3\sigma_{\bar{x}}$$
$$\text{LCL} = \mu - 3\sigma_{\bar{x}}$$
- If a value of $\bar{x}$ is within the LCL-to-UCL interval, we will assume that the process is in control.

Control Limits for an $\bar{x}$ Chart: Process μ and σ Unknown

- Usually, the process mean and standard deviation must be estimated by using samples that are selected from the process when it is assumed to be operating in control.
- The upper control limit (UCL) and lower control limit (LCL) are:

$$UCL = \bar{\bar{x}} + A_2\bar{R}$$

$$LCL = \bar{\bar{x}} - A_2\bar{R}$$

> where: $\bar{\bar{x}}$ = overall sample mean
> $\bar{R}$ = average range
> A_2 = a constant that depends on n; taken from
>   Factors for Control Charts table

- We can think of A_2 as a multiplier (coefficient) for $\bar{R}$ to make it approximately equal to $3\sigma_{\bar{x}}$.

R Chart

- An R chart is used to monitor and control the variability of a process.
- It is more common to monitor the variability of the process by using the range instead of the standard deviation because the range is easier to compute.
- If the sample size is greater than 10, a standard deviation chart (s chart) is generally preferred.
- If the R chart indicates that the process is out of control, the $\bar{x}$ Chart should not be interpreted until the R chart indicates the process variability is in control.

Control Limits for an *R* Chart

- The upper control limit (UCL) and lower control limit (LCL) are:

$$UCL = \bar{R}D_4$$

$$LCL = \bar{R}D_3$$

> where: D_3 and D_4 are constants that depend on n; taken from
> Factors for Control Charts table

p Chart

- Control charts that are based on data indicating the presence of a defect or the number of defects are attribute control charts.
- A p chart is an attribute control chart. It is used to monitor the proportion of defective items.
- The decision to continue or to adjust the production process will be based on $\bar{p}$, the proportion of defective items found in a sample of the output.

Control Limits for a *p* Chart

- The sampling distribution of $\bar{p}$ can be used to determine the variation that can be expected in $\bar{p}$ values for a process that is in control.
- The standard deviation of $\bar{p}$ is called the standard error of the proportion and is denoted as $\sigma_{\bar{p}}$.

- If p is known, the formula for $\sigma_{\bar{p}}$ is:

$$\sigma_{\bar{p}} = \sqrt{\frac{p(1-p)}{n}}$$

- If p is unknown, we treat all the data as one large sample and compute the overall sample proportion, denoted here as $\bar{\bar{p}}$. In this case, the formula for $\sigma_{\bar{p}}$ is:

$$\sigma_{\bar{p}} = \sqrt{\frac{\bar{\bar{p}}(1-\bar{\bar{p}})}{n}}$$

- The sampling distribution of $\bar{p}$ can be approximated by a normal distribution if the following conditions are met: $np \geq 5$ and $n(1-p) \geq 5$.
- The upper control limit (UCL) and lower control limit (LCL) are:
- If p is known: $\quad\quad\quad$ UCL $= p + 3\sigma_{\bar{p}}$ and LCL $= p - 3\sigma_{\bar{p}}$
- If p is unknown: $\quad\quad\quad$ UCL $= \bar{\bar{p}} + 3\sigma_{\bar{p}}$ and LCL $= \bar{\bar{p}} - 3\sigma_{\bar{p}}$

np Chart

- An *np* Chart is an attribute chart developed for the number of defective items observed in a sample.
- The information provided by an *np* chart is equivalent to the information provided by a *p* chart.
- If a particular process is judged to be out of control on the basis of a *p* chart, the same conclusion about the process would result based on an *np* chart.

Control Limits for an *np* Chart

- Whenever the sample size is large ($np \geq 5$ and $n(1-p) \geq 5$), the distribution of the number of defective items observed in a sample size n can be approximated by a normal distribution with mean np and standard deviation $\sqrt{np(1-p)}$.
- The upper control limit (UCL) and lower control limit (LCL) are:

$$UCL = np + 3\sqrt{np(1-p)}$$
$$UCL = np - 3\sqrt{np(1-p)}$$

Note: If computed LCL is negative, set LCL = 0

Interpretation of Control Charts

- The location and pattern of points in a control chart enable us to determine, with a small probability of error, whether a process is in statistical control.
- A primary indication that a process may be out of control is a data point outside the control limits.
- Certain patterns of points within the control limits can be warning signals of quality problems. These patterns include: a large number of points on one side of center line, or six or seven points in a row that indicate either an increasing or decreasing trend.

Acceptance Sampling
- Acceptance sampling is a statistical method that enables us to base the accept-reject decision on the inspection of a sample of items from the lot.
- A lot might be an incoming shipment of raw material or purchased parts for example.
- Acceptance sampling has advantages over 100% inspection including: less expensive, less product damage, fewer inspectors involved, . . . and more.

- The general steps of acceptance sampling are:
  - After a lot is received, a sample is selected for inspection.
  - The inspection results are compared to quality specifications.
  - If the quality is satisfactory, the lot is accepted.
  - If the quality is not satisfactory, the lot is rejected and managers must decide the disposition of the lot.
- Acceptance sampling is based on hypothesis-testing methodology.
- The hypothesis are: H_0: Good-quality and H_a: Poor-quality lot
- As with other hypothesis-testing procedures, both a Type I error (rejecting a good-quality lot) and a Type II error (accepting a poor-quality lot) are possible.
- Because the probability of a Type I error creates a risk for the producer of the lot, it is known as the producer's risk.
- Because the probability of a Type II error creates a risk for the consumer of the lot, it is known as the consumer's risk.

Probability of Accepting a Lot
- The number of defective items in a sample of n from a large lot has a binomial probability distribution.
- The probability of x defectives in the sample is:

$$f(x) = \frac{n!}{x!(n-x)!} p^x (1-p)^{(n-x)}$$

where: p = proportion of defective items in lot

- A graph of the probability of accepting the lot versus the percent defective in the lot, for a given n value and given c value, is called the operating characteristic (OC) curve.

Selecting an Acceptance Sampling Plan
- In formulating a plan, managers specify two values for the fraction defective in the lot.
  - α = the probability that a lot with p_0 defectives will be rejected.
  - β = the probability that a lot with p_1 defectives will be accepted.
- Then the values of n and c are selected that result in an acceptance sampling plan that comes closest to meeting both the α and β requirements specified.

Multiple Sampling Plans
- A multiple sampling plan uses two or more stages of sampling.
- At each stage the decision possibilities are: a) stop sampling and accept the lot, b) stop sampling and reject the lot, or c) continue sampling.
- The specifics of the plan are as follows:
  - Initially a sample of n_1 items is selected.
  - If the number of defective items x_1 is less than or equal to c_1, accept the lot.
  - If x_1 is greater or equal to c_2, reject the lot.

- If x_1 is between c_1 and c_2, select a second sample of n_2 items.
- Determine the total number of defectives from the first sample (x_1) and the second sample (x_2).
- If $x_1 + x_2 \leq c_3$, accept the lot; otherwise reject the lot.
- Multiple sampling plans often result in a smaller total sample size than single-sample plans with the same Type I error and Type II error probabilities.

KEY CONCEPTS

CONCEPT	EXAMPLES	EXERCISES
Control Charts		
$\bar{x}$ Chart: μ and σ Known	1	1
R Chart	②	2
$\bar{x}$ Chart	③	2
p Chart	④	3
np Chart	⑤	3
Acceptance Sampling		
Probability of Accepting a Lot	6	4
Selecting an Acceptance Sampling Plan	7	4
Constructing an OC Curve	⑧	5
Producer's Risk and Consumer's Risk	6,7,8	4,5

◯ Excel Used

EXAMPLES

EXAMPLE 1

$\bar{x}$ Chart: μ and σ Known

The weight of bags of cement filled by Granite Rock Company's packaging process is normally distributed with a mean of 50 pounds and a standard deviation of 1.5 pounds when the process is in control. What should the control limits be for a sample mean, $\bar{x}$, chart if 9 bags are sampled at a time?

SOLUTION 1

The sampling distribution (mean and standard deviation) of $\bar{x}$ is used to determine what values of $\bar{x}$ are reasonable if the process is in control. Because the filling weights (x) are normally distributed, the sampling distribution of $\bar{x}$ is normal for any sample size. Thus, the sampling distribution of $\bar{x}$ is a normal probability distribution with mean μ and standard deviation $\sigma_{\bar{x}}$

The standard error of the mean, $\sigma_{\bar{x}}$, is a function of the population standard deviation, σ, and the sample size, n. The standard error of the mean is computed as follows:

$$\sigma_{\bar{x}} = \sigma / \sqrt{n} = 1.5 / \sqrt{9} = 0.5$$

The general practice in quality control is to define as reasonable any value of $\bar{x}$ that is within 3 standard deviations above or below the mean value of $\bar{x}$. Thus, the upper and lower control limits for the $\bar{x}$ chart for Granite Rock Co. are computed as follows:

$$UCL = \mu + 3\sigma_{\bar{x}} = 50 + 3(.5) = 51.5$$
$$LCL = \mu - 3\sigma_{\bar{x}} = 50 - 3(.5) = 48.5$$

EXAMPLE 2

R Chart

Granite Rock Company produces masonry cement and packages it in bags that have the label "50 pounds." Granite does not know the true mean and standard deviation for the weights of the output from the bag-filling process. Nevertheless, It wants to develop control charts for monitoring the variation in the weight. Granite has taken twenty 5-bag samples while the process was believed to be in control. The weights of the five bags in each of the twenty samples have been entered into a worksheet as shown below. Construct an appropriate R chart for the bag-filling process..

Data Worksheet:

	A	B	C	D	E	F
1	**Sample**	**Observ. 1**	**Observ. 2**	**Observ. 3**	**Observ. 4**	**Observ. 5**
2	1	50.22	49.91	50.05	50.12	49.79
3	2	50.13	50.09	50.17	50.23	50.04
4	3	50.30	50.11	49.91	49.89	50.09
5	4	49.91	50.20	50.16	50.05	50.24
6	5	50.11	49.89	49.94	50.17	49.88
7	6	49.78	50.07	49.78	49.79	50.04
8	7	49.84	49.92	50.11	50.04	49.81
9	8	50.08	49.88	49.90	49.97	49.78
10	9	49.89	50.10	50.14	49.99	49.90
11	10	50.11	50.16	50.20	50.06	50.06
12	11	49.86	49.79	50.06	50.11	49.97
13	12	49.99	50.03	49.92	50.17	50.19
14	13	50.20	49.81	49.89	49.88	50.11
15	14	49.84	49.97	50.08	50.22	49.82
16	15	50.30	49.83	50.04	49.78	50.23
17	16	50.04	50.19	49.92	50.17	50.01
18	17	49.90	50.16	49.86	49.98	49.83
19	18	49.95	50.02	50.13	49.91	49.89
20	19	50.07	49.85	49.89	50.27	49.78
21	20	50.03	49.94	50.00	49.79	50.07

SOLUTION 2

Using Excel's Chart Wizard

Enter Data: The data for the bag weights for the 20 samples selected by Granite Rock are entered into a worksheet we will call <u>Data</u>. We will refer to the Data worksheet in the process of constructing a second worksheet for developing our *R* chart. The discussion that follows pertains to the second worksheet.

Enter Functions and Formulas: Column A contains the sample numbers 1-20. Column B contains the formulas needed to compute the range for each sample from the data in cells B2:F21 of the Data worksheet. In these formulas we use the MAX and MIN functions and we refer to cell addresses in the Data worksheet. (Note that the worksheet name followed by an exclamation point, Data!, must precede a cell reference when the cells referred to are in another worksheet.) The AVERAGE function is used in cell B22 to compute the average of the ranges for the 20 samples.

In order to compute the LCL and UCL, we must know D_3 and D_4. These values are obtained from the table below (in the $n = 5$ row) and entered into cells D23 and D24, respectively. The formulas in cells C2:C21 are identical; they compute the LCL by multiplying D_3 (cell D23) times the average range (cell B22). The formulas in cells D2:D21 are also identical; they provide the average range. Finally, the formulas in cell E2:E21 (also identical) are used to compute the UCL by multiplying D_4 (cell D24) times the average range (cell B22).

\multicolumn{6}{c}{**Factors for x bar and R Control Charts**}
n	d_2	A_2	d_3	D_3	D_4
2	1.128	1.880	0.850	0	3.267
3	1.693	1.023	0.888	0	2.574
4	2.059	0.729	0.880	0	2.282
5	2.326	0.577	0.864	0	2.114
6	2.534	0.483	0.848	0	2.004
7	2.704	0.419	0.833	0.076	1.924
8	2.847	0.373	0.820	0.136	1.864
9	2.970	0.337	0.808	0.184	1.816
⋮	⋮	⋮	⋮	⋮	⋮

Formula Worksheet:

	A	B	C	D	E
1	Samp.	R	LCL	Mean	UCL
2	1	=MAX(Data!B2:F2)-MIN(Data!B2:F2)	=$D$23*$B$22	=$B$22	=$D$24*$B$22
3	2	=MAX(Data!B3:F3)-MIN(Data!B3:F3)	=$D$23*$B$22	=$B$22	=$D$24*$B$22
4	3	=MAX(Data!B4:F4)-MIN(Data!B4:F4)	=$D$23*$B$22	=$B$22	=$D$24*$B$22
5	4	=MAX(Data!B5:F5)-MIN(Data!B5:F5)	=$D$23*$B$22	=$B$22	=$D$24*$B$22
6	5	=MAX(Data!B6:F6)-MIN(Data!B6:F6)	=$D$23*$B$22	=$B$22	=$D$24*$B$22
20	19	=MAX(Data!B20:F20)-MIN(Data!B20:F20)	=$D$23*$B$22	=$B$22	=$D$24*$B$22
21	20	=MAX(Data!B21:F21)-MIN(Data!B21:F21)	=$D$23*$B$22	=$B$22	=$D$24*$B$22
22	Rbar	=AVERAGE($B$2:$B$21)			
23			D_3	0	
24			D_4	2.114	

Note: Rows 7-19 are hidden.

Value Worksheet:

	A	B	C	D	E
1	Samp.	*R*	LCL	Mean	UCL
2	1	0.43	0	0.32	0.6807
3	2	0.19	0	0.32	0.6807
4	3	0.41	0	0.32	0.6807
5	4	0.33	0	0.32	0.6807
6	5	0.29	0	0.32	0.6807
20	19	0.49	0	0.32	0.6807
21	20	0.28	0	0.32	0.6807
22	*R* bar	0.322			
23			D_3	0	
24			D_4	2.114	

We see in the resulting worksheet above the values for the upper limit, lower limit, and center line in our *R* chart. Now we are ready to draw the *R* chart.

Apply Tools: We will use Excel's Chart Wizard to construct the *R* chart from the data in cells A2:E21 of our worksheet.

Step 1 Select cells A2:E21
Step 2 Select the **Chart Wizard** button on main toolbar
Step 3 When the Chart Wizard-Step 1 0f 4-**Chart Type** dialog box appears:
    Choose **XY (Scatter)** in the **Chart Type** list
    Choose **Scatter with data points connected by lines** from the Chart Subtype display
    Click **Next >**
Step 4 When the Chart Wizard-Step 2 of 4- **Chart Source Data** dialog box appears:
    Click **Next >**
Step 5 When the **Chart Wizard-Step 3 of 4-Chart Options** dialog box appears:
    Select the **Titles** tab and then
      Type **R Chart for Granite Rock Co.** in the **Chart title** box
      Type **Sample Number** in the **Value (X)** axis box
      Type **Sample Range R** in the **Value (Y)** axis box
    Select the **Legend** tab and then
      Remove the check in the **Show Legend** box
    Select the **Gridlines** tab and then
      Remove the check in the **Major Gridlines** box
      Click **Next >**
Step 6 When the **Chart Wizard- Step 4 of 4 – Chart Location** dialog box appears:
    Specify a location for the chart
    Click **Finish**

With practice and patience, you can alter the chart initially produced by Excel to look like the one below or to suit your personal preferences. A right-click on almost any item in the chart will bring up a menu of alteration options.

***R* Chart:**

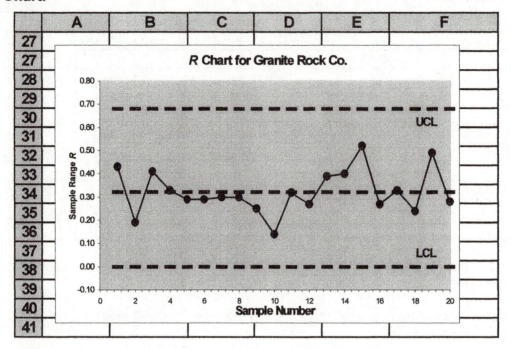

EXAMPLE 3

$\bar{x}$ Chart

Refer again to the background information and data for the Granite Rock Co. in Example 2. Construct an appropriate $\bar{x}$ chart for the bag-filling process.

SOLUTION 3

Using Excel's Chart Wizard

Enter Data: The data for the bag weights for the 20 samples selected by Granite Rock are entered into a worksheet we will call <u>Data</u>. We will refer to the Data worksheet in the process of constructing a second worksheet for developing our $\bar{x}$ chart. The discussion that follows pertains to the second worksheet. Our second worksheet is a continuation of the worksheet we developed for Example 2; for this reason we start here with row 28.

Enter Functions and Formulas: Column A contains the sample numbers 1-20. Column B contains the formulas needed to compute the mean for each sample from the data in cells B2:F21 of the Data worksheet. In these formulas we use the AVERAGE function and we refer to cell addresses in the Data worksheet. (Note that the worksheet name followed by an exclamation point, Data!, must precede a cell reference when the cells referred to are in another worksheet.) The AVERAGE function is used in cell B49 to compute the average of the 20 sample means.

In order to compute the LCL and UCL, we must know A_2. This value (0.577) is obtained from the Control Chart Factors table (shown in Solution 2) and entered into cell D50. The formulas in cells C29:C48 are identical; they compute the LCL by multiplying A_2 (cell D50) times the overall sample mean (cell B49). The formulas in cells D29:D48 are also identical; they provide the overall sample mean. Finally, the formulas in cell E29:E48 (also identical) are used to compute the UCL by multiplying A_2 (cell D50) times the overall sample mean (cell B49).

Formula Worksheet:

	A	B	C	D	E
28	Sample	*x* bar	LCL	Mean	UCL
29	1	=AVERAGE(Data!B2:F2)	=$B$49-$D$50*$B$22	=$D$50	=$B$49+$D$50*$B$22
30	2	=AVERAGE(Data!B3:F3)	=$B$49-$D$50*$B$22	=$D$50	=$B$49+$D$50*$B$22
31	3	=AVERAGE(Data!B4:F4)	=$B$49-$D$50*$B$22	=$D$50	=$B$49+$D$50*$B$22
32	4	=AVERAGE(Data!B5:F5)	=$B$49-$D$50*$B$22	=$D$50	=$B$49+$D$50*$B$22
33	5	=AVERAGE(Data!B6:F6)	=$B$49-$D$50*$B$22	=$D$50	=$B$49+$D$50*$B$22
47	19	=AVERAGE(Data!B20:F20)	=$B$49-$D$50*$B$22	=$D$50	=$B$49+$D$50*$B$22
48	20	=AVERAGE(Data!B21:F21)	=$B$49-$D$50*$B$22	=$D$50	=$B$49+$D$50*$B$22
49	Mean	=AVERAGE(B29:B48)			
50				A_2 0.577	

Note: Rows 34-46 are hidden.

Value Worksheet:

	A	B	C	D	E
28	Sample	*x* bar	LCL	Mean	UCL
29	1	50.018	49.824	50.01	50.195
30	2	50.132	49.824	50.01	50.195
31	3	50.060	49.824	50.01	50.195
32	4	50.112	49.824	50.01	50.195
33	5	49.998	49.824	50.01	50.195
47	19	49.972	49.824	50.01	50.195
48	20	49.966	49.824	50.01	50.195
49	Mean	50.010			
50					
51				A_2 0.577	

We see in the resulting worksheet above the values for the upper limit, lower limit, and center line for our $\bar{x}$ chart. Now we are ready to draw the $\bar{x}$ chart.

Apply Tools: We will use Excel's Chart Wizard to construct the $\bar{x}$ chart from the data in cells A29:E48 of our worksheet. The steps to follow are nearly identical to those we outlined in Solution 2 where we were constructing an *R* chart. Refer to Solution 2 for details. You can alter the chart initially produced by Excel to look like the one below or to suit your personal preferences. A right-click on almost any item in the chart will bring up a menu of alteration options.

$\bar{x}$ **Chart:**

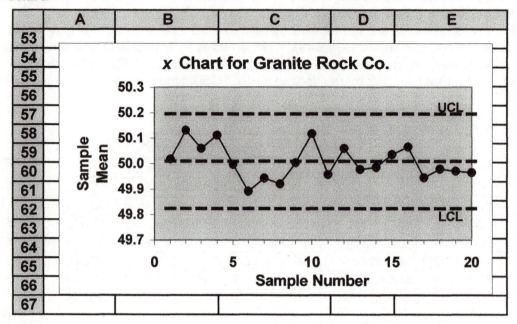

EXAMPLE 4

p Chart

Every check cashed or deposited at Norwest Bank must be encoded with the amount of the check before it can begin the Federal Reserve clearing process. The accuracy of the check encoding process is of utmost importance. If there is any discrepancy between the amount a check is made out for and the encoded amount, the check is defective.

Twenty samples, each consisting of 250 checks, were selected and examined when the encoding process was known to be operating correctly. The numbers of defective checks found in the twenty samples are listed below.

4	1	5	3	2	7	4	5	2	3
2	8	5	3	6	4	2	5	3	6

Construct a *p* chart for the check encoding process, assuming each sample has 250 checks.

SOLUTION 4

Using Excel's Chart Wizard

Enter Data: The identifying sample number and the number of defective checks for the 20 samples selected by Norwest Bank are entered into the worksheet in columns A and B.

Enter Functions and Formulas: We compute the proportion of checks that are defective in each sample by entering the formula =B2/250 into cell C2 and then copying it to cells C3:C21. The overall proportion of defective checks for the 20 samples, the estimate of *p*, is computed by entering the formula =AVERAGE(C2:C21) into cell C22. The estimated standard error of the proportion, $\sigma_{\bar{p}}$, is computed by entering the following formula into cell C23:

$$=SQRT(C22*(1-C22)/250)$$

The formulas in cells D2:D21 are identical; they compute the lower control limit. The LCL generally equals the estimated *p* <u>minus</u> three times the standard error of the proportion ($C$22-3*$C$23). However, if this calculation results in a negative value, the LCL is set equal to zero. For this reason we use the MAX function to select the greater of the two values: 0 and ($C$22-3*$C$23).

The formulas in cells E2:E21 are also identical; they provide the overall proportion of defective checks. Finally, the formulas in cell F2:F21 (also identical) are used to compute the UCL which equals the estimated *p* <u>plus</u> three times the standard error of the proportion ($C$22-3*$C$23).

Formula Worksheet:

	A	B	C	D	E	F
1	Sample	Number Defect.	Proportion Defective	LCL	CL	UCL
2	1	4	=B2/250	=MAX(0,$C$22-3*$C$23)	=$C$22	=$C$22+3*$C$23
3	2	1	=B3/250	=MAX(0,$C$22-3*$C$23)	=$C$22	=$C$22+3*$C$23
4	3	5	=B4/250	=MAX(0,$C$22-3*$C$23)	=$C$22	=$C$22+3*$C$23
5	4	3	=B5/250	=MAX(0,$C$22-3*$C$23)	=$C$22	=$C$22+3*$C$23
20	19	3	=B20/250	=MAX(0,$C$22-3*$C$23)	=$C$22	=$C$22+3*$C$23
21	20	6	=B21/250	=MAX(0,$C$22-3*$C$23)	=$C$22	=$C$22+3*$C$23
22	Estimated *p*		=AVERAGE(C2:C21)			
23	Estim. Std. Error		=SQRT(C22*(1-C22)/250)			

Note: Rows 6-19 are hidden.

Value Worksheet:

	A	B	C	D	E	F
1	Sample	Number Defect.	Proportion Defective	LCL	CL	UCL
2	1	4	0.016	0	0.0160	0.0398
3	2	1	0.004	0	0.0160	0.0398
4	3	5	0.020	0	0.0160	0.0398
5	4	3	0.012	0	0.0160	0.0398
20	19	3	0.012	0	0.0160	0.0398
21	20	6	0.024	0	0.0160	0.0398
22	Estimated *p*		0.016			
23	Estim. Std. Error		0.00794			

Note: Rows 6-19 are hidden.

We see in the resulting worksheet above the values for the upper limit, lower limit, and center line for our *p* chart. Now we are ready to draw the *p* chart.

Apply Tools: We will use Excel's Chart Wizard to construct the *p* chart from the data in cells A2:A21 and C2:C21 of our worksheet. (We will not be graphing the number of defectives data in column B.) The steps to follow are outlined below.

Constructing an *p* Chart

    Step 1 Select cells A2:A21 and D2:F21

    Step 2 Select the **Chart Wizard** button on main toolbar

    Step 3 When the Chart Wizard-Step 1 Of 4-**Chart Type** dialog box appears:

            Choose **XY (Scatter)** in the **Chart Type** list

            Choose **Scatter with data points connected by lines** from the Chart subtype display

            Click **Next >**

    Step 4 When the Chart Wizard-Step 2 of 4- **Chart Source Data** dialog box appears:

            Click **Next >**

    Step 5 When the **Chart Wizard-Step 3 of 4-Chart Options** dialog box appears:

            Select the **Titles** tab and then

                Type **p Chart for Norwest Bank** in the **Chart title** box

                Type **Sample Number** in the **Value (X)** axis box

                Type **Sample Proportion p** in the **Value (Y)** axis box

            Select the **Legend** tab and then

            Remove the check in the **Show Legend** box

            Select the **Gridlines** tab and then

            Remove the check in the **Major Gridlines** box

            Click **Next >**

    Step 6 When the **Chart Wizard- Step 4 of 4 – Chart Location** dialog box appears:

            Specify a location for the chart

            Click **Finish**

    With practice and patience, you can alter the chart initially produced by Excel to look like the one below or to suit your personal preferences. A right-click on almost any item in the chart will bring up a menu of alteration options.

p Chart:

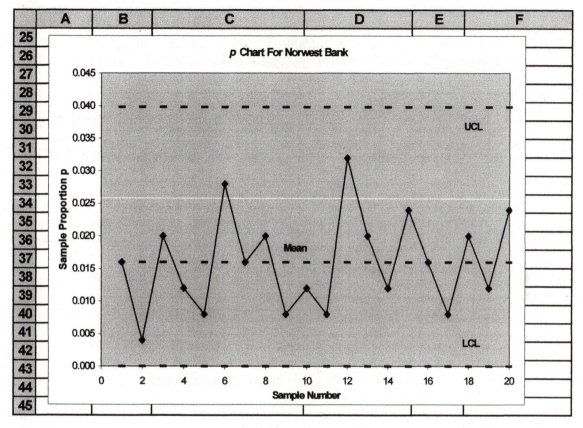

EXAMPLE 5

np Chart

Refer again to the background information and data for Norwest Bank in Example 4. Construct an appropriate *np* chart for the check encoding process..

SOLUTION 5

Using Excel's Chart Wizard

With just a few modifications to the worksheet developed in Solution 4, we can construct an *np* chart for Norwest Bank.

Enter Data: The data is already entered. See Solution 4 for details.

Enter Functions and Formulas: The proportion of checks that are defective in each sample, as well as the overall proportion of defective checks, are already computed. The estimated standard error is computed by entering the following formula into cell C23:

=SQRT(250*C22*(1-C22))

The one new item in this worksheet is the estimated average number of defective checks per sample of 250, denoted *np*. We compute the estimated *np* by entering the formula =250*C22 into cell C24.

The formulas in cells D2:D21 are identical; they compute the lower control limit. The LCL generally equals the estimated *np* <u>minus</u> three times the standard error ($C$24-3*$C$23). However, if this calculation results in a negative value, the LCL is set equal to zero. For this reason we use the MAX function to select the greater of the two values: 0 and ($C$24-3*$C$23).

The formulas in cells E2:E21 are also identical; they provide the expected number of defective checks. Finally, the formulas in cell F2:F21 (also identical) are used to compute the UCL which equals the estimated *p* <u>plus</u> three times the standard error ($C$24-3*$C$23).

Formula Worksheet:

	A	B	C	D	E	F
1	Sample	Number Defect.	Proportion Defective	LCL	CL	UCL
2	1	4	=B2/250	=MAX(0,$C$24-3*$C$23)	=$C$24	=$C$24+3*$C$23
3	2	1	=B3/250	=MAX(0,$C$24-3*$C$23)	=$C$24	=$C$24+3*$C$23
4	3	5	=B4/250	=MAX(0,$C$24-3*$C$23)	=$C$24	=$C$24+3*$C$23
5	4	3	=B5/250	=MAX(0,$C$24-3*$C$23)	=$C$24	=$C$24+3*$C$23
20	19	3	=B20/250	=MAX(0,$C$24-3*$C$23)	=$C$24	=$C$24+3*$C$23
21	20	6	=B21/250	=MAX(0,$C$24-3*$C$23)	=$C$24	=$C$24+3*$C$23
22	Estimated *p*		=AVERAGE(C2:C21)			
23	Estim. Std. Error		=SQRT(250*C22*(1-C22))			
24	Estimated *np*		=250*C22			

Note: Rows 6-19 are hidden.

We see in the resulting worksheet below the values for the upper limit, lower limit, and center line in our *np* chart. Now we are ready to graph the *np* chart.

Value Worksheet:

	A	B	C	D	E	F
1	Sample	Number Defect.	Proportion Defective	LCL	CL	UCL
2	1	4	0.016	0	4.00	9.952
3	2	1	0.004	0	4.00	9.952
4	3	5	0.020	0	4.00	9.952
5	4	3	0.012	0	4.00	9.952
20	19	3	0.012	0	4.00	9.952
21	20	6	0.024	0	4.00	9.952
22	Estimated *p*		0.0160			
23	Estim. Std. Error		1.9839			
24	Estimated *np*		4.0000			

Note: Rows 6-19 are hidden.

Apply Tools: We will use Excel's Chart Wizard to construct the *n* chart from the data in cells A2:B21 and D2:F21of our worksheet. (We will not be graphing the proportion defective data in column C.) . The steps to follow are nearly identical to those we outlined in Solution 4 where we were constructing a *p* chart. Refer to Solution 4 for details. You can alter the chart initially produced by Excel to look like the one below or to suit your personal preferences. A right-click on almost any item in the chart will bring up a menu of alteration options.

np **Chart:**

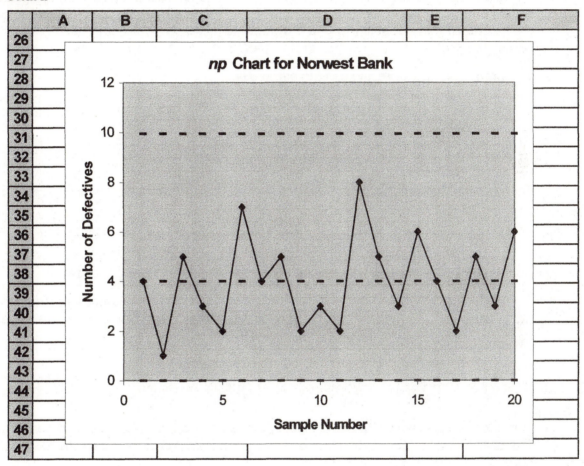

EXAMPLE 6

Probability of Accepting a Lot

Ledd Electronics has received a large shipment of power supply units for the desktop computers being assembled. The units are coming from a new supplier and Ledd is not sure what the actual defect rate will be for this component. Ledd is considering an acceptance sampling plan with $n = 30$ and $c = 1$.

a) Find the probability of accepting a lot when the defect rate is 2%, 4%, and 6%.

b) What happens to the producer's risk as the defect rate increases?

c) What happens to the consumer's risk as the defect rate increases?

SOLUTION 6

a) The maximum number of defective units that can be found in a sample of 30 units and still deem the shipment as being acceptable is 1. Therefore, the probability of accepting the lot equals the probability of 0 or 1 defectives. The probability of rejecting the lot equals the probability of there being 2 or more defectives in the sample.

The probability of x defectives in the sample is:

$$f(x) = \frac{n!}{x!(n-x)!} p^x (1-p)^{(n-x)}$$

where: p = the proportion of defectives in the lot
n = the sample size

For example, the probability of 0 defectives when $n = 30$ and $p = .02$ is computed as:

$$f(0) = \frac{30!}{0!(30!)} .02^0 (.92)^{30} = .54548$$

Continuing in this manner, the calculations can be summarized as follows:

Defect Rate p	$P(x = 0)$	$P(x = 1)$	Probab. of Accepting (Consumer's Risk, β) $P(x \le 1)$	Probab. of Rejecting (Producer's Risk, α) $P(x \ge 2)$
.02	.54548	.33397	.87945	.12055
.04	.29386	.36732	.66118	.33882
.06	.15626	.29921	.45547	.54453

b) Refer to the table above where the acceptance criterion, c, has been held constant at 1. The chance that a lot will contain 2 or more defectives will increase as the expected number of defectives in the lot increases.

c) We see that the consumer's risk decreases as the defective rate increases.

EXAMPLE 7

Selecting an Acceptance Sampling Plan

An acceptance sampling plan with $n = 20$ and $c = 1$ has been designed with a producer's risk of .12.

a) Was the value of p_0 equal to .02, .03, .04, or .05?

b) What is the consumer's risk associated with this plan if p_1 is .08?

c) Assume the consumer's risk found in (b) is unacceptably high. Which modification of the sampling plan will result in the greater reduction of the consumer's risk, increasing n to 30 or decreasing c to 0?

SOLUTION 7

a)

Defect Rate p	$P(x = 0)$	$P(x = 1)$	Probab. of Accepting (Consumer's Risk, β) $P(x \le 1)$	Probab. of Rejecting (Producer's Risk, α) $P(x > 1)$
.02	.66761	.27249	.94010	.05990
.03	.54379	.33637	.88016	.11984
.04	.44200	.36834	.81034	.18966
.05	.35848	.37735	.73583	.26417

b) $n = 20$, $c = 1$, $p_1 = .08$

$P(x = 0) = .188693$
$P(x = 1) = .328162$
$P(x \le 1) = .516855 = $ Consumer's Risk

c) $n = 30$, $c = 1$ $P(x \le 1) = .081966 + .213825 = .295791$
$n = 20$, $c = 0$ $P(x = 0) = .188693$
Decreasing c to 0 results in the lowest consumer's risk.

EXAMPLE 8

Constructing an Operating Characteristic Curve

Dock 4 Exports receives a particular style of candle holder in large lots from a wholesaler. When Dock 4 receives a shipment, a random sample of 20 candle holders are inspected to determine if they meet the product quality specifications. If any defectives are detected in the sample, the lot is rejected and returned to the wholesaler.

Graph the operating characteristic curve for this acceptance sampling plan. Using the graph, determine the approximate probability (producer's risk) that the plan will reject a lot that has a .03 defective rate.

SOLUTION 8

Using Excel's BINOMDIST Function and Chart Wizard

Enter Data: The integer values 0, 1, 2, ..., 29, 30 are entered into cells A4:A34. These represent the percentage of defectives in a lot, ranging from 0% to 30%. (Generally, it is not necessary to graph the OC curve beyond a 30% defective rate because the curve is essentially flat at that point.) Next, the value of n, which is 20, is entered into cell D1 and the value of c, which is 1, is entered into cell D2. Finally, identifying labels should be entered into cells A1:A3, C1, and C2.

Enter Functions and Formulas: We will compute the cumulative probability of accepting a lot with each of the defective rates listed in cells A5:A34 by using the BINOMDIST function in cells B5:B34. (We simply enter the value 0 into cell B4 because the BINOMDIST function returns an error message when we try to enter a value of 0 for p.)

The BINOMDIST function's first argument is the value of x for which we are computing a cumulative probability. Dock 4 Exports will accept a lot if the number of defectives, x, is less than or equal to c, the acceptance criterion. For this reason, we use the value of c, in cell D2, as the first argument in the function. The second argument is the value of n which is in cell D1. The third argument is the lot defect rate whose value is in cell A5 (we must convert it from a percentage to a proportion by dividing by 100). We will input TRUE as the last argument because we want a cumulative probability returned by the function. To summarize, the following formula is entered into cell B5 and then copied to cells B6:B34.

$$=BINOMDIST(\$D\$2,\$D\$1,A5/100,TRUE)$$

Formula Worksheet:

	A	B	C	D
1	Percent	Probability	$n =$	20
2	Defective	of Accepting	$c =$	1
3	in the Lot	the Lot		
4	0	1.00000		
5	1	=BINOMDIST($D$2,$D$1,A5/100,TRUE)		
6	2	=BINOMDIST($D$2,$D$1,A6/100,TRUE)		
7	3	=BINOMDIST($D$2,$D$1,A7/100,TRUE)		
8	4	=BINOMDIST($D$2,$D$1,A8/100,TRUE)		
9	5	=BINOMDIST($D$2,$D$1,A9/100,TRUE)		
30	26	=BINOMDIST($D$2,$D$1,A30/100,TRUE)		
31	27	=BINOMDIST($D$2,$D$1,A31/100,TRUE)		
32	28	=BINOMDIST($D$2,$D$1,A32/100,TRUE)		
33	29	=BINOMDIST($D$2,$D$1,A33/100,TRUE)		
34	30	=BINOMDIST($D$2,$D$1,A34/100,TRUE)		

Note: Rows 10-29 are hidden.

Value Worksheet:

	A	B	C	D
	Percent	**Probability**	*n =*	20
1				
2	**Defective**	**of Accepting**	*c =*	1
3	**in the Lot**	**the Lot**		
4	0	1.00000		
5	1	0.98314		
6	2	0.94010		
7	3	0.88016		
8	4	0.81034		
9	5	0.73584		
30	26	0.01946		
31	27	0.01551		
32	28	0.01230		
33	29	0.00972		
34	30	0.00764		

Note: Rows 10-29 are hidden.

We now have the data needed to plot an OC curve for an acceptance sampling plan with $n = 20$ and $c = 1$.

Apply Tools: The following steps describe how to use the Chart Wizard to graph an OC curve from the data in our worksheet.

Step 1 Select cells A4:
Step 2 Select the **Chart Wizard** button
Step 3 When the **Chart Wizard-Step 1 of 4-Chart Type** dialog box appears:
      Choose **XY (Scatter)** in the **Chart type** list
      Choose **Scatter with data points connected by lines** from the
        Chart sub-type display
      Click **Next >**
Step 4 When the **Chart Wizard-Step 2 of 4-Chart Source Data** dialog box appears
      Click **Next >**
Step 5 When the **Chart Wizard-Step 3 of 4-Chart Options** dialog box appears:
      Select the **Titles** tab and then
        Type **Operating Characteristic Curve** in the **Chart title** box
        Enter **Percent Defective in the Lot** in the **Value (X)** axis box
        Enter **Probability of Accepting the Lot** in the **Value (Y)** axis box
      Select the **Legend** tab and then
        Remove the check in the **Show Legend** box
        Click **Next >**
Step 6 When the **Chart Wizard-Step 4 of 4-Chart Location** dialog box appears:
      Specify the location for the new chart
      Click **Finish** to display the ogive

Using the OC curve below, we see that the probability of rejecting a lot with .03 defective is approximately .06.

Operating Characteristic (OC) Curve:

	B	C	D	E	F	G	H	I
1	Probability	*n* =	20					
2	of Accepting	*c* =	1					
3	the Lot							
4	1.00000							
5	0.98314							
6	0.94010							
7	0.88016							
8	0.81034							
9	0.73584							
10	0.66045							
11	0.58686							
12	0.51686							
13	0.45160							
14	0.39175							
15	0.33757							
16	0.28910							
17	0.24615							
18	0.20843							
19	0.17556							
20	0.14713							
21	0.12269							
22	0.10183							

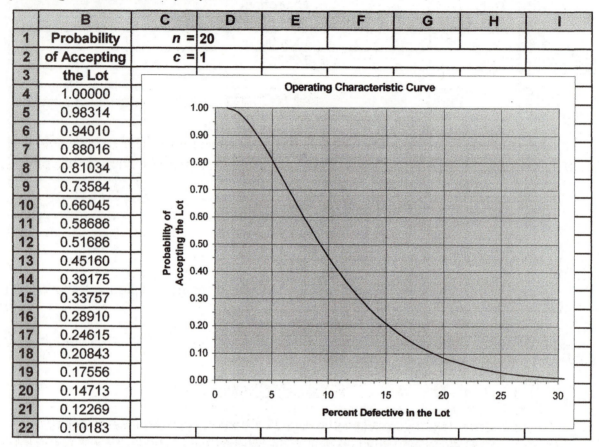

You can alter the chart initially produced by Excel to look like the one above or to suit your personal preferences. A right-click on almost any item in the chart will bring up a menu of alteration options.

EXERCISES

EXERCISE 1

$\bar{x}$ Chart: μ and σ Known

A process that is in control has a mean of $\mu = 56.5$ and a standard deviation of $\sigma = 3.4$. What should the control limits be for a sample mean chart if samples of size 8 are taken?

EXERCISE 2

$\bar{x}$ and R Charts

A process sampled 30 times with a sample of size nine resulted in $\bar{\bar{x}}$ = 12.7 and $\bar{R}$ = 0.8. Compute the upper and lower control limits for the $\bar{x}$ and $\bar{R}$ charts for this process.

EXERCISE 3

p and np Charts

Snipper, Inc. manufactures lawnmowers that require minor, final assembly by the customer. A sealed plastic bag containing the hardware (nuts, bolts, washers, and so on) needed for final assembly is included with each lawnmower shipped.

During a week of normal, in-control operation, twenty samples of 200 bags of hardware were examined for content (hardware type and count) accuracy. A total of 104 bags of the 4000 examined failed to have the correct contents.

a) Compute the upper limit, center line, and lower limit for a p chart.

b) Compute the upper limit, center line, and lower limit for an np chart.

EXERCISE 4

Selecting an Acceptance Sampling Plan

To inspect incoming shipments of components, a manufacturer is considering samples of sizes 12, 15, and 18. Use binomial probabilities to select a sampling plan that provides a producer's risk of $\alpha = .12$ when p_0 is .04 and a consumer's risk of $\beta = .08$ when p_1 is .25.

EXERCISE 5

Constructing an OC Curve

A U.S. manufacturer of video cassette recorders purchases a circuit board from a Taiwanese firm. The circuit boards are shipped in lots of 2000. The acceptance sampling procedure uses 12 randomly selected circuit boards. The acceptance number is 1.

a) Construct an operating characteristic curve for this acceptance sampling plan.

b) If p_0 is .03 and p_1 is .20, what are the producer's and consumer's risks for this plan?

SELF-TEST

TRUE/FALSE

___ 1. No corrective action is necessary when output variations are due to common causes.

___ 2. The consumer's risk is the probability of rejecting good-quality lot.

___ 3. If the R chart indicates that the process is out of control, the $\bar{x}$ chart should not be interpreted until the R chart indicates the process variability is in control.

___ 4. If we were to conclude that a particular process is out of control on the basis of a p chart, we might <u>not</u> come to the same conclusion on the basis of an *np* chart.

___ 5. If all data points plotted on a control chart lie inside the control limits, the process is in statistical control.

FILL-IN-THE-BLANK

1. _____ refers to the entire system of policies, procedures, and guidelines established by an organization to achieve and maintain quality.

2. Operator error and incorrect machine settings are examples of _____ causes.

3. An operating characteristic curve is based on a _____ probability distribution.

4. A control chart that is based on data indicating the presence of a defect or the number of defects is called a(n) _____ control chart.

5. In the context of statistical process control, the _____ hypothesis is formulated in terms of the process being out of control.

MULTIPLE CHOICE

___ 1. If the value of c in a single-stage acceptance sampling plan is increased, with n remaining constant, the probability of accepting the lot
   a) increases
   b) decreases
   c) remains the same
   d) might increase or decrease, depending on the percent defective in the lot

___ 2. The general practice in quality control is to set the control chart's upper and lower control limit values equal to the variable's mean value +/-
   a) 1 standard deviation
   b) 2 standard deviations
   c) 2.5 standard deviations
   d) 3 standard deviations

___ 3. The sample result plotted on an *np* control chart is
   a) *n*
   b) *p*
   c) *np*
   d) the number of defectives in the sample

___ 4. The second stage of a two-stage acceptance sampling plan is executed (additional items are sampled) when the first-stage result is
   a) $x_1 > c_1$
   b) $c_1 < x_1 < c_2$
   c) $x_1 \geq c_2$
   d) $x_1 \geq c_1 + c_2$

___ 5. The producer's risk is the probability of
   a)   a Type I error
   b)   a Type II error
   c)   accepting a poor quality lot
   d)   not rejecting a null hypothesis that is false

ANSWERS

EXERCISES

1) UCL = 60.11, CL = 56.5, LCL = 52.89

2) $\bar{x}$ chart: UCL = 12.97, LCL = 12.43; $\bar{R}$ chart: UCL = 1.453, LCL = 0.147

3) a) UCL = .0598, CL = .0260, LCL = 0
   b) UCL = 11.952, CL = 5.200, LCL = 0

4) *n* = 15, *c* = 1

5) b) $\alpha = .05$, $\beta = .275$

TRUE/FALSE

1) True
2) False
3) True
4) False
5) False

FILL-IN-THE-BLANK

1) Quality assurance
2) assignable
3) binomial
4) attributes
5) alternative

MULTIPLE CHOICE

1) a
2) d
3) d
4) b
5) a

Appendix

TABLE 1   <u>Cumulative Probabilities for the Standard Normal Distribution</u>

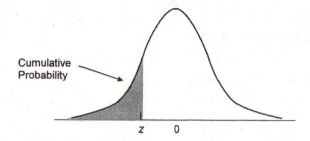

Cumulative
Probability

Entries in the table give the area under the curve to the left of the *z* value.
For example, for *z* = -.85 the cumulative probability is .1977.

z	.00	.01	.02	.03	.04	.05	.06	.07	.08	.09
-3.0	.0013	.0013	.0013	.0012	.0012	.0011	.0011	.0011	.0010	.0010
-2.9	.0019	.0018	.0018	.0017	.0016	.0016	.0015	.0015	.0014	.0014
-2.8	.0026	.0025	.0024	.0023	.0023	.0022	.0021	.0021	.0020	.0019
-2.7	.0035	.0034	.0033	.0032	.0031	.0030	.0029	.0028	.0027	.0026
-2.6	.0047	.0045	.0044	.0043	.0041	.0040	.0039	.0038	.0037	.0036
-2.5	.0062	.0060	.0059	.0057	.0055	.0054	.0052	.0051	.0049	.0048
-2.4	.0082	.0080	.0078	.0075	.0073	.0071	.0069	.0068	.0066	.0064
-2.3	.0107	.0104	.0102	.0099	.0096	.0094	.0091	.0089	.0087	.0084
-2.2	.0139	.0136	.0132	.0129	.0125	.0122	.0119	.0116	.0113	.0110
-2.1	.0179	.0174	.0170	.0166	.0162	.0158	.0154	.0150	.0146	.0143
-2.0	.0228	.0222	.0217	.0212	.0207	.0202	.0197	.0192	.0188	.0183
-1.9	.0287	.0281	.0274	.0268	.0262	.0256	.0250	.0244	.0239	.0233
-1.8	.0359	.0351	.0344	.0336	.0329	.0322	.0314	.0307	.0301	.0294
-1.7	.0446	.0436	.0427	.0418	.0409	.0401	.0392	.0384	.0375	.0367
-1.6	.0548	.0537	.0526	.0516	.0505	.0495	.0485	.0475	.0465	.0455
-1.5	.0668	.0655	.0643	.0630	.0618	.0606	.0594	.0582	.0571	.0559
-1.4	.0808	.0793	.0778	.0764	.0749	.0735	.0721	.0708	.0694	.0681
-1.3	.0968	.0951	.0934	.0918	.0901	.0885	.0869	.0853	.0838	.0823
-1.2	.1151	.1131	.1112	.1093	.1075	.1056	.1038	.1020	.1003	.0985
-1.1	.1357	.1335	.1314	.1292	.1271	.1251	.1230	,1210	.1190	.1170
-1.0	.1587	.1562	.1539	.1515	.1492	.1469	.1446	.1423	.1401	.1379
-.9	.1841	.1814	.1788	.1762	.1736	.1711	.1685	.1660	.1635	.1611
-.8	.2119	.2090	.2061	.2033	.2005	.1977	.1949	.1922	.1894	.1867
-.7	.2420	.2389	.2358	.2327	.2296	.2266	.2236	.2206	.2177	.2148
-.6	.2743	.2709	.2676	.2643	.2611	.2578	.2546	.2514	.2483	.2451
-.5	.3085	.3050	.3015	.2981	.2946	.2912	.2877	.2843	.2810	.2776
-.4	.3446	.3409	.3372	.3336	.3300	.3264	.3228	.3192	.3156	.3121
-.3	.3821	.3783	.3745	.3707	.3669	.3632	.3594	.3557	.3520	.3483
-.2	.4207	.4168	.4129	.4090	.4052	.4013	.3974	.3936	.3897	.3859
-.1	.4602	.4562	.4522	.4483	.4443	.4404	.4364	.4325	.4286	.4247
-.0	.5000	.4960	.4920	.4880	.4840	.4801	.4761	.4721	.4681	.4641

TABLE 1 Cumulative Probabilities for the Standard Normal Distribution (continued)

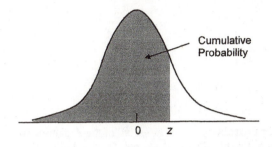

Cumulative
Probability

Entries in the table give the area under the curve to the left of the z value.
For example, for z = 1.25 the cumulative probability is .8944.

z	.00	.01	.02	.03	.04	.05	.06	.07	.08	.09
.0	.5000	.5040	.5080	.5120	.5160	.5199	.5239	.5279	.5319	.5359
.1	.5398	.5438	.5478	.5517	.5557	.5596	.5636	.5675	.5714	.5753
.2	.5793	.5832	.5871	.5910	.5948	.5987	.6026	.6064	.6103	.6141
.3	.6179	.6217	.6255	.6293	.6331	.6368	.6406	.6443	.6480	.6517
.4	.6554	.6591	.6628	.6664	.6700	.6736	.6772	.6808	.6844	.6879
.5	.6915	.6950	.6985	.7019	.7054	.7088	.7123	.7157	.7190	.7224
.6	.7257	.7291	.7324	.7357	.7389	.7422	.7454	.7486	.7517	.7549
.7	.7580	.7611	.7642	.7673	.7704	.7734	.7764	.7794	.7823	.7852
.8	.7881	.7910	.7939	.7967	.7995	.8023	.8051	.8078	.8106	.8133
.9	.8159	.8186	.8212	.8238	.8264	.8289	.8315	.8340	.8365	.8389
1.0	.8413	.8438	.8461	.8485	.8508	.8531	.8554	.8577	.8599	.8621
1.1	.8643	.8665	.8686	.8708	.8729	.8749	.8770	.8790	.8810	.8830
1.2	.8849	.8869	.8888	.8907	.8925	.8944	.8962	.8980	.8997	.9015
1.3	.9032	.9049	.9066	.9082	.9099	.9115	.9131	.9147	.9162	.9177
1.4	.9192	.9207	.9222	.9236	.9251	.9265	.9279	.9292	.9306	.9319
1.5	.9332	.9345	.9357	.9370	.9382	.9394	.9406	.9418	.9429	.9441
1.6	.9452	.9463	.9474	.9484	.9495	.9505	.9515	.9525	.9535	.9545
1.7	.9554	.9564	.9573	.9582	.9591	.9599	.9608	.9616	.9625	.9633
1.8	.9641	.9649	.9656	.9664	.9671	.9678	.9686	.9693	.9699	.9706
1.9	.9713	.9719	.9726	.9732	.9738	.9744	.9750	.9756	.9761	.9767
2.0	.9772	.9778	.9783	.9788	.9793	.9798	.9803	.9808	.9812	.9817
2.1	.9821	.9826	.9830	.9834	.9838	.9842	.9846	.9850	.9854	.9857
2.2	.9861	.9864	.9868	.9871	.9875	.9878	.9881	.9884	.9887	.9890
2.3	.9893	.9896	.9898	.9901	.9904	.9906	.9909	.9911	.9913	.9916
2.4	.9918	.9920	.9922	.9925	.9927	.9929	.9931	.9932	.9934	.9936
2.5	.9938	.9940	.9941	.9943	.9945	.9946	.9948	.9949	.9951	.9952
2.6	.9953	.9955	.9956	.9957	.9959	.9960	.9961	.9962	.9963	.9964
2.7	.9965	.9966	.9967	.9968	.9969	.9970	.9971	.9972	.9973	.9974
2.8	.9974	.9975	.9976	.9977	.9977	.9978	.9979	.9979	.9980	.9981
2.9	.9981	.9982	.9982	.9983	.9984	.9984	.9985	.9985	.9986	.9986
3.0	.9987	.9987	.9987	.9988	.9988	.9989	.9989	.9989	.9990	.9990

TABLE 2   *t* Distribution

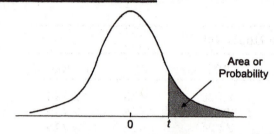

Area or
Probability

Entries in the table give *t* values for an area or probability in the upper tail of the *t* distribution.
For example, with 10 degrees of freedom and a .05 area in the upper tail, $t_{.05} = 1.812$.

Degrees of Freedom	Area in Upper Tail					
	.20	.10	.05	.025	.01	.005
1	1.376	3.078	6.314	12.706	31.821	63.657
2	1.061	1.886	2.920	4.303	6.965	9.925
3	.978	1.638	2.353	3.182	4.541	5.841
4	.941	1.533	2.132	2.776	3.747	4.604
5	.920	1.476	2.015	2.571	3.365	4.032
6	.906	1.440	1.943	2.447	3.143	3.707
7	.896	1.415	1.895	2.365	2.998	3.499
8	.889	1.397	1.860	2.306	2.896	3.355
9	.883	1.383	1.833	2.262	2.821	3.250
10	.879	1.372	1.812	2.228	2.764	3.169
11	.876	1.363	1.796	2.201	2.718	3.106
12	.873	1.356	1.782	2.179	2.681	3.055
13	.870	1.350	1.771	2.160	2.650	3.012
14	.868	1.345	1.761	2.145	2.624	2.977
15	.866	1.341	1.753	2.131	2.602	2.947
16	.865	1.337	1.746	2.120	2.583	2.921
17	.863	1.333	1.740	2.110	2.567	2.898
18	.862	1.330	1.734	2.101	2.552	2.878
19	.861	1.328	1.729	2.093	2.539	2.861
20	.860	1.325	1.725	2.086	2.528	2.845
21	.859	1.323	1.721	2.080	2.518	2.831
22	.858	1.321	1.717	2.074	2.508	2.819
23	.858	1.319	1.714	2.069	2.500	2.807
24	.857	1.318	1.711	2.064	2.492	2.797
25	.856	1.316	1.708	2.060	2.485	2.787
26	.856	1.315	1.706	2.056	2.479	2.779
27	.855	1.314	1.703	2.052	2.473	2.771
28	.855	1.313	1.701	2.048	2.467	2.763
29	.854	1.311	1.699	2.045	2.462	2.756
30	.854	1.310	1.697	2.042	2.457	2.750
31	.853	1.309	1.696	2.040	2.453	2.744
32	.853	1.309	1.694	2.037	2.449	2.738
33	.853	1.308	1.692	2.035	2.445	2.733
34	.852	1.307	1.691	2.032	2.441	2.728

TABLE 2   *t* Distribution (continued)

Degrees of Freedom	Area in Upper Tail					
	.20	**.10**	**.05**	**.025**	**.01**	**.005**
35	.852	1.306	1.690	2.030	2.438	2.724
36	.852	1.306	1.688	2.028	2.434	2.719
37	.851	1.305	1.687	2.026	2.431	2.715
38	.851	1.304	1.686	2.024	2.429	2.712
39	.851	1.304	1.685	2.023	2.426	2.708
40	.851	1.303	1.684	2.021	2.423	2.704
41	.850	1.303	1.683	2.020	2.421	2.701
42	.850	1.302	1.682	2.018	2.418	2.698
43	.850	1.302	1.681	2.017	2.416	2.695
44	.850	1.301	1.680	2.015	2.414	2.692
45	.850	1.301	1.679	2.014	2.412	2.690
46	.850	1.300	1.679	2.013	2.410	2.687
47	.849	1.300	1.678	2.012	2.408	2.685
48	.849	1.299	1.677	2.011	2.407	2.682
49	.849	1.299	1.677	2.010	2.405	2.680
50	.849	1.299	1.676	2.009	2.403	2.678
51	.849	1.298	1.675	2.008	2.402	2.676
52	.849	1.298	1.675	2.007	2.400	2.674
53	.848	1.298	1.674	2.006	2.399	2.672
54	.848	1.297	1.674	2.005	2.397	2.670
55	.848	1.297	1.673	2.004	2.396	2.668
56	.848	1.297	1.673	2.003	2.395	2.667
57	.848	1.297	1.672	2.002	2.394	2.665
58	.848	1.296	1.672	2.002	2.392	2.663
59	.848	1.296	1.671	2.001	2.391	2.662
60	.848	1.296	1.671	2.000	2.390	2.660
61	.848	1.296	1.670	2.000	2.389	2.659
62	.847	1.295	1.670	1.999	2.388	2.657
63	.847	1.295	1.669	1.998	2.387	2.656
64	.847	1.295	1.669	1.998	2.386	2.655
65	.847	1.295	1.669	1.997	2.385	2.654
66	.847	1.295	1.668	1.997	2.384	2.652
67	.847	1.294	1.668	1.996	2.383	2.651
68	.847	1.294	1.668	1.995	2.382	2.650
69	.847	1.294	1.667	1.995	2.382	2.649
70	.847	1.294	1.667	1.994	2.381	2.648
71	.847	1.294	1.667	1.994	2.380	2.647
72	.847	1.293	1.666	1.993	2.379	2.646
73	.847	1.293	1.666	1.993	2.379	2.645
74	.847	1.293	1.666	1.993	2.378	2.644

TABLE 2   *t* Distribution (continued)

Degrees of Freedom	Area in Upper Tail					
	.20	.10	.05	.025	.01	.005
75	.846	1.293	1.665	1.992	2.377	2.643
76	.846	1.293	1.665	1.992	2.376	2.642
77	.846	1.293	1.665	1.991	2.376	2.641
78	.846	1.292	1.665	1.991	2.375	2.640
79	.846	1.292	1.664	1.990	2.374	2.639
80	.846	1.292	1.664	1.990	2.374	2.639
81	.846	1.292	1.664	1.990	2.373	2.638
82	.846	1.292	1.664	1.989	2.373	2.637
83	.846	1.292	1.663	1.989	2.372	2.636
84	.846	1.292	1.663	1.989	2.372	2.636
85	.846	1.292	1.663	1.988	2.371	2.635
86	.846	1.291	1.663	1.988	2.370	2.634
87	.846	1.291	1.663	1.988	2.370	2.634
88	.846	1.291	1.662	1.987	2.369	2.633
89	.846	1.291	1.662	1.987	2.369	2.632
90	.846	1.291	1.662	1.987	2.368	2.632
91	.846	1.291	1.662	1.986	2.368	2.631
92	.846	1.291	1.662	1.986	2.368	2.630
93	.846	1.291	1.661	1.986	2.367	2.630
94	.845	1.291	1.661	1.986	2.367	2.629
95	.845	1.291	1.661	1.985	2.366	2.629
96	.845	1.290	1.661	1.985	2.366	2.628
97	.845	1.290	1.661	1.985	2.365	2.627
98	.845	1.290	1.661	1.984	2.365	2.627
99	.845	1.290	1.660	1.984	2.364	2.626
100	.845	1.290	1.660	1.984	2.364	2.626
∞	.842	1.282	1.645	1.960	2.326	2.576